CONNECTED **C**OMMUN
Creating a new knowledge lan

AFTER URBAN REGENERATION

Communities, policy and place

Edited by
Dave O'Brien and Peter Matthews

First published in Great Britain in 2016 by

Policy Press
University of Bristol
1-9 Old Park Hill
Bristol
BS2 8BB
UK
t: +44 (0)117 954 5940
pp-info@bristol.ac.uk
www.policypress.co.uk

North America office:
Policy Press
c/o The University of Chicago Press
1427 East 60th Street
Chicago, IL 60637, USA
t: +1 773 702 7700
f: +1 773-702-9756
sales@press.uchicago.edu
www.press.uchicago.edu

British Library Cataloguing in Publication Data
A catalogue record for this book is available from the British Library

Library of Congress Cataloging-in-Publication Data
A catalog record for this book has been requested

ISBN 978-1-4473-2416-4 paperback
ISBN 978-1-4473-2415-7 hardcover

The right of Dave O'Brien and Peter Matthews to be identified as editors of this work has
been asserted by them in accordance with the Copyright, Designs and Patents Act 1988.

Cover design by Hayes Design
Front cover image: Joe Decie
Printed and bound in Great Britain by CMP, Poole
Policy Press uses environmentally responsible print partners

Contents

Notes on contributors

Clyde Ancarno completed her PhD in Linguistics in 2011 (Cardiff University). Her experience and understanding of co-production and public engagement in academic research (including the development of bespoke evaluation tools) find their roots in a Knowledge Exchange research project she designed and managed and for which she engaged tourism businesses in London (UCL – 2012). She worked on an AHRC-funded research project specifically concerned with how academics in the humanities engage with communities (Cardiff University – 2013). She is currently interested in participatory approaches to applied linguistics research and works as a researcher on the People, Products, Pests and Pets: The Discursive Representation of Animals project (King's College London).

Rebecca Bernstein is an editorial photographer based in Bristol. She works for a number of publications including *The Telegraph Magazine* and *Gardens Illustrated*, and specialises in portraiture and garden photography. For this project Beki photographed residents of St Werburghs and Patchway, Bristol, at various community events including a storytelling event 'Tasty Tales' at the St Werburgh's cafe in Bristol.

Sue Cohen is Co-Investigator on the Productive Margins programme based in the Law School at the University of Bristol. This five-year Connected Communities initiative is developing co-produced research with marginalised communities in Bristol and South Wales on the theme of regulation. Sue has been involved in participatory initiatives combating poverty and discrimination at a local, national and European level. Sue was CEO of Single Parent Action Network from 1990 to 2013, working to support one-parent families to improve their life chances. Sue helped to develop a network of grassroots groups from many different cultures and backgrounds across the UK.

Stephen Connelly is Senior Lecturer at the Department of Town and Regional Planning, University of Sheffield, UK. His research interests are broadly in the politics of policy making, and in particular of stakeholder involvement in governance in both the global North and South. Taking an interpretive approach, and drawing in part on social psychological insights, recent research has taken him into institutional issues of welfare service integration and its evaluation, and investigating how research is translated between academic and policy domains.

Oliver Davis is Lecturer in Archaeology at Cardiff University and Co-director of the CAER (Caerau and Ely Rediscovering) Heritage Project. His main archaeological research interests lie in the understanding of later prehistoric settlement (particularly hillforts), farming and social patterns. He is passionate about working with communities and using archaeological themes and debates to explore contemporary issues.

Catherine Durose is Senior Lecturer in the Institute of Local Government Studies and Director of Research and Knowledge Transfer for the School of Government and Society at the University of Birmingham. Catherine's research explores the intermediation of relationships between the state, communities and citizens, recently focusing on the politics and practice of community work participation and co-production. She has a passionate interest in how research can support progressive social change.

Dave Harte is Senior Lecturer in Media and Communications and Award Leader for the MA in Social Media at Birmingham City University. His main research interests are on the role that community news websites play in fostering citizenship. His research into the scale and scope of hyperlocal publishing in the UK was part of a large Connected Communities research project focused on Creative Citizenship. He has a background in working with local and regional policy-makers on developing the creative economy and has managed projects with a focus on supporting creative businesses.

Phil Jones is Senior Lecturer in Cultural Geography at the University of Birmingham and Principal Investigator on a £1.5 million AHRC-funded project Cultural Intermediation and the Creative Urban Economy (2012–16). He has published widely on cities, including work on sustainability and regeneration as well as arts and creative methods. Along with James Evans, Phil is co-author of the book *Urban regeneration in the UK* (second edition, 2013) and has co-edited the collection *Creative economies, creative communities: Rethinking place, policy and practice* (2015) with Saskia Warren.

Amadu Wurie Khan has been Research Associate in the AHRC-funded Connected Communities project Community Hacking and Web 2.0 at the University of Edinburgh, UK. He is currently reviewing the social design and functionality issues around co-production of the *Digital Sentinel* newspaper, which is one of the community-generated digital outputs of the project. His research interests include the sociology and ethnography of the design and applications of digital media and public artwork by and among 'disadvantaged' communities.

Antonia Layard is Professor of Law at the University of Bristol. Her research is in law and geography where she explores how law, legality and maps construct space, place and 'the local'. She has particular interests in 'urban law", and the legal provisions and practices involved in large-scale regeneration and infrastructure projects. Antonia teaches courses on property, planning and environmental law and has been involved in a number of AHRC Connected Communities projects. More information on her research and copies of pre-publication papers can be found at http://antonialayard.com.

Colin Lorne is an urban and cultural geographer who has undertaken his PhD at the University of Birmingham, UK. His research brings together interests in architecture and the built environment, changing working practices and contemporary urban society. His recent research brings a critical geographic perspective to the 'entrepreneurial' spaces and practices of co-working. Other interests involve engaging with architects who are expanding the role of design beyond buildings as well as the Localism Act 2011 in the UK, with particular focus upon how communities are engaging in Neighbourhood Planning exercises with minimal resources.

Peter Matthews is Lecturer in Social Policy in the School of Applied Social Science, University of Stirling, UK. In his research he is particularly interested in urban policy, urban inequalities and community engagement and empowerment. Research projects have focused on co-producing engagement and research with communities within marginalised neighbourhoods and understanding the motivations and consequences of engagement by the affluent.

Martin Maudsley is a professional storyteller based in Dorset working across the UK in theatres, festivals, schools, village halls, museums and often outdoors. Martin also works with national organisations providing storytelling performances, commissioned projects and creative workshops. Recent clients include the BBC, Bristol Festival of Nature, Cheltenham Festivals of Science and Literature, the Eden Project, English Heritage, the National Trust, River Cottage HQ and the Soil Association.

Morag McDermont is Professor of Socio-legal Studies at the University of Bristol Law School, and Principal Investigator for two research programmes: New Sites of Legal Consciousness: A Case Study of UK Advice Agencies and Productive Margins: Regulating for Engagement. Her research has been shaped by 15 years' working in local government and voluntary sector housing organisations. She has published two books: *Regulating social housing: Governing decline* (Glasshouse, 2006) with Dave Cowan; and *Governing, independence and expertise: The business of housing associations* (Hart, 2010), a study of the historical role played by the National Housing Federation in the governance of social housing

Max Nathan is Deputy Director of the What Works Centre for Local Economic Growth, a collaboration between the London School of Economics and Political Science (LSE), the Centre for Cities and Arup, which aims to improve the use of evidence and impact evaluation in local economic development. He is also a Senior Research Fellow at the National Institute of Economic and Social Research. Max has over 15 years' public policy experience in think tanks, consultancy and government, most recently at Department for Communities and Local Government (DCLG) as an ESRC–DCLG-funded policy advisor. Max also co-founded the Centre for Cities, where he ran the research programme for the Centre's first three years. He writes in a personal capacity, not that of the What Works Centre.

Dave O'Brien is Senior Lecturer in Cultural Policy at Goldsmiths, University of London. He has worked on several Connected Communities projects, exploring early career researchers' experiences, dementia and imagination, and the creative economy. His most recent book is *Cultural policy*, published by Routledge.

Kate Pahl is Professor of Literacies in Education at the University of Sheffield. She is interested in everyday literacies in home and community contexts. Her most recent book *Materializing Literacies in Communities* is published by Bloomsbury Academic Press. Her work is currently concerned with the role of artists in community projects, and with the cultural context of civic engagement.

Martin Phillips is Professor of Human Geography at the University of Leicester. His research interests involve four broad areas of geography: rural social and cultural geography, historical geography, society/environment relations, and philosophy in geography. Much of his recent work has focused on the material and symbolic constructions of rural space, with particular regard to the social relations and identities of class and gender. He is also conducting work on museum geographies, retail-led gentrification, filmic geographies and adaptations to climate change.

Sheffield-based artist **Steve Pool** originally trained as a sculptor. He now works as a visual artists in multiple media to help people realise ideas, often making physical objects or changing environments. For the past 25 years he has worked on many initiatives including Creative Partnerships, Public Understanding of Science, and regeneration through area-based renewal programmes. He has an interest in stories, objects and research. He works in varied settings including art galleries, communities and more recently universities through the AHRC Connecting Communities programme. Central to his work is the belief that access to new technologies offers many opportunities for people to produce as well as consume culture.

Hilary Ramsden is Senior Lecturer in Drama and Performance at the Faculty of Creative Industries, University of South Wales. Hilary's arts-led research practice involves participatory and collaborative experiments to interrupt our assumptions and perceptions about our relationship with our surroundings and wider environment. Since 2000 she has been exploring everyday walking habits and creating interventions that open our eyes and hearts to the potential alternative use of public spaces.

Liz Richardson is Senior Lecturer in Politics and Director of Undergraduate Studies for Politics at the University of Manchester. She is a Visiting Fellow in the Centre for Analysis of Social Exclusion (CASE) at LSE, and a board member for national charities the National Association of Neighbourhood Management and the National Communities Resource Centre. Her work is dedicated to trying out ways in which academics, practitioners, and citizens can develop more democratic and participatory ways of doing politics.

Robert Rutherfoord is Principal Research Officer in the Department of Communities and Local Government (DCLG). He is responsible for analysis on neighbourhood decentralisation and neighbourhood planning, and has a particular interest in linking up the civil service with academic research, to share insights and solve problems. Previous roles included research on regeneration, spatial analysis and small business studies.

Chris Speed is Chair of Design Informatics at the University of Edinburgh where his research focuses upon the Network Society, Digital Art and Technology, and The Internet of Things. At present Chris is working on funded projects that engage with the social opportunities of crypto-currencies, an internet of toilet roll-holders, and a persistent argument that chickens are actually robots. Chris is co-editor of the journal *Ubiquity* and leads the Design Informatics Research Centre that is home to a combination of researchers working across the fields of interaction design, temporal design, anthropology and software engineering.

Jerome Turner is Research Assistant at the Birmingham Centre for Media and Cultural Research, Birmingham City University. His research interests are in online community media and social media, typically explored through ethnographic or participatory/co-creative research methods – he is currently engaged in an ethnographic study of south Birmingham hyperlocal community media audiences for his PhD.

Dave Vanderhoven has worked intensively within marginalised communities, developed services and worked with public bodies and policymakers; this includes community development and therapeutic support to individuals, organisational development with Irish Travellers to secure rights and policy change, and managing a Therapeutic Community. Dave completed a PhD at University of Sheffield exploring informal political representation in urban development within an artists' community in Johannesburg. He is focusing on the intersections between knowledge, policy and the artistry of practice; conducting research with 14 local authorities and several government departments. Dave is on the board of a local domestic violence support organisation and the *Community Development Journal*.

Stuart Wilks-Heeg is Head of Politics and a Reader in Politics at the University of Liverpool. He has published widely on issues concerned with urban policy and local communities as well as on a range of topics connected with the UK democratic process. Stuart was also the Director of the Democratic Audit of the UK from 2009 to 2012 and provides regular media commentary on current political events.

Dave Wyatt is Senior Lecturer in History and Community Engagement Co-ordinator in the School of History, Archaeology and Religion (SHARE) at Cardiff University. Dave's research specialises in the history of slavery in the societies of early medieval Britain. He also co-ordinates SHARE's engagement activities, developing formal and informal learning opportunities and promoting a culture of engagement and co-production. Dave is project PI (Principal Investigator) and is involved in the delivery and management of all key aspects of the CAER Heritage Project.

ONE

Introduction

Peter Matthews and Dave O'Brien

This edited collection has emerged from studies funded through the UK Arts and Humanities Research Council's (AHRC's) 'Connected Communities' programme. It uses the evidence and knowledge created by a range of projects to explore two theses: first, that the UK, and England in particular, has now entered a 'post-regeneration era'; and, second, that new relationships are being developed between academics, universities and 'communities', producing new kinds of knowledge. These two propositions are explored throughout the book, but are related to global challenges.

Most obviously, the international push towards government austerity, with the UK government spearheading a global charge since 2010, has ended the era of public spending largesse that kept previous urban regeneration policies sustained (Sullivan, 2012). In England, the previous structures of area-based partnerships intended to deliver holistic regeneration have been replaced by a hotchpotch of initiatives, most notably, the range of powers included in the Localism Act, including neighbourhood planning, and the vague commitments and partial policy implementation associated with the much-discredited 'Big Society' (Allmendinger and Haughton, 2012).

Elsewhere in the UK, similar trends have emerged. While the Scottish government still has a small amount of central government funding that may be classed as regeneration funding, the focus is primarily on local authorities and health boards, through community planning partnerships, delivering outcomes for the most marginalised and excluded groups and neighbourhoods. The longer-term public service reform agenda sees co-production as a key way to deliver services more efficiently (Christie, 2011). Similarly, in Wales, the ongoing changes to Communities First are seeing the programme of area-based initiatives gradually becoming more mainstream and focused on delivering outcomes (NAWPAC, 2010). Across the UK, policy changes have occurred, or are occurring, that are changing the way in which central government treats the most deprived and marginalised communities. While for 40 years, at least, these neighbourhoods have been the focus of specific initiatives, they are now increasingly left to find their own way in a complex and unfavourable policy environment.

The 'Connected Communities' programme emerged into this policy context in 2009, not without controversy. Changes within the broader context of higher education were challenging arts and humanities research. This was particularly the case regarding the impact agenda embedded in the 2013 Research Excellence Framework, where 'units of assessment' at UK universities had to demonstrate 'an effect on, change or benefit to the economy, society, culture, public policy or services, health, the environment or quality of life, beyond academia' (Research Excellence Framework, 2012: 26). Typical ways of delivering and measuring socio-economic impact – for example, spin-out companies, numbers of patents registered, supporting policy design and policy problem definition; affecting policy design and delivery, and so on – were seen as a challenge for arts and humanities subjects.

At the time of writing, the 'Connected Communities' programme has invested over £30 million in over 300 projects. However, the nascent programme was controversial – the 2010 AHRC delivery plan suggested that 'Connected Communities will enable the AHRC to contribute to the government's initiatives on localism and the "Big Society"' (AHRC, 2010: 9). This commitment was seen as a political act by the AHRC and a dangerous incursion on the Haldane Principle that decisions on the allocation of research funding to UK universities must remain an apolitical decision. As a result, a number of members of the AHRC's peer review college resigned in protest following a high-profile campaign.

Parallels can be drawn between the Economic and Social Research Council's strategic focus on research on social exclusion in the late 1990s and early 2000s as a response to the contemporary policy context, or the current Engineering and Physical Sciences Research Council's 'Digital Economy' programme, paralleling the 'Connected Communities' programme. These examples suggest that the Haldane Principle is a line toed, not a line in the sand. Arguably, the furore over the AHRC 2010 strategy also reflects the broader debate on the 'crisis in the humanities'. While applied social science and science, technology, engineering and mathematics (STEM) subjects may be comfortable with impact-focused research strategies aligned to current government policy, this is new territory for many scholars within the arts and humanities.

While the 'Connected Communities' programme was critiqued for its pragmatic, impact-focused agenda, the programme itself rapidly became something with much greater radical intent, simply stated in research call documents as 'doing research with communities, not on communities'. While many social scientists were quick to highlight the basic problem, and a perennial debate in many disciplines, of how one defines 'community', this core principle was a radical departure from research practice across disciplines and for the research councils themselves. Very early in the programme, issues arose around the power differentials between community partners and universities created by the bureaucracy of the research councils and the universities themselves; paying community partners for their time and commitment was an early issue that was not entirely resolved. Ultimately, this radical intent aligned research practice in 'Connected Communities' with current policy mood music – like Big Society policy, research was now to be co-produced *with* communities. This added to the broader debate challenging what a university is in our current time, with the increasing pressures of marketisation and research performance management through the Research Excellence Framework.

Structure of the book

The book is divided into four parts, which take us through the preceding narrative in greater depth through broad evidence, theoretical and methodological reviews, and specific case studies from 'Connected Communities' projects. Part One focuses on urban regeneration policy and how we are moving to a 'post-regeneration' era. In Chapter Two, Wilks-Heeg takes us through the history of urban regeneration policy since 1945, with a particular focus on communities and the relationship between communities and the knowledge about them. The chapter highlights how communities have variously been problematised by policy – for example, with the pathologisation of the 'inner city' in the 1960s' Community Development Projects – and also placed in the position as political leaders of regeneration – for example, in the New Deal for Communities programme. In Chapter Three, Matthews and O'Brien continue this history into the narrative of 'post-regeneration' today. With a particular focus on England, they explore how communities have now been set adrift with little financial support into a new world of neighbourhood planning and local enterprise partnerships with even greater challenges in the future following to May 2015 General Election. Chapter Four, a dialogue between a leader of a third-sector activist organisation, Sue Cohen, and an academic, Morag McDermont, describes in emotional detail the complexities of what dry policy narratives have meant for thousands of similar initiatives across the UK. This narrative of complex regulation, distrust and the collapse of partnership working shows what 'post-regeneration' means for the most marginalised and deprived communities and neighbourhoods in the UK.

A theme in Chapter Two is how the long history of urban regeneration in the UK has been paralleled by a history of its 'knowing' by academic research and the growth of the social sciences. The early Community Development Projects were twinned with university research partners, who famously ended up producing the Marxist critique of this failed urban policy, *Gilding the ghetto* (CDP Interdisciplinary Team, 1977). As discussed earlier, the modern impact agenda for UK universities is pushing the 'Connected Communities' programme; for the Economic and Social Research Council, a similar drive is present in its various 'What Works' centres. To start Part Two, and taking a reflexive turn, in Chapter Five, Max Nathan discusses the epistemological and practical barriers to knowing what works in urban regeneration policy from a social science perspective. The 'Connected Communities' programme brought new epistemologies into research with communities and these are explored in the following two chapters. First, in Chapter Six, Steve Pool and Kate Pahl talk about the process of producing representations to policymakers in the UK government Department for Communities and Local Government with young people in Rotherham, South Yorkshire, and the challenges of getting these differing representations heard by policymakers. Similarly, focusing on the methodology of their research project, in Chapter Seven, Rebecca Bernstein and co-authors highlight how storytelling revealed new knowledges of the 'local' beyond those used in policy rhetoric.

The final two parts of the book seek to answer the question: what do these changes mean in practice for communities and for academic inquiry? The era of regeneration created a proliferation of hard and soft spaces and places – area-based initiatives most typically would delineate a neighbourhood as being subject to a specific intervention, and if you were resident outside of the neighbourhood, then you would not benefit, often creating artificial 'postcode lotteries'. Soft spaces were also created around partnership working and community development activities: a community media initiative delimiting a newspaper circulation area as a 'community' or a partnership office or community flat being a safe, affordable place for residents to use (Jupp, 2008). Forming Part Three, Chapters Eight, Nine and Ten report on how these places are being explored and (re)created by 'Connected Communities' projects. In Chapter Eight, Clyde Ancarno, Oliver Davis and David Wyatt use their example of the Caer project in Cardiff, working with the deprived neighbourhoods of Caerau and Ely, to highlight the new ways of working among academics that have been engendered by the 'Connected Communities' programme. This has enabled communities to know themselves differently – in this case, to understand their history as linked to an Iron Age hill fort that is the archaeological foundation of the settlement of Cardiff, while also developing skills and confidence within the community. In Chapter Nine, David Harte and Jerome Turner focuses on research with residents in Castle Vale on hyper-local news, dealing with a combined legacy of stigma and distrust of communication channels as being part of the Housing Action Trust regeneration programme. In Chapter Ten, Amadu Wurie Khan, Chris Speed and Martin Phillips present their case study of working with Wester Hailes, a deprived neighbourhood in Edinburgh, in order to use structures and organisations that emerged out of over 40 years of resident and state-led regeneration to 'hack' the very idea of the Big Society that has been so central to the 'post-regeneration' policy process.

In Part Four, the final two chapters by Phil Jones et al and Steve Connelly et al take a clear epochal break with earlier periods of urban regeneration and 'knowing' about urban communities. While urban regeneration policy created spaces and places, so the new governance structures being rolled out through localism are creating new places and spaces at the micro-level. In Chapter Eleven, Jones et al critically engage with the neighbourhood planning agenda in this regard, using the example of their optimistic 'MapLocal' project, which sought to give communities the ability to know their area and to then write a plan. However, the inequalities and barriers to successfully engaging in neighbourhood planning, including the fact that it is inherently and paradoxically a highly centralising policy initiative, mean that the new places of urban policy are ultimately unequal and riven by power differentials. Finally, in Chapter Twelve, Connelly et al focus at the macro-level on how these new knowledges being created by the 'Connected Communities' programme might be used by policymakers. Using the concept of 'translation' and theoretical work from translation studies, the chapter argues that most academic research on the challenges of 'knowledge exchange' or getting academic evidence into policymaking processes ultimately falls short by not fully exploring how both academics and policymakers communicate and use evidence.

The book presents, and concludes, by suggesting that we are in a new policy era. The New Labour era of regeneration expenditure was known about, and also critically engaged with, by the social sciences (for an evaluation of the New Deal for Communities, see, eg, Imrie and Raco, 2003; Lawless, 2011). The emergent initiatives springing up across the UK in the wake of the withdrawal of the state and the rhetoric of co-production, asset transfer and the Big Society is being known in very different ways: through archaeology, arts practice, history and co-produced research. This poses a challenge to the academy: what is the role of expert knowledge of communities in a world where research is done *with* communities, not *on* communities, particularly a world where the regeneration funding that previously supported many such activities has long ceased?

References

AHRC (Arts and Humanities Research Council) (2010) *Arts & Humanities Research Council delivery plan 2011–2015*, Swindon: AHRC.

Allmendinger, P. and Haughton, G. (2012) 'The evolution and trajectories of English spatial governance: "neoliberal" episodes in planning', *Planning Practice & Research* 28(1): 6–26.

CDP (Community Development Project) Interdisciplinary Team (1977) *Gilding the ghetto: the state and the poverty experiments*, London: CDP Inter-Project Editorial Team.

Christie, C. (2011) *Commission on the future delivery of public services*, Edinburgh: Commission on the Future Delivery of Public Services.

Imrie, R. and Raco, M. (eds) (2003) *Urban renaissance? New Labour, community and urban policy*, Bristol: The Policy Press.

Jupp, E. (2008) 'The feeling of participation: everyday spaces and urban change', *Geoforum* 39: 331–43.

Lawless, P. (2011) 'Understanding the scale and nature of outcome change in area-regeneration programmes: evidence from the New Deal for Communities programme in England', *Environment and Planning C: Government and Policy* 29(3): 520–32.

NAWPAC (National Assembly for Wales Public Accounts Committee) (2010) *Communities first*, Cardiff: National Assembly for Wales.

Research Excellence Framework (2012) *Assessment framework and guidance on submissions*, Bristol: REF.

Sullivan, H. (2012) 'DEBATE: a Big Society needs an active state', *Policy & Politics* 40(1): 141–4.

Part One
After regeneration?

TWO

Urban policy and communities

Stuart Wilks-Heeg

Introduction

In one form or another, all UK governments since 1945 have pursued policies aimed at addressing urban problems. A concern with community has been evident throughout, although the assumptions about how communities would be engaged with, and benefit from, these policies have varied enormously. In the first two decades after the end of the Second World War, communities were regarded as the passive beneficiaries of planned decentralisation to new towns and the replacement of 'slums' with modern public housing. Partly due to the backlash against such policies, the late 1960s witnessed the emergence of neighbourhood-based, often experimental, urban policy initiatives designed to address what Home Secretary James Callaghan described as the 'deadly quagmire of need and apathy' in some inner-city communities.[1] Since then, there have been numerous shifts in the way in which communities are framed by urban policies, with some initiatives framing 'communities' as the solution and others promoting them as the problem. As this chapter demonstrates, this shifting approach to community reflects a deeper set of long-run tensions in urban policy, with policy change tending to emerge as a response to previous policy failure.

The chapter is divided into three main sections. The first section provides an overview of urban policy, with an emphasis on understanding the key shifts in policy since the first area-based initiatives (ABIs) were established in the late 1960s. The tendency for urban policy experiments to serve as a barometer of political and ideological change is noted and the consequences for policymaking are highlighted, with particular emphasis on the circular nature of urban policy debate. The second section examines in more detail the turn, or, more accurately, return, to community in urban policy from the early 1990s onwards. It is shown how community involvement, and ultimately community leadership, came to be seen as the solution to previous policy failure.

Yet, it is argued, urban policies continued to repeat the mistakes of past initiatives by misrepresenting the causes of neighbourhood decline. The final, short section briefly examines the contemporary urban policy context. For the first time since 1968, there are effectively no ABIs in England and national government policy has shifted from targeted intervention to a philosophy of general 'facilitation'. In many ways, this abandonment of urban policy experiments is the biggest regeneration experiment to date. The outcome is almost certain to be that the gap between affluent and deprived neighbourhoods continues to grow.

Urban policy and communities

There is a long history of UK governments adopting policies aimed specifically at addressing urban and regional problems. Indeed, it is possible to argue that regional policies were pioneered in the UK during the 1930s, when measures were introduced in response to the rise of mass unemployment in many core industrial areas (Forthergill, 2005). Many authors also highlight the historical significance of post-war planning frameworks in driving the reconstruction of British cities within the context of the broad political consensus associated with the Keynesian welfare state (Thornley, 1991; Atkinson and Moon, 1994). However, it was the late 1960s that served as the key starting point for most accounts of the development of what has become known as 'urban policy'. It was at this time that the then Labour government launched the first special programmes targeted at a small number of neighbourhoods deemed to be suffering from concentrated urban social problems. Introducing the government's proposals to the House of Commons on 22 July 1968, Home Secretary James Callaghan explained:

> There remain areas of severe social deprivation in a number of our cities and towns—often scattered in relatively small pockets. They require special help to meet their social needs and to bring their physical services to an adequate level. The Government propose to initiate an urban programme to help tackle the social problems of the communities concerned. (Callaghan, 1968)

Callaghan's framing of the new Urban Programme captures many of the recurrent and defining, although not necessarily constant, features of urban policy. First, urban policies tend to take the form of ABIs operating in a limited number of localities. Second, this spatial targeting has generally been determined on the basis of social need (although sometimes on other criteria) and involves initiatives that operate in addition to mainstream state provision. Third, the social problems that these initiatives are designed to address are assumed to be present in particular localities, or communities, and therefore essentially absent from others.

These long-term continuities in many of the defining characteristics of urban policy should not, however, be taken as an indicator of policy stability. There have been dramatic shifts in the objectives and character of urban policy initiatives over time. Moreover, since the creation of the Urban Programme in 1968, a bewildering array of initiatives that could legitimately be classified as urban policies have come and gone. By the mid-1990s, accounts of urban policy were already replete with an 'alphabet soup' of abbreviations: CDPs (Community Development Projects), SRB (Single Regeneration Budget) and UDCs (Urban Development Corporations). After New Labour came to power in 1997, the number of ABIs proliferated dramatically (Rhodes et al, 2005). Indeed, if we cast the net a little wider than the core features of urban policy outlined earlier, it is possible to identify around 200 policy programmes with 'some relevance to urban policy' operating during the early 2000s (Imrie and Raco, 2003: 14–16).

Given the sheer number of initiatives involved, this chapter makes no attempt to present a full history of urban policy, not least because numerous detailed accounts already exist (see Atkinson and Moon, 1994; Tallon, 2010). Instead, it will suffice to summarise five key phases through which urban policy passed after 1968, and the dominant features of policy, as well as examples of key policy initiatives, in each of these (developments since 2010 are considered in the final part of the chapter).

In the first phase, from 1968 to 1976, urban policy initiatives arose as a response to the so-called 'rediscovery of poverty' in the 1960s and to growing concerns about racial and ethnic tensions in a number of inner-city areas. These programmes were largely premised on what became known as a 'social pathology' perspective. Essentially, it was assumed that given the existence of full employment and a 'cradle to grave' welfare state, the persistence of poverty and other social problems in some inner-city areas must be the product of the dysfunctional character of the communities concerned. As well as the Urban Programme, initiatives such as the CDPs and the Inner Area Studies reflected this approach. There was a particular focus on policymakers and other 'experts', including university researchers, seeking to work with local communities to generate 'solutions' to social problems.

There were growing criticisms of the 'social pathology' perspective during the 1970s, many of them voiced from key players in the programmes themselves. In response, a brief second phase of urban policy, from 1977 to 1978, saw the focus shift towards efforts to devise strategic policy responses to the impact of structural economic change, particularly deindustrialisation and manufacturing job loss, on inner-city areas. Based on the analysis contained in the Labour government's (Department of the Environment, 1977), six Inner City Partnerships were created as mechanisms for coordinating local and central government efforts to tackle urban decline. While these programmes were short-lived, the new emphasis on the causes of inner-city problems being primarily economic, rather than social, was to mark a significant change in direction.

Thus, from 1979 to 1990, under Margaret Thatcher's governments, problems associated with urban decay came to be seen as manifestations of the lack of an enterprise culture in inner-city areas. This third phase of urban policy resulted in programmes designed to 'lever in' private sector investment in order to bring about physical regeneration and drive job creation. It was assumed that economic benefits would subsequently 'trickle down' to local communities, primarily through improved employment opportunities. This policy shift was underpinned by significant institutional changes. Many urban policy initiatives circumvented local authorities, which the Thatcher governments saw as part of the problem, and, in some cases, involved the establishment of new organisational structures giving business representatives a leading role. The UDCs were the dominant policy initiative of the period. Other key programmes included Enterprise Zones and Derelict Land Grants.

However, under the Major governments of the early to mid-1990s, urban policy again shifted in response to a growing body of criticism. By the early 1990s, evidence was mounting that while the property-led regeneration programmes of the previous decade had brought about the physical transformation of some urban areas, the impact on levels of unemployment and poverty had been negligible. At the same time, the previous proliferation of programmes and the poor coordination of regeneration initiatives was widely held to have created an ineffectual 'patchwork quilt' of agencies and initiatives. New policy programmes from 1991 to 1996 sought to address urban social and economic problems in an integrated way, to promote partnership-working between the public, private and voluntary sectors, and to facilitate the involvement of local communities in urban policy. At the same time, there was a move away from allocating funding solely on the basis of social need. In particular, the key initiatives launched during this period – City Challenge and the SRB – were based on a new model of competitive bidding between areas seeking regeneration funding.

A fifth distinctive phase of urban policy, from 1997 to 2010, was marked by Labour's return to power under Tony Blair in 1997 and the rise of 'third way' ideas in shaping the party's economic and social policies. With respect to urban policy, the 'New Labour' approach was underpinned by the objective of tackling 'social exclusion' and a renewed emphasis on community-based solutions at the neighbourhood level. The New Deal for Communities (NDC) was the centrepiece of Labour's urban policy agenda, which also saw a return to targeting policies towards areas with the greatest social need. Meanwhile, other Labour initiatives focused on economic development at a regional scale, through the creation of Regional Development Agencies. There was also a proliferation of regeneration and economic development partnerships, particularly at local authority and sub-regional scales.

Despite the sheer number of urban policy initiatives operating in each of these periods, and the bold claims made about their potential to tackle urban problems, they have never accounted for more than a fraction of public expenditure. As selective and spatially targeted programmes, the budgets for urban policy initiatives are dwarfed by mainstream social policy expenditure. Nonetheless, urban policy has always been a high-profile, and much-studied, area of public policy. A key reason for the disproportionate attention it has received is that urban policy starkly reflects broader political and ideological shifts with respect to pressing questions of social and economic policy. There are a number of good reasons why urban policy operates as such an effective barometer of wider public policy change. First, and foremost, as urban policies operate beyond mainstream programmes, radical shifts in policy are relatively easy to bring about, not least because they rarely require primary legislation. Second, as urban policy initiatives tend to be spatially targeted, they are also amenable to experimental approaches and can be used to trial new approaches before they are rolled out more widely. Third, the relatively low cost and flexible and experimental nature of urban policies makes them highly suitable for new ministers seeking to make their mark politically. Perhaps more so than in any other policy area, urban policy programmes tend to be identified as the 'pet projects' of particular secretaries of state, as other contributors to this volume highlight.

The highly politicised nature of urban policy exemplifies, and arguably exaggerates, a number of tensions that are widely observed in public policy more generally. Regular policy shifts take place despite a broad consensus that tackling urban social problems requires a sustained, long-term approach. Moreover, while a great deal has been invested in evaluating urban policies and in schemes to promote policy learning, it is the political and ideological factors identified earlier that serve as the primary drivers of policy change. Finally, urban policies tend to be characterised by failure, or, perhaps more charitably, it tends to be very difficult to find evidence of their success, particularly in the short term (Lawless, 2010).

Of course, there is no reason to assume that urban policy should offer any greater prospect of lasting cross-party consensus, evidence-based policymaking or unambiguously successful policy outcomes than other policy areas. However, when combined with a tendency for each experimental urban policy to be announced as a virtual panacea for urban decline, these shortcomings have created a very particular set of temporal policy dynamics. Despite the vast array of urban policy initiatives, there are, in truth, a limited range of options for spatial targeting. Essentially, policy can attempt to improve the lives of people or improve the look of places, or, under the most ambitious variants, both. Yet, these modestly resourced, experimental programmes always tend to founder in the face of deep-rooted urban problems, prompting policy to switch continually from one of these broad approaches to another. As a result, urban regeneration exhibits a cyclical tendency, whereby 'wheels have to be reinvented and long-established truths have to be rediscovered' (Wilks-Heeg, 1996: 1264).

This cycle has had significant consequences for how communities have been defined with respect to urban policy. It is certainly true that community has represented 'a recurrent theme' in urban policy since the late 1960s (Tallon, 2010: 140) and that ABIs 'have always had some measure of community involvement' (Dargan, 2009: 306). However, the way in which policies have viewed the role of communities has been far from stable. As the preceding summary of the history of urban policy illustrated, communities have been seen variously as the problem that needs fixing, as the passive recipients of 'trickle-down' from inward investment, or as the unique possessors of the local knowledge that will help provide the solutions. It is also evident, however, that there was a growing emphasis on community involvement in urban policy from the early 1990s, which reached its peak during the 2000s. Writing with reference to the failings of property-led regeneration in the 1980s, Robinson and Shaw (1991) noted some initial signs of community involvement in urban policy and argued for far stronger emphasis on community as part of a balancing of place-based and people-based regeneration. Reflecting a decade and a half later on their 1991 account, Robinson et al (2005: 14) noted that 'the change has been substantial – even, perhaps, remarkable'. How, then, did this (re)turn to community come about?

Understanding the (re)turn to community

As noted earlier, the 'turn to community' was not new to urban policy as attempts had already been made to embed urban policy initiatives in specific communities through the ABIs of the late 1960s and early 1970s. In this sense, it is more accurate to speak of a 'return to community', albeit with some important distinctions to note in the way in which community participation was framed (see later). Equally, community involvement was not unique to urban policy and neither was it a specifically British development. Similar trajectories were evident in wide range of other policy areas, such as health and education, and not just in Britain, but internationally (Mathers et al, 2008). As Lawless and Pearson (2012: 510) suggest: 'it is now virtually impossible to find any government in a democratic society not claiming to be enhancing citizen engagement in public policy'.

The reasons for this promotion of public engagement are not difficult to identify. Against a backdrop of concerns about falling levels of political participation and declining faith in public bodies, the engagement of residents and users in the policy process was seen to offer the potential to bolster democratic legitimacy. It was also widely argued that community involvement offered distinct policy advantages, in particular, with respect to ensuring the effective design and implementation of social policy interventions. Of course, there are numerous pitfalls associated with citizen engagement, as well as widely articulated doubts about the extent to which such efforts provide for meaningful participation or influence in shaping decisions. These issues have been debated extensively in the literature on urban policy, as is illustrated in the following.

While far from unique, there are some good reasons to pay particular attention to the experience of community involvement in regeneration programmes. There was a distinctive set of drivers behind the return to community in urban policy, and efforts to engage citizens began earlier, and went further, than in other policy areas. A vital trigger was provided by the mounting evidence in the early 1990s that physical regeneration brought about by the UDCs had not resulted in the promised 'trickle down' of economic benefits to local residents. The high-profile national evaluation of urban policy initiatives conducted by Robson et al (1993) found little evidence of improvements in socio-economic conditions and recommended, among other changes, that future policy be based on closer partnership-working with local communities. The point was brought home even more dramatically by events in the London Docklands, where Olympia and York, the developer of Canary Wharf, went bankrupt amid desperate attempts to divert transport and urban policy funds to connect the vast office complex to central London. The symbolism, at that time, of Canary Wharf as a towering and costly white elephant in one of the most deprived parts of the country was all the more powerful given the concerns of the Major government to dissociate itself from the most controversial policies of the Thatcher years. With the failure of the UDCs to tackle local poverty levels being 'blamed on the lack of resident participation' (Dargan, 2009: 307), and the UK economy entering a deep recession, policy shifted rapidly away from property-led regeneration. The concern to engage communities, which had already been apparent from the launch of the City Challenge in 1991, grew progressively stronger with subsequent policy initiatives.

The return to community culminated in the design of NDC as a community-led programme under the incoming Labour government after 1997. By this stage, community involvement in regeneration had become axiomatic. The benefits were seen as largely self-evident and to support it was 'to be on the side of the angels' (Robinson et al, 2005: 15). As Dargan (2009: 307) suggests, community involvement therefore came to be seen not only as inherently valuable, but, more broadly, 'as a panacea to regeneration failure'. In line with my earlier observations about the cyclical nature of urban policy, a number of authors have noted the irony of these developments. Taylor (2000) notes how NDC served to bring policy full circle, returning to the community-based, participatory approaches of the late 1960s and early 1970s. However, there are some important contrasts between the two periods. Under the initial urban policy programmes, communities were engaged as the *subjects* of regeneration, but over time, they came to be seen as the *managers* of regeneration, through partnership and, later, community leadership (cf Dargan, 2009). The justifications for this latter approach were manifold, and reflected the wider rationale, noted earlier, for policymakers to reach out to residents and service users. In particular, community-led regeneration would ensure that policy benefitted from the insider knowledge of local communities, it would secure community 'buy in' to the regeneration process and it would help rebuild stocks of social capital locally, thereby ensuring the sustainability of regeneration (Amin, 2005; Tallon, 2010).

In many ways, therefore, the approach to community involvement in urban policy that evolved from the early 1990s onwards turned the rationale for the urban policy initiatives of the late 1960s on its head. The CDPs and other initiatives from that period had been underpinned by the assumption that social problems were inherent to the communities themselves and that expert interventions were required to enable communities to break out of what Keith Joseph termed a 'cycle of poverty'. Thus, the objective was to tackle personal and collective failings 'to re-socialize the poor, bringing them into line with the mores and values of the day' (Dargan, 2009: 307). However, by the late 1990s, the logic had, apparently, been reversed. In principle, the NDC was designed to ensure that communities were actively 'doing regeneration' rather than having it 'done to them'. It was urban policy that was to be brought into line with the needs of the community, not the other way around.

The NDC provided a crucial test of the assumption that community leadership was the missing link in urban policy. At the time of its launch, the NDC was presented by government as 'the most concerted attack on area deprivation this country has ever seen' (Social Exclusion Unit, 1998). Despite the hyperbole generally associated with the introduction of urban policy programmes, this was not an empty claim. The NDC represented a step-change in urban policy, with the programme being consciously designed to address a number of the long-standing criticisms of previous programmes. In response to evidence that past initiatives had been too short-term to enable effective community engagement and bring about lasting change, NDC programmes were funded for a 10-year period. The level of expenditure was unprecedented and there was a stronger emphasis on multi-agency working than at any time since the late 1970s. To assist in the identification and dissemination of 'good practice', the programme was supported by policy learning mechanisms, underpinned by a £25 million evaluation programme. Given the scale and ambitions of the intervention, there are legitimate grounds to regard the NDC as 'one of the most significant ABIs ever devised in England, and conceivably anywhere' (Lawless, 2010: 25). The significance of the NDC was certainly not lost on the academic community. The programme provided the basis for dozens of books, reports and articles, including assessments of the programme as a whole and numerous case studies of individual NDC areas, notably, Salford (Wallace, 2010), Bristol (MacLeavy, 2009) and Newcastle (McCulloch, 2004; Dargan, 2009).

Across this large body of research, there is general agreement that the NDC failed to transform the neighbourhoods in which it operated

(Tallon, 2010). There was no evidence across a range of indicators that NDC areas fared better than comparable areas without the NDC (Lawless and Pearson, 2012). In particular, there was limited impact on levels of worklessness (Crowley et al, 2012) and there was little change in the key indicators of social capital (Lawless, 2010). Levels of resident participation tended to be modest. Mathers et al (2008) note that survey evidence found that only 11% of residents in NDC areas had become actively engaged with their local partnership in 2003 (although the figure was slightly higher, at 15%, the following year). While there were clear variations in levels of participation in different NDC areas, there was no indication that areas in which community engagement was greater achieved better than average outcomes (Lawless and Pearson, 2012). Reflecting on the overall outcomes, Lawless (2010) suggests that the NDCs proved more effective in improving places than the lives of the people who live in them.

A number of potential factors have been put forward to explain these findings. Crowley et al (2012) point to the possibility that the benefits realised within the programme areas were subject to 'leakage', with many of those whose lives had been improved through the interventions opting to move out of NDC areas. The same authors suggest that this tendency for population 'churn' to reduce the apparent impact of NDC programmes was exacerbated by the focus on small geographical areas. In this respect, it is significant that there is some evidence that larger NDC areas tended to do better (Lawless, 2010). Other explanations centre on the dynamics of decision-making. Lawless (2010) points to the difficulties caused by intra-community conflicts in some cases, as well as substantial variations in how committed local agencies were to NDC partnership-working and a general set of tensions in the balance between central government direction and local leadership and control. A further possible explanation for weak policy outcomes, posited by Lawless and Pearson (2012), is that the evidence base is simply deficient. Not only is it difficult to answer the 'counterfactual question' of what would have happened without the policy intervention (NDC interventions may have prevented further neighbourhood decline), but there is also the difficulty that evaluations tend not to extend beyond the life of the programmes and thus offer no scope to assess longer-term legacies (an issue with which the Connected Communities programme has also grappled).

There have been two broad responses to the evidence that community-led regeneration appears to have brought limited benefits. The first response has been to reaffirm the principle of community engagement in urban policy while also making recommendations for changes in policy and practices that could make community leadership more effective. Typically, such accounts advocate a variety of steps to eradicate barriers between communities and local power-holders. These include measures to address the uneven capacity of individual partners, to make further provisions to build the capacity of the local community and to reduce the extent of central direction in regeneration programmes (Taylor, 2003, 2007; Robinson et al, 2005).

The second strand of work has been more critical and has tended to raise fundamental concerns about the conception of community on which community-led regeneration has been based. Dargan (2009) captures the essence of this critique in her observation that the understanding of community that underpinned the design of the NDC was sociologically naive. As she notes, the rationale for NDC is that residents of a neighbourhood have a common set of concerns and a shared view of how the area should be regenerated, and that, as a result, they 'will pull together to raise their area out of poverty' (Dargan, 2009: 309). Yet, the problematic nature of such assumptions has long been highlighted in the literature (Brent, 1997; Hoggett, 1997; Amin; 2005; Wallace, 2010). As Brent (1997: 83) notes, community is 'as much about struggle as it is about unity'.

Dargan's (2009) study of Newcastle NDC reinforces this picture of community engagement as a process of contestation rather than consensus generation. She highlights that among the minority of residents who became involved, there was little evidence of common understanding about the nature or purpose of their involvement. Rather than acting in unison, residents advanced contrasting perspectives on the regeneration process and about their role within it. Thus, what emerged was that multiple 'advocates of different discourses of participation were locked into a struggle for power and authority that threatened the progress of the regeneration' (Dargan, 2009: 315). If the minority of active residents could not find common cause, what about the non-participants, who clearly made up the majority? In the context of wider community divisions, it seems simplistic to dismiss the non-engaged as apathetic. Indeed, it can even be argued, following Mathers et al (2008), that non-participation by residents is often rational. Given the variety of 'survival strategies' that residents in deprived areas adopt, many may well have obvious reasons to seek to avoid the 'gaze of the state'; as such, the dominant approaches to community participation may well be 'fundamentally flawed' (Mathers et al, 2008).

However, the problem extends beyond the fact that neighbourhood residents fail to conform to policymakers' romanticised notions of local community. There is also a tendency for policy discourses to present contradictory approaches to the role of communities. As Amin (2005: 614) observes, local communities have come to be seen, simultaneously, as 'cause, consequence and remedy of social and spatial inequality'. The source of this contradiction, in Amin's view, is that New Labour's focus on community served to redefine the social by localising it (at the neighbourhood level). This conflation of society, community and neighbourhood is then 'thrown back at hard-pressed areas as both cause and solution' (Amin, 2005: 620). In practice, what this means in policy terms is that 'the problem of "failed" places becomes a problem of eliminating bad community and replacing it with good community' (Amin, 2005: 620). These contradictory conceptions of community are, moreover, all the more problematic because of the assumption that restoring community will provide the basis for regeneration. As Amin notes, there are obvious flaws to the logic that communities defined to be in deficit, owing to a lack of social capital, participation and cohesion, are the key to policy programmes that aim to harness the very same resources of community to achieve regeneration.

At the heart of this logical fallacy is a failure to consider why some neighbourhoods came to experience such concentrations of poverty and other social problems in the first place. The vast majority of neighbourhoods experiencing social breakdown today are those that suffered most severely from the economic restructuring of the 1970s and 1980s. These economic changes were, in turn, compounded by key government policies, notably, those that led to the residualisation of social housing as a tenure for the poorest in society, leading to the emergence of neighbourhoods in which as many as half of working-age residents were without employment. Yet, despite evident institutional failures to respond to the dynamics of neighbourhood decline, these same areas have come to be blamed for their own dysfunctionality, in much the same way as they were when social pathology perspectives dominated urban policy. The critique of the CDPs, which briefly led to the reframing of urban policy in the late 1970s, remains as valid as ever. There is no starker reminder of this point than the enormous 'jobs gap' that continues to exist in almost all city-regions outside London (Crowley et al, 2012). There would have to be around 60,000 extra jobs in the former coalfield areas of South Yorkshire, another 64,000 in the Welsh Valleys and a further 100,000 additional jobs in Merseyside for these areas to have employment levels typically found in the South of England (Beatty and Fothergill, 2011).

Placed against this backdrop, the potential explanations for the shortcomings of the NDCs highlighted earlier can be seen in a different light. Virtually all the issues held to have limited the success of community-led regeneration have been identified in studies of previous urban policy programmes. In particular, the tendency for place-based initiatives to either 'fail' by empowering some residents to leave only to be replaced by the disempowered, or to 'succeed' by facilitating the displacement of poorer residents by richer ones, has been well-documented in previous studies. It is for this reason that urban policy programmes, including the NDC, are frequently judged to have a greater impact on places than the people who live in them. The crucial question that then arises is what conclusions we should draw from this evidence with respect to the focus of urban policy. As the final section of this chapter underlines, UK governments since 2010 have clearly provided one possible answer to this question: they have abandoned ABIs entirely.

Regeneration without communities or communities without regeneration?

Lawless (2010) notes that proposals for regeneration policies did not feature in the policy statements published by any of the three main parties in the run-up to the 2010 election. Subsequently, under the Conservative–Liberal Democrat coalition which governed from 2010 to 2015 the nature of urban policy bacame far clearer. In essence, we have entered a phase of post-urban policy. For the first time in 40 years, there are no ABIs in England targeted at the most deprived areas. Following the election of a Conservative majority administration in May 2015, there are no signs of such initiatives being reintroduced. What this abandonment of urban policy means with respect to communities and regeneration is slightly less certain, however. Are deprived areas simply being abandoned or has government policy instead shifted from a place-based to a people-based approach to regeneration (Crowley et al, 2012)? To put it another way, are we now in an era of communities without regeneration or one of regeneration without communities?

Although dated, perhaps the most useful summary of the new approach to regeneration is provided by the Department of Communities and Local Government's (2011) publication *Regeneration to enable growth: what government is doing in support of community-led regeneration*. The title is something of a misnomer. What the document really highlights is that central government is retreating from regeneration as part of a wider Conservative agenda emphasising 'localism' and the 'Big Society'. Community-led regeneration means, in this view, that regeneration is not a task for government. Instead, the role of government is to provide the relevant freedoms and frameworks for local responses, but it is for others to develop initiatives. Yet, another shift is also evident. Whereas 'community' had, misleadingly, become synonymous with 'neighbourhood' in regeneration policy from the early 1990s onwards, the use of 'community' after 2010 has tended to refer variously to residents' groups, voluntary sector bodies, the local authority or even the city-region. This approach has been underpinned by a range of other initiatives, including City Deals, Community Budgeting, Whole Place Budgeting, and Tax Increment Financing. At the same time, the resources being directed to deprived areas have been cut substantially. It is not just that spatially targeted ABIs have come to an end. Changes to the way in which central grants are allocated to local authorities have had a far greater impact, disproportionally affecting the most deprived areas (Wilks-Heeg, 2011). It is therefore virtually certain that post-regeneration policies founded on localism and the Big Society will widen the gaps between places and communities (Crowley et al, 2012). These policy trajectories will continue under the Conservative majority government elected in 2015.

Conclusion

Despite 40 years of ABIs designed to tackle the problem, the persistence of urban social problems remains all too evident. In this light, it is difficult to argue with Lawless's (2010: 24) conclusion that the assumptions that policies have made about what can be achieved are generally unrealistic and that 'the whole policy area needs to be given a sense of realism'. Yet, such a call for realism only serves to remind us of the absence of any political agreement about the most effective means of tackling concentrated urban social deprivation. Where these contrasting political and ideological approaches were previously reflected in the contrasting phases, and partial circularity, of urban policy experimentation, they are now played out in other policy debates, notably, those associated with welfare reform, austerity and the devolution of powers to city-regions.

This chapter has also highlighted some paradoxes about the role which academic research, and other forms of knowledge, have played in the urban policy context. While academic knowledge has often been instrumental in highlighting shortcomings and bringing about policy shifts, urban policy programmes have generally ignored the overwhelming evidence presented in academic research about persistent policy failure. Many academic commentators would agree with the conclusions reached by Amin (2005: 630) that regeneration cannot be tackled through initiatives at the local level, but instead requires an approach that is located in 'a wider political economy of decentred power and redistributive justice'.

However, the likelihood of such an approach being adopted in the short term seems remote. Certainly, there have been some moves under the Coalition to decentre power, but this process has taken place alongside major reductions in central government funding to local authorities and, in effect, an abandonment of the principle that deprivation indicators should determine the distribution of such funds. Where New Labour localised the social through its approach to urban policy, the Coalition localised responsibility for urban social problems, and this looks set to continue. However, it would be a mistake to regard the end of ABIs as the end of urban policy experimentation. In effect, the current governmental approach to urban problems is the largest, and riskiest, urban policy experiment to date. If it fails, it will be the residents of Britain's most deprived neighbourhoods who will, once again, pay the price.

Note

[1] Early UK government urban policy interventions applied to England and Wales. Following devolution in the late 1990s, urban policies diverged across England, Wales, Scotland and Northern Ireland. Accounting for these differences is beyond the scope of this chapter, which primarily considers the English experience.

References

Amin, A. (2005) 'Local community on trial', *Economy and Society*, 34(4): 612–33.

Atkinson, R. and Moon, G. (1994) *Urban policy in Britain: the city, the state and the market*, London: Macmillan.

Beatty, C. and Fothergill, S. (2011) 'The prospects for worklessness in Britain's weaker local economies', *Cambridge Journal of Regions, Economy and Society* 4(3): 401–17.

Brent, J. (1997) 'Community without unity', in P. Hoggett (ed) *Contested communities*, Bristol: Policy Press, pp 68–83.

Callaghan, J. (1968) Statement to the House of Commons, HC Deb, 22 July 1968, vol 769, c40.

Crowley, L., Balaram, B. and Lee, N. (2012) *People or place? Urban policy in the age of austerity*, Lancaster: The Work Foundation.

Dargan, L. (2009) 'Participation and local urban regeneration: the case of the New Deal for Communities (NDC) in the UK', *Regional Studies* 43(2): 305–17.

Department of Communities and Local Government (2011) *Regeneration to enable growth: what government is doing in support of community-led regeneration*, London: DCLG.

Department of the Environment (1977) *Policy for the inner cities*, Cmnd 6845, London: HMSO.

Fothergill, S. (2005) 'A new regional policy for Britain', *Regional Studies* 39(5): 659–67.

Hoggett, P. (ed) (1997) *Contested communities: experiences, struggles, policies*, Bristol: The Policy Press.

Imrie, R. and Raco, M. (2003) *Urban renaissance? New Labour, community and urban policy*, Bristol: The Policy Press.

Lawless, P. (2010) 'Urban regeneration: is there a future?', *People, Place and Policy Online* 4(1): 24–8.

Lawless, P. and Pearson, S. (2012) 'Outcomes from community engagement in urban regeneration: evidence from England's New Deal for Communities programme', *Planning Theory & Practice* 13(4): 509–27.

MacLeavy, J. (2009) '(Re)Analysing community empowerment: rationalities and technologies of government in Bristol's New Deal for Communities', *Urban Studies* 46(4): 849–75.

Mathers, J., Parry, J. and Jones, S. (2008) 'Exploring resident (non-) participation in the UK Deal for Communities regeneration programme', *Urban Studies* 45(3): 591–606.

McCulloch, A. (2004) 'Localism and its neoliberal application: a case study of West Gate New Deal for Communities in Newcastle upon Tyne, UK', *Capital & Class* 28(2): 133–65.

Rhodes, J., Tyler, P. and Brennan, A. (2005) 'Tackling social exclusion at the neighbourhood level: new findings from the national evaluation of the single regeneration budget', *Urban Studies*, October 42(11): 1919–46.

Robinson, F. and Shaw, K. (1991) 'Urban regeneration and community involvement', *Local Economy* 6(1): 61–73.

Robinson, F., Shaw, K. and Davidson, G. (2005) '"On the side of the angels": community involvement in the governance of neighbourhood regeneration', *Local Economy* 20(1): 13–26.

Robson, B., Bradford, M., Deas, I., Hall, E., Parkinson, M., Evans, R., Garside, P. and Harding, A. (1993) *Assessing the impact of urban policy*, London: HMSO.

Social Exclusion Unit (1998) *Bringing Britain together: national strategy for neighbourhood renewal*, London: Cabinet Office.

Tallon, A. (2010) *Urban regeneration in the UK*, London: Routledge.

Taylor, M. (2000) 'Communities in the lead: power, organisational capacity and social capital', *Urban Studies* 37(5/6): 1019–35.

Taylor, M. (2003) *Public policy in the community*, Basingstoke: Palgrave Macmillan.

Taylor, M. (2007) 'Community participation in the real world: opportunities and pitfalls in new governance spaces', *Urban Studies* 44(2): 297–317.

Thornley, A. (1991) *Urban planning under Thatcherism*, London: Routledge.

Wallace, A. (2010) *Remaking community: New Labour and the governance of poor neighbourhoods*, Aldershot: Ashgate.

Wilks-Heeg, S. (1996) 'Urban experiments limited revisited: urban policy comes full circle?', *Urban Studies* 33(8): 1263-80.

Wilks-Heeg, S. (2011) '"You can't play politics with people's jobs and people's services": localism and the politics of local government finance', *Local Economy* 26(8): 635–51.

THREE

Connecting community to the post-regeneration era

Peter Matthews and Dave O'Brien

Introduction

This chapter aims to bridge the discussion of the history of community in urban regeneration with the rest of the book. It does this by advancing a central argument: that urban policy has entered a post-regeneration era. This argument runs alongside a specific discussion of the 'Connected Communities' programme. The chapter begins by outlining how and why the era of urban regeneration came to an end, building on the discussion in Chapter Two, with a specific focus on the combination of broader socio-economic structures and ideological decisions that have shaped urban policy since 2010. The ideas of localism, city mayors, Big Society and decentralisation are considered, along with practical developments such as the National Planning Policy Framework. These agendas and events are then used to understand the 'Connected Communities' programme and the way that its focus, specifically on co-production and co-development with communities, has come to represent the leading edge of academic research in this area. The chapter concludes by looking forward to the rest of the book, arguing that we are now in a post-regeneration era, and what is more, we need new ways of knowing this.

The chapter does this in three ways. In the first instance, it questions the sustainability of discussing regeneration in the current policy context. It therefore introduces the idea that the UK, but England in particular, may be in a 'post-regeneration' state, based on current academic definitions of the term. This builds on discussions of the post-political that featured in both the scoping for 'Connected Communities' (Tsouvalis and Waterton, 2011) and discussions of urban regeneration itself (Deas et al, 2013). In this context, the unquestioned dominance of much of the 'What works?' approach to urban policy (as discussed in Chapter Five), along with the insistence on the primacy of economic growth, has led policy narratives away from what have traditionally been seen as the defining features of urban regeneration: both spatially targeted initiatives in specific neighbourhoods (Matthews, 2012; Deas et al, 2013) and as linked to major building and development projects (Miles, 2010; Plaza, 1999). The argument here is that the lack of public and private funding, along with the marginalisation of those elements adding value to regeneration projects, such as culture or community development, means that a different era is facing those involved in the practice of, or research on, regeneration. It is also, much more importantly, facing those living with the consequences of what comes after the great regeneration boom under New Labour, most notably, people facing immediate hardships in the most deprived neighbourhoods in the UK.

Second, the argument for post-regeneration is continued in the extension of the discussion of the history of community in urban regeneration begun in Chapter Two. We present a brief overview of policy and practice under the Coalition government, particularly the National Planning Policy Framework (NPPF) and Local Enterprise Partnerships (LEPs), showing how continuity in the form of competition and central control sits uneasily with important developments in the funding afforded to the local level and the narrative of 'empowering' communities and individuals at the most local spatial scale.

Finally, this chapter uses lessons from a range of Arts and Humanities Research Council (AHRC) 'Connected Communities' scoping studies to engage with the policy developments outlined in the previous sections of the chapter. The chapter shows both how policy and practice can be characterised as post-regeneration and how the 'Connected Communities' programme, in the form of best practice lessons drawn from the extensive set of literature reviews commissioned by the AHRC, has played a part in bringing post-regeneration policy into being. The *practice* of post-regeneration is thus an important point of dialogue for the set of case studies that follow in the rest of the book.

Are we in a post-regeneration era?

Current policy practices that are privileging the role of communities helping themselves over and above other forms of development, such as large area-based initiatives or spending on large buildings (eg museums or libraries), immediately suggest that we are in an era of post-regeneration. The various meanings of urban regeneration also suggest that this is the case. This can be shown by considering three definitions found in two introductory texts. For Tallon (2013: 4), urban regeneration 'in the 1980s focused on economic growth and property development, and used public funds to lever in largely undirected market investment, as exemplified in London's Docklands'. Here, urban regeneration is contrasted with ideas of state-led urban renewal in the 1960s and 1970s or the much wider concern with community and social exclusion found in urban regeneration policy in the New Labour era of the 1990s and 2000s. Turok (2005, cited in Tallon, 2013: 5) offers a tripartite understanding of urban regeneration, whereby it: changes the nature of a place by involving communities and local agencies; cuts across the departmental expertise and capabilities of government based on the problems needing to be solved; and involves partnerships between different stakeholders. For Turok, urban regeneration is, ultimately, the bringing together of people, business and place. This is consistent with the New Labour narrative of urban regeneration, as reflected in policy approaches that sought to cut across both levels and sectors of government activity.

However, Jones and Evans (2013) highlight how regeneration is most usually associated with the built environment, rather than questions of community. They draw the distinction between community-focused forms of *renewal* under New Labour in England and *regeneration*, which is more closely linked to both building projects and economic activity. This distinction is important as we argue that the dominant focus on organic community activism is one of the important forms of contemporary urban policy that is distinct from previous regeneration policy in England, among a broader collection of changes associated with the election of the UK Coalition in 2010.

Indeed, this cuts across party lines. There are many parallels between the communitarian co-production and cooperative agenda being pursued by Ed Miliband as leader of the Labour Party and localism and the Big Society (Sage, 2012). These parallels are intertwined with the quiescence of Labour to the view that there is no alternative to austerity, suggesting that a permanent shift in policy framing has occurred in the UK. The 'good times' of regeneration in the decade of growth will never return. Definitional questions aside, the divergence between transformations of the urban fabric and community-focused projects gestures towards a more fundamental change in the landscape of urban policymaking. There has been a continued rescaling of the grounds upon which policy interventions take place for communities and government at all levels.

Where are we now? Urban policy in an age of austerity

As Stuart Wilks-Heeg discussed in Chapter Two, urban policy in England has now moved into a new era. The New Labour era, which focused on spatial redistribution through strong interventions at a variety of levels, has ceased (Allmendinger and Haughton, 2012). These included: Regional Development Agencies (RDAs) and regional planning; neighbourhood renewal; and initiatives such as TotalPlace (Bailey and Pill, 2011; Baker and Wong, 2012; Matthews, 2012). In 2011, the Communities and Local Government Committee sternly criticised the eponymous department, stating that its regeneration strategy 'gives us little confidence that the Government has a clear strategy for addressing the country's regeneration needs' (Communities and Local Government Committee, 2011: 3). It seems that we have returned to the 'patchwork quilt' of regeneration, as famously criticised in a report of the Audit Commission (1989).

Current policy may best be described as a 'mixed economy' of interventions. At the neighbourhood level, the Localism Act has provided a legislative framework for communities to be empowered to run their own local services and own assets to become more sustainable (Department of Communities and Local Government, 2010). In practice, this has often meant deprived communities taking over services such as libraries, leisure centres and community centres that would otherwise close (Hastings et al, 2015). At the regional level, regional planning and economic development has been replaced by LEPs and the 'duty to cooperate' placed upon local authorities when they develop their Local Development Frameworks (Baker and Wong, 2012). At its best, this is leading to striking examples of partnership-working, such as in Greater Manchester. Elsewhere, the failure to cooperate is preventing economic development. Cities such as Manchester and Glasgow are signing City Deals to take advantage, through increased business rates income and reductions in welfare benefits, of any economic development that they deliver.

However, as we began to suggest earlier, the policy change is most marked by its focus on the 'local' through localism. Localism is, of course, not a singular concept, nor does it have a well-defined core. Moreover, as Hildreth (2011) identifies, the Localism Act itself contains at least three forms of localism: conditional, community and representative. However, there is a clear contrast between Coalition localism and the approaches adopted by New Labour, even the later concepts of 'double-devolution' used during the Brown era (Durose, 2009). The ideological drive behind this change is the view that the New Labour era was one of 'Big Government' (as described in Conservative Party discourses), particularly under Gordon Brown (for detail of these debates in the North East of England, see Shaw and Robinson, 2012). This 'Big Government', according to the Conservatives, took responsibility away from individuals and communities and left them dependent on the state. Thus, the policy solution is focused on reducing the state in order to allow a 'Big Society' to flourish in its place, whereby government is left to act as 'a leading force for progress in social responsibility ... by breaking [open] state monopolies, allowing charities, social enterprises, and companies to provide public services, devolving power down to neighbourhoods, making government more accountable' (Cameron, 2010: 1, cited in Raco, 2013: 46).

The differential, unequal implementation of this ideology can be explored through two policy areas that were synonymous with the regeneration era of the Labour governments: land-use planning and regional economic development in the form of LEPs. In the former, in their pre-election 'Green Paper', *Open source planning*, the Conservative Party (2009) placed the blame for low housing development levels at a regional planning system that was top-down and forced communities to accept massive new developments with little local benefit. Rather, *Open source planning* would lead to a development of good Conservative values and 'will engage local communities and foster a spirit of innovation and entrepreneurship' (Conservative Party, 2009: 2). If communities could, first, be economically incentivised and, second, be empowered through neighbourhood planning to choose how much new housing they wanted and where, then new home completions would increase. Arguably, this misunderstood opponents to new housing as rational economic actors, but it did empower the vocal, affluent communities that are particularly against new housing development and are effective at stopping it (Matthews et al, 2015). The contradictions of this policy in implementation were exemplified by successive Conservative planning ministers, and the Chancellor of the Exchequer himself, supporting opponents of new development within their own constituencies while favouring massive increases in housing development nationally, with the presumption in favour of sustainable development in the NPPF.

The implementation of the NPPF also exemplified this ongoing tension between localism and centralisation, which has been a marker of UK policy for decades (Allmendinger and Haughton, 2012). Given statutory weight by the Localism Act, the NPPF sought to combine the numerous previous central government planning policy documents into a single document. This, in itself, was not that controversial;

however, the document also contained a 'presumption in favour of sustainable development'. That is, if a local area did not have an up-to-date Local Development Framework or Neighbourhood Plan in place, then development had to be allowed if it met a test for sustainability (Department for Communities and Local Government, 2012). In legal terms, this was merely a reiteration of an existing position. However, the furore, particularly in the right-wing press, over the belief that the presumption in favour of development would lead to vast swathes of rural Southern England being concreted over stung the Coalition and the consultation had to be extended. While the legal points of the presumption in favour of development can be discussed at length, in its presentation, this policy looked like the government centralising decision-making, on the one hand, while devolving responsibility for planning to neighbourhoods, on the other (Allmendinger and Haughton, 2012).

Further, all subsidiary plans have to be in agreement with the NPPF, including any Neighbourhood Plans produced under the other provisions of the Localism Act. This meant that neighbourhoods could not oppose all development – they had to allow sufficient land for all types of development based on the technical tools of planners, such as housing market needs and demand assessments, as well as any international and national environmental designations. This was a highly circumscribed localism that could only be successfully negotiated by those with the necessary skills and knowledge. Moreover, it is a circumscribed localism with direct dependence on local power differentials, as shown by case studies in Chapters Seven and Eleven.

This iteration of localism, with its problematic power differentials, is displayed in the other example from Coalition policy, the LEPs. The LEPs were designed to fill the gap between the rescaled urban policy following the removal of the regional level, but also reflected the partial development of cross-agency working at the local level under Labour. The LEPs were set up on a voluntary basis, with the initial 39 LEPs replacing eight RDAs. The move from regional development to LEPs is reflected in the spatial scale of the LEP, with most of the 39 LEPs consisting of cross-local authority conglomerates mapping onto metropolitan or smaller sub-regional levels, for example, Derby and Nottingham, Greater Manchester, The Leeds City-Region, and Croydon to Brighton. There is no single model for LEPs, although the Northern cities reflect both the economic footprint of the city at the core of the LEP and the pre-1980s' county council areas (though this is not the case in the West Midlands, with several LEPs outside of Birmingham). Back to the future, as it were, for sub-regional policy.

In some ways, LEPs return to older long-standing themes in urban policy, with their role in delivering economic growth, the competitive nature of LEP funding and the overrepresentation of business on LEP boards (Pugalis and Shutt, 2012; Ward and Hardy, 2013). Indeed, the focus of almost all 39 of the LEPs was economic growth, in particular, based on partnership with businesses (Pugalis and Shutt, 2012).

This focus on partnership activity to deliver economic growth raises a question for this chapter's post-regeneration thesis. On the one hand, the dominance of business and the focus on LEPs competing for funding reflects very traditional Conservative urban policy, in keeping with much of the regeneration era identified by Tallon (2013; see also Deakin and Edwards, 1993). However, on the other hand, LEPs have been starved of funding and reflect the deeply uneven set of policy outcomes associated with localism (Pike et al, 2013), which, much like the NPPF, involves devolving the responsibility to cross-local authority partnerships but, in the grand tradition of English policy, keeping the finances firmly centralised. Indeed, it is easy to agree with Haughton and Allmendinger's (2013: 2) assessment that:

> With every new government for the past 20 years proclaiming its supposed allegiance to greater local empowerment and repudiation of past centralist approaches, it is hard not to be skeptical about the current claims that are being made about radical changes in approach. Such skepticism is not assuaged by the none-too-subtle criticisms of planning as a 'burden on business' by some in Government, the dusting off of repackaged initiatives such as enterprise zones and the deployment of centralizing and growth driven policies under a thin veneer of localism in the National Planning Policy Framework.

Moreover, Peck et al (2013) argue that, perversely, LEPs have led to the need for more central command and control in terms of industrial policy as they lack the capacity to do effective industrial policy at the scale upon which they were created. This centralising thrust is supported by Deas et al's (2013) research on the capacity of LEPs, suggesting an uneven set of resources across the 39 LEPs, contradicting the insistence that LEPs will be a nationally comprehensive urban policy focused on growth in their respective areas.

What is notable about LEPs is that the structures foregrounding both business and economic growth exist at the same time as LEP policy rhetoric is framed very strongly by ideas of removing power from the centre, bringing levels of government closer to individuals and place-based communities, and making those same sets of actors responsible for the success or failure of local area economic policy. This idea, albeit ambivalent in terms of an argument for post-regeneration, has been crucial in the critiques of regeneration and the subsequent forms of best practice constructed by community-focused academic interventions.

The unequal nature of localism

The unequal nature of the responsibilisation and empowerment agenda is part of a much wider suite of changes to social policy pursued by the Coalition government. The context matters as, following Raco's (2013) assessment of the relationship between broader social policy and New Labour's planning policy, the form that ideas such as localism take is shaped by the larger narratives of state–society relations displayed in the Coalition's general approach to social issues. Just as the state, in planning, will be reconfigured to allow for citizen control, a package of reforms, including the cap on welfare benefits, the 'bedroom tax' (or 'removal of the spare room subsidy') and Universal Credit, have been explicitly designed to lessen welfare 'dependency', witnessed by the Secretary of State for Work and Pensions Iain Duncan-Smith in his Easterhouse epiphany (Slater, 2014; Macdonald et al, 2014). Focused on those groups that were typically the subject of spatial urban regeneration policies – the long-term unemployed, young unemployed people and lone parents – these reforms derived from the view that people had become dependent on an overly generous welfare state, trapped on benefits that paid more than employment. The system had to be changed to make work pay; even if the work was casual, insecure, on zero-hours contracts and left households in extreme poverty.

This is both a continuation of and contrast to urban policy from 1997 to 2008, which was predicated on macroeconomic growth and the associated expansion of public funds (Jones and Evans, 2013). A rising tide of gross domestic product (GDP) would pour into the most deprived cities and neighbourhoods, producing new economic opportunities in derelict inner cities (Atkinson and Eckardt, 2004). Regeneration programmes and labour market interventions in deprived neighbourhoods would connect residents to these new economic opportunities – trendy coffee shops provided the millennial generation with semi-skilled employment (Whitehead, 2004). The the recession following the 2007/8 financial crisis destroyed this model. The narrative of austerity emerging afterwards turned a crisis of private debt – exemplified by the empty city-centre buy-to-let flats in places such as Manchester and Leeds – into a crisis of public debt as banks were nationalised.

Discursively, this was used to drive the policy changes described earlier. Welfare benefits were no longer affordable because of austerity. Neighbourhood planning, and the presumption in favour of development, were needed to restore the UK economy to its previous dependence on the construction sector, and to depress ever-increasing house prices that stretched out of reach of a population with falling incomes. However, while public funds were afforded to some local areas, the revanchist nature of much of urban policy did not go unnoticed in academic work (for a summary of this continuity, see Lees, 2014).

While the ideological nature of localism and the Big Society has been noted (Bednarek, 2011; Buser, 2012; Sage, 2012), a continued criticism of these policies at the local level is that austerity has meant that they are simply not resourced sufficiently to be successful. Analysis of where the cuts to the local government budget in England are falling have demonstrated that those areas that are seeing the biggest cuts are those that received substantial quantities of discretionary regeneration, economic development and sports and cultural funding under the New Labour governments. Deprived local authorities saw their budgets cut by up to 21% compared to 15% in the most affluent local authorities, and even increases in some of the richest areas of the country (Hastings et al, 2013). Four years into the unprecedented period of austerity for local government, basic services such as street-sweeping are being ended as luxuries that cannot be afforded (Hastings et al, 2015). Raco (2013) further highlights that the simplistic state–society dualism that was present in much of the Coalition's planning policy ignores the need for state support for capital growth.

The point here is that regeneration policy, in localism and the LEPs, will be useless without robust links to areas of policy such as transport and social welfare. The NPPF and LEPs have conspicuously left out cross-cutting, cross-departmental policy working from the devolution of responsibility, provided little direct financing, and burdened the local level with responsibility for successful delivery. This is a major break with New Labour's *attempts* at joined up policymaking. Further, basic services to support the Big Society and put localism, or community empowerment, into action in a meaningful way are the very services that are seen as the 'low-hanging fruit' for cash-strapped local authorities to cut across the UK: community education and development; community arts and cultural policy; museums and art galleries; and libraries.

'Connected Communities' and urban policy: critical voices and best practices

In the previous section, localism is essentially an elite form, whereby local 'leaders' are charged with responsibility for economic growth. This, of course, is in keeping with local democracy, previous 'community leadership' policies and the Westminster tradition (Rhodes, 1997; Sullivan, 2007). However, it is largely untroubled by the growing sound of dissent from academic understandings of what being and doing 'local' is in the modern world, most notably, around the idea of community. These critiques are exemplified in recent work by Lees (2014), a long-standing critic of urban policy in the UK. Regeneration, for Lees, often presented communities with false choices between forms of social exclusion by property development, or the decline and collapse of local housing estates. Most crucially, for Lees, residents' views and ideas were commonly misrepresented in the process of consultation and involvement, raising profound questions for the policy process associated with regeneration. In this respect, 'the mode of governance ... remains as top down as it did in the 1960s' urban renewal schemes, despite new processes of public participation' (Lees, 2014: 932).

This example ties into how the term 'community' was deployed during the height of the regeneration era, as discussed by Wilks-Heeg in Chapter Two of this volume (Wallace, 2010). Lees' recent work is one of many voices showing how the ideas of community were transformed from representation and participation to techniques of financial and risk management (Dicks, 2013), forms of governmental control (Imrie and Raco, 2003), or class-based conflict (and, in some ways, defeat) (Allen, 2008).

Critical voices surrounding the way in which community has been deployed in policy are touched on in Chapter One. The 'Connected Communities' programme raised some controversy during its early phase and some questions have persisted. In the present era, as described earlier, with cuts to services by local and national authorities to the very things that 'Connected Communities' is interested in – community development, co-production, community heritage and participatory arts practice – one major criticism has to be voiced as to whether the AHRC has merely stepped into a funding void left by others. Is 'Connected Communities' a very expensive community development project that should be provided for not by academic research funding, but rather by mainstream funding?

If 'Connected Communities' did replace some of this expenditure, then it was distributed not necessarily according to need, as with former regeneration expenditure, but rather by whether the research application met the characteristics of rigorous, high-quality research as defined by the AHRC. Allocation of scarce resources, then, becomes a lottery based on the social or geographic propinquity of a community to a university with access to funding (as one 'Connected Communities' grant recipient openly acknowledged in conversation with one of the authors: "we received the funding and then went looking for a nearby community to work with"), or on whether the community had an existing relationship with a university (see Chapter Six). It could even be the case that the funding was not supporting communities – ordinarily those most economically deprived – that needed help in co-producing research with academics. Research council funding could have been spent on facilitating relationships with middle-class or more affluent communities that had the existing stock of social and cultural capital to effectively engage with university partners, and perhaps could use this relationship to further their own aims, even if this exacerbated existing socio-economic inequalities.

One part of 'Connected Communities' that may be able to offer clues as to how to move beyond these criticisms, as well as critically engaging with core policy terms such as community, co-production and localism, are the series of scoping studies funded during the initial phase of 'Connected Communities'. The first wave funded and published 44 studies (with a further 31 ongoing in a second round focusing on arts and humanities perspectives), including work on ethics, time, authority, transnationalism and the historic environment. Given the discussion of the definitional issues associated with regeneration that opened this chapter, it is difficult to demarcate those studies that are and those that are not relevant to thinking about best practice, or the state of the art, in this area. Examples such as online social networking, schools policy, place-specific histories or sport volunteering could all be seen to fit with some aspect of regeneration in its widest sense. However, in light of the policy focus on economic growth and its elision with often punitive welfare policy, the remainder of the discussion is confined to those areas that are directly relevant to this set of ideas.

This leaves 11 studies, with a focus on: co-production (as an important tool in both research and policy); power; the Big Society or localist political agendas; and urban policy or politics. The 11 exclude policy-focused reviews in areas such as policing, migration and health care. The scoping studies offer clues as to the state of the art in community research, as to the meaning of community and, in addition, as to the relationship between the academy and society.

There are five key points to be drawn from the 11 selected studies. First, the question of power is never absent from any form of research, whether co-produced, participatory or merely aimed at communities. Indeed, new models of 'power to', as opposed to 'power over', are needed to negotiate work in contexts that 'are not homogeneous, egalitarian social spaces where people are just waiting for the government to hand over power so that they can pursue pre-formed agendas' (Pearce, 2011: 6). 'Power to' thus requires capacity-building and needs to move beyond the simplistic dichotomy between an over-mighty state and communities as its subjects or, indeed, its victims.

Second, the dominant policy model for community involvement is one that aims at getting citizens to be involved in the existing practices of the local and national state. This misses the opportunity to develop independent (and alternative) community action of the type demanded in the Coalition's rhetoric of localism and Big Society (Goodson et al, 2011; Laffin et al, 2011; Painter et al, 2011). Most notable in this context is the need for government to relinquish funds and control and to create supportive legal environments, all of which are important lessons in the case studies that follow.

Third, there is, to a lesser or greater extent, still the danger of an elision, even where consciously avoided, between 'community' and social problems. This was a core characteristic of New Labour policy (Lees, 2014) and thus even colours some of the reviews (for a summary of the problems with this discourse, see Hamalianen and Jones, 2011). 'Community' can be used positively to represent social belonging, collective well-being, solidarity and support, but also negatively in relation to social problems and problem populations (Crow and Mah, 2011: 3). It is here that work needs to be done in reclaiming the positive associations of community from the negative focus, which is how it has ended up playing out in policy.

Fourth, Tsouvalis and Waterton (2011) stress that notions of participation are used to depoliticise questions of urban policy. This has parallels in the discussion of both the NPPF and LEPs, whereby shifts to more localised forms of decision-making are accompanied both by major funding cuts (or the reallocation of funds in ways that make them more unevenly spread) and the retention of specific decision-making powers by the centre, paying lip service to localism and participation. While this new approach is not co-opting citizens' participation to justify often preordained policy approaches, it is some distance from the rhetoric and promise of localist discourse.

Finally, three of the reviews (DCRT, 2011; Durie, 2011; Durose et al, 2011) looked at co-production from a variety of perspectives, identifying the multiple nature of this idea. It can apply to a range of activities: some of which are about the sharing of power; some of which are about the recognition of expertise; and some of which are about neither, ending up replicating the issues that co-production is being used to alleviate or challenge. There is little or nothing in any of the reviews that is about economic growth. Thus, 'communities', 'co-production' and 'localism' are all ultimately, in the ways outlined in 'Connected Communities', very distant from the purpose of how policy has imagined these words and the discourses associated with them.

Conclusion

This chapter was an attempt to introduce the idea of 'post-regeneration' as a way of framing current urban policy. It did this by exploring two of the Coalition's core policies, in the form of neighbourhood planning and the NPPF/LEPs. These two policies were framed by the context of state restructuring around the disputed narratives of austerity, localism and the Big Society. These developments were seen as being partially continuations of existing policy themes, such as centralisation, but also marking a break with the past through the stripping away of resources along with the increased claims of the devolution of power and localism. Most notably, the chapter used lessons from 'Connected Communities' work designed to clear the ground for research projects to critique and engage with Coalition policy. The use of this set of 'Connected Communities' work provides a bridge between the discussions in the opening section of the book, around the policy-focused discussions, and the case studies and academically reflective chapters that follow in Parts Three and Four.

References

Allen, C. (2008) *Housing market renewal and social class*, Abingdon: Routledge.

Allmendinger, P. and Haughton, G. (2012) 'The evolution and trajectories of English spatial governance: "neoliberal" episodes in planning', *Planning Practice & Research* 28(1): 6–26.

Atkinson, R. and Eckardt, F. (2004) 'Urban policies in Europe: the development of a new conventional wisdom', in F. Eckardt and P. Kreisl (eds) *City images and urban regeneration*, Oxford: Peter Lang, pp 33–65.

Audit Commission (1989) *Urban regeneration and economic development: the local government dimension*, London: The Audit Commission.

Bailey, N. and Pill, M. (2011) 'The continuing popularity of the neighbourhood and neighbourhood governance in the transition from the "big state" to the "Big Society" paradigm', *Environment and Planning C: Government and Policy* 29(5): 927–42.

Baker, M. and Wong, C. (2012) 'The delusion of strategic spatial planning: what's left after the Labour government's English regional experiment?', *Planning Practice & Research* 28(1): 83–103.

Bednarek, A. (2011) 'Responsibility and the Big Society', *Sociological Research Online* 16(2): 17.

Buser, M. (2012) 'Tracing the democratic narrative: Big Society, localism and civic engagement', *Local Government Studies* 39(1): 3–21.

Communities and Local Government Committee (2011) *Regeneration: sixth report of session 2010–12*, London: House of Commons.

Conservative Party (2009) *Open source planning: Green Paper*, London: The Conservative Party.

Crow, G. and Mah, A. (2011) *Conceptualisations and meanings of 'community'*, Swindon: AHRC. Available at: http://www.ahrc.ac.uk/Funding-Opportunities/Research-funding/Connected-Communities/Scoping-studies-and-reviews/Pages/Scoping-Studies-first-round.aspx (accessed 1 April 2015).

Durham Community Research Team (2011) *Community-based participatory research: ethical challenges*, Swindon: AHRC. Available at: http://www.ahrc.ac.uk/Funding-Opportunities/Research-funding/Connected-Communities/Scoping-studies-and-reviews/Pages/Scoping-Studies-first-round.aspx (accessed 1 April 2015).

Deakin, E. and Edwards, J. (1993) *The enterprise culture and the inner city*, London: Routledge.

Deas, I., Hincks, S. and Headlam, N. (2013) 'Explicitly permissive? Understanding actor relationships in the governance of economic development', *Local Economy* 28(7/8): 718–37.

Department for Communities and Local Government (2010) *Decentralisation and Localism Bill: an essential guide*, London: HM Government.

Department for Communities and Local Government (2012) *The National Planning Policy Framework*, London: CLG.

Dicks, B. (2013) 'Participatory community regeneration: A discussion of risks, accountability and crisis in devolved Wales', *Urban Studies*, 51(5): 959–77.

Durie, R., Lundy, C. and Wyatt, K. (2011) *Researching with communities*, Swindon: AHRC. Available at: http://www.ahrc.ac.uk/Funding-Opportunities/Research-funding/Connected-Communities/Scoping-studies-and-reviews/Pages/Scoping-Studies-first-round.aspx (accessed 1 April 2015).

Durose, C. (2009) 'Front-line workers and "local knowledge": neighbourhood stories in contemporary UK local governance', *Public Administration* 87(1): 35–49.

Durose, C., Beebeejaun, Y., Rees, J., Richardson, J. and Richardson, L. (2011) *Towards co-production in research with communities*, Swindon: AHRC. Available at: http://www.ahrc.ac.uk/Funding-Opportunities/Research-funding/Connected-Communities/Scoping-studies-and-reviews/Pages/Scoping-Studies-first-round.aspx (accessed 1 April 2015).

Goodson, L., Coaffee, J. and Rowlands, R. (2011) *Resilient, mutual self-help in cities of growing diversity*, Swindon: AHRC. Available at: http://www.ahrc.ac.uk/Funding-Opportunities/Research-funding/Connected-Communities/Scoping-studies-and-reviews/Pages/Scoping-Studies-first-round.aspx (accessed 1 April 2015).

Hamalainen, L. and Jones, K. (2011) *Conceptualising community as a social fix*, Swindon: AHRC. Available at: http://www.ahrc.ac.uk/Funding-Opportunities/Research-funding/Connected-Communities/Scoping-studies-and-reviews/Pages/Scoping-Studies-first-round.aspx (accessed 1 April 2015).

Hastings, A., Bailey, N., Besemer, K., Bramley, G., Gannon, M. and Watkins, D. (2013) *Coping with the cuts? Local government and poorer communities*, York: Joseph Rowntree Foundation.

Hastings, A., Bailey, N., Besemer, K., Bramley, G., Gannon, M. and Watkins, D. (2015) *The cost of the cuts? The impact on local government and poorer communities*, York: Joseph Rowntree Foundation.

Haughton, G. and Allmendinger, P. (2013) 'Spatial planning and the new localism', *Planning Practice and Research* 28(1): 1–5.

Hildreth, P. (2011) 'What is localism and what implications do different models have for managing the local economy?', *Local Economy* 26(8): 702–14.

Imrie, R. and Raco, M. (2003) 'Community and the changing nature of urban policy', in R. Imrie and M. Raco (eds) *Urban renaissance? New Labour, community and urban policy*, Bristol: The Policy Press, pp 3–36.

Jones, P. and Evans, J. (2013) *Urban regeneration in the UK: theory and practice*, London: Sage.

Laffin, M., Mawson, J. and Ormston, C. (2011) *Connecting communities to the nation*, Swindon: AHRC. Available at: http://www.ahrc.ac.uk/Funding-Opportunities/Research-funding/Connected-Communities/Scoping-studies-and-reviews/Pages/Scoping-Studies-first-round.aspx (accessed 1 April 2015).

Lees, L. (2014) 'The urban injustices of New Labour's "New Urban Renewal": the case of the Aylesbury Estate in London', *Antipode* 46(4): 921–47.

Macdonald, R., Shildrick, T. and Furlong, A. (2014) 'In search of "intergenerational cultures of worklessness": hunting the yeti and shooting zombies', *Critical Social Policy* 34(2): 199–220.

Matthews, P. (2012) 'From area-based initiatives to strategic partnerships: have we lost the meaning of regeneration?', *Environment and Planning C: Government and Policy* 30(1): 147–61.

Matthews, P., Bramley, G. and Hastings, A. (2015) 'Homo economicus in a Big Society: understanding middle-class activism and NIMBYism towards new housing developments', *Housing, Theory and Society* 32(1): 54–72.

Miles, S. (2010) *Spaces for consumption: pleasure and placelessness in the post-industrial city*, London: Sage.

Painter, J., Dominelli, L., MacLeod, G., Orton, A. and Pande, R. (2011) *Connecting localism and community empowerment*, Swindon: AHRC. Available at: http://www.ahrc.ac.uk/Funding-Opportunities/Research-funding/Connected-Communities/Scoping-studies-and-reviews/Pages/Scoping-Studies-first-round.aspx (accessed 1 April 2015).

Pearce, J. (2011) *Power in community: a research and social action scoping review*, Swindon: AHRC. Available at: http://www.ahrc.ac.uk/Funding-Opportunities/Research-funding/Connected-Communities/Scoping-studies-and-reviews/Pages/Scoping-Studies-first-round.aspx (accessed 1 April 2015).

Peck, F., Connolly, S., Durnin, J. and Jackson, K. (2013) 'Prospects for "place-based" industrial policy in England: the role of Local Enterprise Partnerships', *Local Economy* 28(7/8): 828–41.

Pike, A., Marlow, D., McCarthy, A., O'Brien, P. and Tomaney, J. (2013) *Local institutions and local economic growth*, SERC Discussion Paper 150, London: SERC.

Plaza, B. (1999) 'The Guggenheim–Bilbao Museum effect', *International Journal of Urban and Regional Research* 23(3): 589–92.

Pugalis, L. and Shutt, J. (2012) 'After regions: what next for Local Enterprise Partnerships?', *Regions* 286(2): 23–5.

Raco, M. (2013) 'The new contractualism, the privatization of the welfare state and the barriers to open source planning', *Planning Practice and Research* 28(1): 45–64.

Rhodes, R.A.W. (1997) *Understanding governance: policy networks, governance, reflexivity and accountability*, Buckingham: Open University Press.

Sage, D. (2012) 'A challenge to liberalism? The communitarianism of the Big Society and Blue Labour', *Critical Social Policy* 32(3): 365–82.

Scottish Government (2012) *A consultation on the proposed Community Empowerment and Renewal Bill*, Edinburgh: The Scottish Government.

Shaw, K. and Robinson, F. (2012) 'From "regionalism" to "localism": opportunities and challenges for the North East', *Local Economy* 27(3): 232–50.

Slater, T. (2014) 'The myth of "Broken Britain": welfare reform and the production of ignorance', *Antipode* 46: 948–69.

Sullivan, H. (2007) 'Interpreting "community leadership" in English local government', *Policy & Politics* 35(1): 141–61.

Tallon, A. (2013) *Urban regeneration in the UK* (2nd edn), London: Routledge.

Tsouvalis, J. and Waterton, C. (2011) *Public participation as a process of de-politicisation*, Swindon: AHRC. Available at: http://www.ahrc.ac.uk/Funding-Opportunities/Research-funding/Connected-Communities/Scoping-studies-and-reviews/Pages/Scoping-Studies-first-round.aspx (accessed 1 April 2015).

Wallace, A. (2010) 'New neighbourhoods, new citizens?', *International Journal of Urban and Regional Research* 34(4): 805–19.

Ward, M. and Hardy, S. (2013) 'Introduction', in M. Ward and S. Hardy (eds) *Where next for LEPs?*, London: Smith Institute.

Whitehead, M. (2004) 'The urban neighbourhood and the moral geographies of British urban policy', in C. Johnstone and M. Whitehead (eds) *New horizons in British urban policy: perspective on New Labour's urban renaissance*, Aldershot: Ashgate, pp 59–73.

FOUR

When things fall apart

Sue Cohen and Morag McDermont

Introduction

In this chapter, one of the authors tells the story of when she was chief executive officer (CEO) of the Single Parent Action Network (SPAN) and became involved in an ambitious urban regeneration project in the early 2000s, a venture that then fell apart under the pressures of 'austerity'. SPAN is now a partner in 'Productive Margins: Regulating for Engagement', a collaboration between two universities and nine community organisations that aims to co-produce a series of research projects, and is one of the largest single research programmes to be funded through 'Connected Communities'.

This story illustrates the two different strands enmeshed in this book. In the urban policy context, it can be viewed as a 'post-regeneration' story, showing the ways in which changes in urban policy shape and interact with the lived reality of the organisations, people and social structures that the policy is focused upon. For the 'Connected Communities' programme, it illustrates why community organisations and academics must be concerned with the regulatory mechanisms that enmesh the everyday activities of communities at the margins if the programme is to engage with issues of social justice.

The experiences in the SPAN story are the experiences of many, and have led to the research question that guides the 'Productive Margins' programme: how can we explore ways in which the 'creativity, passions and skills' of communities at the margins are able to produce new ways of thinking and 'new experiments in living'? The 'Productive Margins' partnership intends to explore new imaginings of social space, ways of 'mobilising neighbourhoods' and ways in which digital spaces can and have been harnessed to shift power relations. Perhaps most critically, we aim to both explore *and produce* 'spaces of dissent' in which to challenge dominant discourses of 'austerity' and 'we're all in it together', discourses that are all too frequently used to regulate and control social space, negating dreams of equality, the celebration of difference and of living differently.

The authors of this chapter were both involved in the design of the 'Productive Margins' programme from the outset. One, an academic with research projects on social housing and third sector advice organisations, became the principal investigator responsible for bringing together the bid to the Economic and Social Research Council. The other, the then CEO of SPAN (a national network founded in 1990, creating space for dissenting voices in furthering social and economic justice for families living in poverty), became a co-investigator and 'adviser' to the academics. Sue was one of the founding members of SPAN alongside single-parent volunteers. However, like many involved in the 'Connected Communities' programme, neither Sue nor Morag can be pigeonholed as 'community activist' or 'academic'; both have held multiple identities. Morag had worked in social housing organisations for many years; Sue had previously undertaken a Master's degree at Bristol University while working at SPAN. In part, it was these hybrid origins of many of those involved in the programme that led us to develop a methodology that would challenge existing power relations between academics and communities. In order to move away from models in which *only* academics set the research parameters, a 'Productive Communities Research Forum' has been established, itself a space of experimentation, in which community organisations and academics can together co-produce the research programme, from research questions to data collection, analysis and outputs.

The rest of the chapter falls into three sections. In the first, we explore, through the story of SPAN and its struggles with urban governance, some dimensions of the regulatory environment that dictates urban spaces. This is a case study that is all about praxis – the linking of theory with practice – but theory is seldom given much space in the everyday battles of survival. We therefore use the next section to explore, through a conversation between the authors, some theoretical questions that this story raises about the nature of power relations within urban spaces: about regulatory structures, localism, time, space, dreams and embodiment. It is this intermeshing of theory, policy and praxis that we believe can be made possible in the 'Productive Margins' co-produced research programme. We conclude with some observations on the important role that universities must play in opening up and maintaining safe spaces for reflection, discussion and dissent.

The story

In the early 1990s, SPAN was based in a run-down shop in the inner city of Bristol. With no prospect of expansion, we began to look around for a larger space. Falling school rolls suggested moving into a redundant school might be a good bet. We put our name forward and were unexpectedly offered redundant premises attached to an existing primary school. A helpful council employee brokered the deal with us before she emigrated to Australia, leaving the process of signing the lease to be sorted after the move.

In the event, the lease was never signed. In the 16 years that followed, SPAN's solicitor made intermittent attempts to sort out the details. Men would arrive from Property Services, measure up, go away and nothing would be heard. When we contacted Property Services, the plans had either disappeared or new staff were in charge.

To some extent, this suited us as we could develop our services unimpeded by local council controls. On their part, Property Services expressed the benefit of keeping the building safe. Although the headmistress had feared that single parents would be stalked by violent men, in the 16 years that followed, there was no act of violence and only one reported theft – a coat, returned the same day. There was no vandalism either, except when an unruly school pupil smashed our crèche windows.

We did have to contend with the vacuum left by the helpful council employee. Although the building was rent-free, SPAN was responsible for internal improvements: some officers began to lay down demanding requirements for heating systems, plumbing, electrical works and so on at SPAN's own expense. We rose to the challenge and in the following decade, were left to our own devices, unregulated and sidelined by urban regeneration policies.

Social movements are not necessarily 'bound by the rules of the game and the institutionalisation of dominant values and norms' (Castells, 1983: 294). SPAN had a rare organisational culture, heterogeneous and homogeneous, involving single parents from diverse ethnicities and cultures, who, at the same time, experienced common oppressions – poverty, lack of childcare, unemployment and, for many, the aftermath of fleeing family violence or war. Rather than the stereotype of their inability to cope, more remarkable are the strategies they developed to protect their families. This tenacity and care extended to the organisation, influencing SPAN's long-term struggle to survive. We became experienced in strategies for survival and praxis. Individual and organisational praxis developed through an analysis of different and common oppressions, and by keeping abreast of economic and political change. The very context that threatened the organisation politicised those involved.

In challenging the government-led stigmatisation and increasing poverty of one-parent families, SPAN received no government support in the 1990s. Conversely, SPAN accessed funding from bodies targeting the deepening inequalities in society – the European Commission, the National Lottery and anti-poverty trusts. We supported innovative development projects involving self-organising groups across the UK and were involved in transnational research with groups in most countries of the European Union (EU). We helped to establish the European Anti-Poverty Network in England and the UK Coalition Against Poverty.

Although a national project, SPAN's premises increasingly became a haven for local single-parent families, personally and politically. Projects began organically – we could fulfil dreams. The Single Parent Study Centre, a multicultural crèche and home-grown model action projects were influenced by our embodied knowledge, as well as by our national and international work. We were thinking and acting both locally and globally, unusual for our time. Grace Allen, long-term volunteer and trustee, said recently:

> "We wouldn't have now if we didn't have then: the dedication of the volunteers, the ethos of what we believed in. When Pearl and Yvonne, as black women, gave out those flyers on the streets of Northern Ireland and Scotland, they believed in togetherness. Together, we were a force.... We believed we could be a force in Europe. We took the lead on childcare, food issues, benefits. And it did make a difference. It allowed people to feel they could have a voice on poverty. Those in power were not able to give them what they need because they didn't live it."

Our base was adjacent to an isolated wasteland area riven through by a motorway; a derelict space increasingly used to buy drugs and sex. Our premises, however, were cocooned from the ever-increasing environmental degeneration. Volunteers helped decorate; outside, single parents worked on flower and herb gardens, attracting a wide variety of wildlife. The community architect who came to help us reconfigure the space thought it a sanctuary in the middle of the inner city. SPAN had effectively created its own local urban regeneration programme.

The architect, aware that the expanding childcare and training courses were outgrowing the space, set up an impromptu meeting with the Bristol director of the Scarman Trust and the head of libraries at Bristol City Council (BCC). The three came up with a remarkable proposition – to build a new community library that would include SPAN's increased training and childcare needs. 'Build it over there', I said, pointing in the direction of the wasteland, and so the Junction 3 development was conceived.

There were to be many challenges along the way, but these three were movers and shakers who lived and breathed urban regeneration. Furthermore, this was the turn of the century, the start of a new political and economic era beginning to address endemic poverty and community disintegration, and giving some leaders space to exercise power. SPAN joined the partnership. We gained community empowerment funding from government programmes to draw in local residents, and in 2005, we successfully bid to the Government Office of the South West to take the proposed capital infrastructure project from its groundwork stage to planning permission and practical development on the derelict site.

A major barrier was land ownership – small bits of land owned by individuals, developers and BCC that needed to be brought under common ownership. The head of libraries, now promoted to the head of cultural services, drove this through the BCC. Knightstone Housing Association came in as a major further partner, with a complex capital/ land deal to build homes and small workshops on the site.

Some of us from SPAN began to envision an urban space that would transform lives – a safe, nurturing, experimental space, bringing together fragmented communities, shared by people from different generations, cultures and backgrounds. Could this be possible? I regularly had to suspend my disbelief. Grassroots organisations (including the ones I have worked for) are too often located in spaces that are degenerating, temporary or contentious.

The partnership got down to detail. We developed a business plan and set up the Junction 3 Company to further the vision and manage the community development. The Library Service, with the support of the partners, put in a Big Lottery application for nearly £2 million – a bid that included both the library and SPAN's additional childcare and training needs; SPAN offices, crèche and courses were to continue alongside in the school buildings. The funding bid was successful and a building company was commissioned.

It was around this stage that things began to fall apart. A man sent by Property Services to unblock the drains in our school-based premises remarked casually to one of our administration staff that the BCC would shortly be taking the building back due to increased school rolls – communication was never Property Services' strongest point. A one-line email from the Children and Young People's Services (CYPS) confirmed this – the Compact[1] was clearly not part of their agenda; nor, it seems, were SPAN's training and childcare services, some hundreds of families, 50-plus staff and various community offices. Not only would the Junction 3 development take some years to complete, but it was never intended to house all of our services.

Staff, trustees and volunteers, appalled at the shabby treatment and the prefigured organisational disintegration, sprang into lobbying mode. However, the lobbying of key decision-makers to at least stave off immediate eviction got nowhere. With the support of the trustees, I began to explore a regulatory strategy. Aware that the BCC had failed to adhere to the Public Sector Equality Duty, I approached the London-based Public Law Project to take up the case, knowing that it had already won a successful action for the Southall Black Sisters on similar grounds.

Tramping through the snow from Kings Cross to meet our new solicitor, I wondered at the time and energy expended in threatening to take the BCC to court, energy that surely could have been better directed if it had followed its own regulatory policies?

The Public Law Project proved indispensable. CYPS acknowledged that it had yet to undertake an equalities appraisal. In the time it took to do this and publish the ensuing findings, SPAN gained a breathing space of two years to find temporary accommodation and plan strategically for the future. We negotiated with council officers to locate all SPAN's local services at Junction 3 (they adamantly refused our national/international offices). It was agreed that SPAN would contribute to our fair share of the overhead costs (approximately £17,500 pa) and that we would find the funding needed to deliver our training/childcare services from elsewhere. We then worked with the BCC and the developers to plan the kit-out of the crèche, training rooms and the roof garden, all to be completed with Lottery Funding.

However, as is often the case, unanticipated regulatory delays held up the process. First, two blue tits were found nesting on the site; environmental controls meant that only once their young had flown the nest could the building begin. Then, the bodies gradually emerged, over 70 of them, on the site of an old graveyard. By the time the birds, the bodies and other unforeseen obstacles had been overcome and building could begin, two years had passed. We were 'in different times' and the Junction 3 partnership started to unravel and eventually fell apart.

Different times

If not for the butterfly effect of the bodies and the birds, would SPAN now be based in Junction 3? A lot happens over a two-year period. Restructuring meant a new head of libraries and the closure of the Scarman Trust Bristol office. Austerity foreshadowed huge council cuts to staff and services. Capacity-building support programmes were terminated. Partnerships were no longer the order of the day – by 2011, the Library Service controlled the reins of Junction 3. SPAN was no longer to be a partner in the flagship project, but, instead, a commercial tenant at a rental cost of £57,000 per annum to fill the gaping hole in the overall running costs. No thought was given as to how SPAN would sustain such outgoings. 'We are in different times' became a BCC mantra – and indeed we were.

Once again, SPAN was placed in an adversarial position, foreshadowing another diversionary campaign. Many single parents and community members felt that SPAN had been wronged: "We all felt disillusioned and betrayed by the way we were treated. We were joyous. It turned to ashes in our mouths." We felt driven to address that betrayal.

Then, again, out of the blue, we were approached with an offer that, once explored, we could not refuse. The women's training organisation where SPAN's local services were temporarily accommodated asked if SPAN would consider a merger. With this would come extensive premises for training and childcare, as well as a cafe (we had always dreamed of a cafe at Junction 3), tenants providing ongoing income, and, importantly, space for both SPAN's local *and* national offices. SPAN could hold onto its organisational vision without being completely beholden to the vagaries of BCC decision-making, market forces and haphazard regulatory controls.

However, where did this leave the community vision for the Junction 3 area of the city? Once SPAN decided to relocate, the Library Service wanted the Junction 3 Community Interest Company (CIC) to close down in order "to wipe the slate clean". What was to become of the multicultural crèche, roof garden, cafe and community activities for learning and enjoyment? Were these dreams to evaporate? Furthermore, what of those who had contributed to the plans – the volunteers and local residents led to believe that this would be their space?

When the Junction 3 Library opened in early 2013 with speeches from a range of civic dignitaries, and with the history of its development proudly displayed on the walls, no mention was made of our vision, or, indeed, of SPAN's or the Scarman Trust's involvement in its nine-year development history. Rather, the project was described as a partnership between the Library Service and Knightstone Housing Association. "Herstory" had indeed been wiped clean.

There is, however, a postscript to this tale. A small group of community activists, including a local councillor, decided that we wanted to hold on to what we could of the vision by maintaining the Junction 3 CIC. A petition was placed on the BCC website by a volunteer to keep the CIC going, although it was then taken down by council officers who objected to its content. However, the Lord Mayor Elect had already signed the petition, along with other significant local leaders. So, the Junction 3 CIC remains and, following a small successful external funding application, supports pop-up markets, a gardening group and in the library itself, ESOL (English for Speakers of Other Languages) classes, an occasional crèche and small-scale community activities alongside supportive library front-line staff. More projects are in the pipeline. So, given where this story began and the pressures of austerity, are there any real losers? The Junction 3 housing has proved popular, albeit next to a motorway; the BCC preserved the new library, with 100,000 users in the first year of opening; SPAN has a future in a large multipurpose building.

Meanwhile the small Junction CIC remains productive on the margins. This may not be the vision we had hoped for – so many possibilities were lost along the way – and empowered local residents still jostle with the regulatory agendas of both localism and neoliberalism but neither has the slate been entirely wiped clean.

Reflections on theory and practice

On embodied voices

Sue: "In writing this story, I've really appreciated the opportunity to use my own voice. So much of my writing in my day job was constricted by the requirements of funding applications, reports, etc, disembodied in fact. It's been so important for me to reflect on my embodied experience – I know all stories are partial, but as a feminist, I also know that embodied experience is integral to understanding the politics at play and too often excluded in political analysis.

The interrelationship of thoughts, feelings, passion and voice in informing analysis are what has kept me motivated for so long in working to effect change."

Morag: "Bringing embodied experiences of communities at the margins to the foreground of research is one of the aims of 'Productive Margins'. This led to the framing of the central research question as drawing on 'creativity, passions and skills' of communities at the margins to produce new ways of thinking and 'new experiments in living'. SPAN's story contains so many elements of what we meant when we set up 'Productive Margins' as a research programme on regulation."

Sue: "I hadn't clocked until I worked on the story how much dreams/visions figured in SPAN's and Junction 3's history, successes and survival, but how, when it came to the crunch, we had no substantive way of communicating this. Even our modes of expression were regulated by systems and structures that contained and controlled us. The hegemonic, neoliberal discourse was found wanting when we tried to explain the dreams and vision, leaving many decision-makers baffled: they said, 'Where's the market? What's the business plan?'"

Morag: "Creating 'new experiments in living' is one of our dreams for 'Productive Margins', giving us different spaces for reflection and expression. For me, this has always been one of the assets that academic research can bring, and because 'Productive Margins' is not constrained by academic disciplinary boundaries, the programme will enable us to experiment with different forms of expression through film, drama, storytelling, music and arts practice, which can include dreams. This different mix we hope will be critical, both in providing a new critique and in effecting regulatory change."

Sue: "In developing that critique, we will have the opportunity to consider how projects are affected by post-regeneration policies and politics over time, as well as the hidden history that impacts on the legacy of regeneration. Bureaucratic systems edit out 'herstory' in particular. Local government is always restructuring, especially when responding to current government policies – changes of staff are endemic, documents get lost, agreements become a thing of the past

– creating the illusion that it is possible 'to wipe the slate clean'. In the process, we are negated."

On power, neoliberalism, participation and resistance

Morag: "For me, the scholarship around 'histories of the present' that has come out of Michel Foucault's (1991) work has influenced the way I have theorised practice; what we come to understand in the present as 'truths' – maybe 'common sense' is better – arises out of the many paths we have gone down to get where we are now.

Your story shows that law and regulation only come into play when there are also active mechanisms to enforce them, and actors who are called upon to do that enforcement. Power, as Foucault has said, is only present in action. We often talk about possessing power, but we can only know power when it is embodied in people or things that can act. So, for SPAN, the regulatory power of the Public Sector Equality Duty could only come into play when you found the Public Law Project to act on your behalf.

Opening up ways of seeing law and regulation is an important element of our research programme so that we can come to see the operation of power and regulatory practices, enabling us to challenge what has come to be common sense, to transgress boundaries and so occupy space differently."

Sue: "Structural power and the power of agency have all too often been juxtaposed in critical theory, whereas those involved in social action have to, by necessity, consider how they interrelate. I feel that I am always in the process of unravelling this.

It goes without saying that you can't begin to understand urban development and localism agendas without understanding the structural/global impact of neoliberalism on those agendas. If I were reductionist, I'd say that I experienced the politics of the 1990s in resistance mode, what some view as New Labour communitarianism in partnership mode, and austerity somewhere back on the margins. Structural forces were clearly at play. But the reality was much more multifarious and intricate, forming common patterns and numerous contradictions within and outside of the local authority.

For example, many conspiracy theories run about the way local authorities operate but the story is a much more complex one of 'them' and 'us'. Officers come in with their different briefs and ideological ways of working, often working in silos so that one part of the council does not know what the other is doing, especially when the community are in the picture. This meant that, in my role, I would, on the one hand, be challenging the council, on the verge of taking them to court. On the other hand, I was part of an exceptional flagship partnership with council officials, grounded on the belief that, between us, our vision could contribute to a better life for those living in the neighbourhood. Both council officials and the voluntary sector exercised their power in bringing this vision into play.

This all changed, of course, when the concept of power-sharing fell apart under austerity. It could be argued that the power possessed by market forces, once austerity kicked in, marginalised us all: that a hegemonic environment can be contradictory, amenable, concerned, but when the chips are down, can prove ultimately steadfast. Things may fall apart for others – but neoliberalism holds.

So much energy appeared to have been wasted – isn't this how hegemony works – keeping activists focused on individual campaigns – without the time, space, resources to address the bigger picture? The demands it placed on my role were an inevitable diversion from our national development/partnership work with grassroots organisations.

But then maybe, on reflection, it was not a waste of energy given the outcomes. The Junction 3 site has been successfully regenerated. SPAN remains productive on the margins – perhaps better placed in the face of turbulent and unpredictable times?"

On space

Morag: "Your story is also very much about space/place, and space as a thing that has value in itself. The space that you wanted was not just any old space, it needed certain qualities. So, for example, the fact that Junction 3 could not have housed the national/international part of SPAN could have led to a different type of organisation in the future.

Equally, the story brings into focus many other factors that perhaps we have not considered sufficiently as to how they impact on power relations – the motorway, drains, the dereliction of the site, blue tits – these all impact on the visions and dreams of the future. All too often, urban policy treats the non-human elements of space as objects with no role in the power relations. For SPAN, if it had not been for the blocked drains you would not have been forewarned of the council's intentions; the blue tits held up progress but maybe their presence allowed city-dwellers (for whom 'wildlife' is often absent) to see and pay attention to other elements of the environment?"

Sue: "The 'Disobedient Objects' exhibition in the Victoria & Albert Museum illustrated how non-human elements, whilst not possessing agency themselves, can effect change as part of the ecologies of space (Flood and Grindon, 2014: 14–15)."

Morag: "In your story, it is the quality of the space that is also valuable because it had to enable the enactment of dreams. These dreams might contain elements of 'mobilising neighbourhoods', allowing dissent and harnessing the digital, the three key themes of 'Productive Margins'."

Sue: "For a long time, I've been interested in the colonisation of space (Cohen, 1998). Reflecting on this story, I revisited the symbolic nature of the Junction 3 space to us activists. It was a space rent apart by the M32, dividing the communities of St. Pauls, St. Werburghs, Easton and Lawrence Hill, with those on foot driven into potentially dangerous underpasses (especially for women and young people). It was a junction for cars. We re-imagined it as a junction that reunited communities …"

Morag: "… there are so many stories of urban regeneration where reconfiguring space is assumed to reconfigure community …"

Sue: "I also revisited what happens on the margins of hegemonic spaces, those abandoned territories that are both dangerous and, at the same time, can be reclaimed and made safe. In writing this story, I was struck by the fact that our very marginalisation gave us space to develop our own pocket of urban regeneration. It was also a space where we had the freedom, as bell hooks (1994: 208) puts it, to 'transgress boundaries with no fear of policing – a space of radical openness on the margins'."

Morag: "In my work, I have sought to understand how people, in their everyday lives, understand law and regulation. Often, law is only conceived of in terms of criminal law – in terms of police and of action that takes place in courts. There is a cultural production of law and regulation through the images of law in the media, which are all about crime (whether it is newspaper reporting of murder or television dramas about the police). Even then, it's a narrow view of crime. How often do we see corporate crime, or are accidents at work framed as employers being criminally negligent?

I'm struck that you identify your feeling about SPAN's space as one where there was 'no fear of policing'. When SPAN occupied the disused school, it was still a regulated space, regulated by the physical nature of the space, by the drainage and sewer pipes (probably dating back to the Victorians) and by the power available on site. Although there was no lease, the council was able to enmesh you in a set of legal rules that they would be able to invoke if you decided to not move out of the premises when they required them. But, yet, you were able to feel safe from being 'policed'."

Conclusion: praxis and the role of universities

Part of the ambition that we had for 'Productive Margins' was to turn the university inside out. Universities need to enable safe spaces where academics/practitioners/activists can reflect, explore and debate questions about regulation and how best to open out those structures to communities at the margins. Practitioners and activists in communities, particularly those at the margins constantly struggling to find resources to keep going, are seldom allowed space for reflection; traditionally, this has been what academics are meant to do. In setting up structures to co-produce academic research, we hope to create a still point in a turning world (to paraphrase T.S. Eliot [1966] in 'Burnt Norton'), a space where experience, reflection on that experience and theoretical understandings of power relations co-produce research questions that can challenge those values that have led to (among other things) the closing down of the promise of urban regeneration.

Universities are public spaces. Universities have a responsibility for creating and maintaining such safe spaces for reflection, argument and dissent.

Note

[1] The Compact was first made in November 1998, and renewed in 2010 under the Coalition government. The National Council for Voluntary Organisations (NCVO) promotes the Compact as an agreement between the government and the voluntary and community sector, setting out key principles and ways of working that improve their relationship for mutual advantage. This includes cross-sector working to ensure that organisations are better able to influence and deliver services and policies that will have the most positive impact within their communities.

Bibliography

The following books inspired the thinking that went into this chapter:

Castells, M. (1983) *The city and the grassroots: a cross-cultural theory of urban social movements*, London: Arnold.

Cohen, S. (1998) 'Body, space and presence. Women's social exclusion in the politics of the EU', *European Journal of Women's Studies* 5(3/4): 367–80.

Eliot, T.S. (1966) 'Burnt Norton', in T.S. Eliot, *The four quartets*, London: Faber & Faber [Burnt Norton first published 1935].

Flood, C. and Grindon, G. (eds) (2014) *Disobedient objects*, London: V&A Publishing.

Foucault (1991) 'Governmentality', in G. Birchall, C. Gordon and P. Mitchell (eds) *The Foucault effect*, Chicago, IL: University of Chicago Press.

hooks, b. (1994) *Outlaw culture – resisting representations*, London: Routledge.

Part Two
Exploring epistemologies

FIVE

Microsolutions for megaproblems: what works in urban regeneration policy?

Max Nathan[1]

Introduction

This chapter sets 'Connected Communities' in the context of current thinking on urban regeneration and local economic development, in particular, the state of area-based policies in the current 'post-regeneration' era (see Chapter One, this volume). The chapter first provides a brief run-through of post-1997 state-led regeneration in the UK, tracing the shift in England from holistic neighbourhood-level social inclusion initiatives to economically focused local growth programmes. As noted by Wilks-Heeg in Chapter Two, the role for 'community' in all these programmes is ambiguous. Next, the chapter highlights the political, policy and structural 'shocks' that have hit these regeneration models since 2007, and discusses where this leaves neighbourhood-level activity in particular. In theory, localism should set the scene for a flowering of neighbourhood-level, community-led regeneration activity. However, spending cuts, and regeneration's refocusing on economic outcomes leaves challenges for holistic neighbourhood programmes. The theories of change invoked in such interventions, 'Connected Communities' included, suggests that economic impacts will be small; however, in principle, such programmes can provide crucial public 'goods', and so have an important non-economic rationale. Demonstrating causal impacts on well-being seems beyond much of the existing evidence, however. Getting a sense of 'what works' in urban regeneration is extremely challenging given the multifaceted nature of the programmes and the complex socio-economic processes in which they intervene. The UK's emerging experimentalist paradigm could help generate a convincing evidence base for neighbourhood-level urban regeneration, but there are also real constraints to what localism and the 'what works' agenda can do, particularly under austerity. Structured forms of evidence need to be layered alongside local, contextual knowledge.

Basics

'Regeneration' is surprisingly tough to define. Conceptually, it involves seeking to improve one or more of the social, economic and physical conditions in a given place or places, typically urban, and generally in the context of some economic shock or deeper trend. Real-world regeneration programmes typically try to combine these goals. Roberts and Sykes (2000: 10–17) define such holistic strategies as:

> a comprehensive and integrated vision and action which leads to the resolution of urban problems and which seeks to bring about a lasting improvement in the economic, physical, social and environmental conditions of an area that has been subject to change.

Practitioners' ambitions can go beyond this. As Pugalis and McGuinness (2012: 342) suggest, regeneration is also 'a symbolic process that aims to foster a geography of hope'. Very large 'big push' initiatives conform to this: under the US New Deal, for example, the Tennessee Valley Authority initiative attempted to shift the economic trajectory of an entire region from the 1940s to the 1960s (Kline and Moretti, 2014). More recently, the former East Germany has seen a series of programmes that aim to induce structural convergence with the West (Kluve, 2010). In fact, most regeneration activities assert this transformational quality to some extent; alongside concrete improvements, policies often set out to signal change and/or enrich everyday life.

The regeneration policy toolkit is large, encompassing land remediation, remodelling physical property, investment in transport or other infrastructure, training and active labour market initiatives, business advice, tax breaks and other fiscal measures, policing, neighbourhood management, and a range of community development activities – which encompass many of the engagement and social capital-building activities covered under 'Connected Communities'.

This structural breadth explains some of the definitional difficulty. Regeneration budgets and tools tend to be distributed across government scales and functions, making it harder for policymakers and the public to 'see' it as a coherent function. In England, for instance, 'regeneration' lives simultaneously in the planning, business, policing, employment, transport and housing functions of central and local government, as well as in the Treasury. Regeneration was only formally defined for England in 2009 (DCLG, 2009), and more narrowly than in Scotland and Wales (see McGuinness et al, 2015; see also Chapter Two, this volume).

State-led regeneration in the UK has evolved from anti-poverty initiatives in the 1960s, to physically oriented business-led programmes, such as the Urban Development Corporations, in the 1980s, and then towards a joined-up approach in the 1990s, beginning with City Challenge and the Single Regeneration Budget (SRB) programme before shifting into multiple area-based initiatives (ABIs) under New Labour (see Chapter Two, this volume). The next section considers these policy evolutions in more detail.

Policy typologies, shifts and shocks

We can group state-led urban regeneration activities in the UK into three broad types. 'Type 1' is estate renewal, largely carried out by local authorities, with social landlords and private developers taking an increasingly large role. Labour's Decent Homes programme is the most obvious example of this approach. 'Type 2' programmes involve joined-up activity at the large estate or neighbourhood level, coordinated by local partnerships (often led by councils or social landlords). The aims of such programmes are holistic, combining economic, social and physical/environmental goals. The New Deal for Communities (NDC), Neighbourhood Renewal Fund (NRF) and some smaller SRB programmes fall into this category. 'Type 3' programmes are larger ABIs with economic objectives, operating on large urban sites or city-wide. City Challenge, larger SRB programmes, the Local Enterprise Growth Initiative (LEGI) and Housing Market Renewal (HMR) are all examples of this type, as are Enterprise Zones (EZs) and the Regional Growth Fund (RGF).

'Connected Communities' research can be placed – loosely – within this typology.[2] The agenda sits most closely with Type 2 activity, both in terms of scale and in terms of its social welfare focus. However, there are also important differences. Type 2 programmes have clear geographical boundaries, often administrative, while 'Connected Communities' initiatives are more likely to work through social networks and structures, which are not always spatially bounded. Equally, neighbourhood regeneration under Labour was 'concrete' and concerned with mainstream public services and specialised local initiatives; 'Connected Communities' activity has been largely outside the scope of state activity and is more exploratory/participatory in the methods adopted. Notably, the focus on emancipatory processes of co-production is very different in ethos from the state-led emphasis on service delivery and outcomes.

Arguably, 'community' is only present in the background of such initiatives, if at all. One logic model in Type 3 initiatives is that fiscal incentives induce firms into a deprived area, thus creating job opportunities for local residents. Alternatively, physical improvements operate as a signal of confidence in a locale, attracting (net) inward investment that feeds through to greater local employment (Tyler, 2011). This rationale was predominantly used with office/commercial property, although a variant was used in HMR: a more middle-class residential 'offer' was intended to improve the neighbourhood fabric, change the resident mix and attract local shops and services (Leather and Nevin, 2013).

Under Labour, Type 1 and 2 programmes were broadly linked to the social inclusion and neighbourhood renewal agendas (Social Exclusion Unit, 1998); Type 3 programmes were linked to 'urban renaissance' (Urban Task Force, 1999) and the regional growth agenda (HM Treasury, 2007). Under the Coalition, the remaining Type 3 programmes are linked to the 'rebalancing' agenda and to city-regional initiatives. Type 2 programmes technically continue as part of the Big Society, but, as we shall see, they barely exist in practice.

Shifts and shocks

From 1997 to 2001, a 'holistic' phase of urban regeneration policy (Lupton, 2013) combined Type 1 and Type 2 initiatives. Programmes aimed to address severe inequalities of outcome and opportunity by 'bending' mainstream services towards the poorest, trying to ensure that 'no-one should be seriously disadvantaged by where they live' (Social Exclusion Unit, 1998: 3). Neighbourhood-level programmes were seen as central to tackling spatially concentrated disadvantage. Importantly, programme *targets* were also spatial, so that success was defined as narrowing area-level differences. 'Communities' were typically defined in terms of administrative or physical boundaries (such as a single estate), but on-the-ground action was necessarily more involved.

The 2007 sub-national review of regeneration (HM Treasury, 2007) marked a change in direction, proposing a shift of resources into more narrowly focused economic regeneration (DCLG, 2009). As Lupton (2013) points out, this policy 'shock' highlighted *political* differences between Blair and Brown, but also involved a *spatial* upscaling of activity towards the regional level. In practice, much of the spend was at city-regional level, reflecting cities' role as economic cores (Centre for Cities, 2009).

The financial crisis of 2007 and the subsequent recession led to further shocks. The initial credit crunch collapsed the forward-funding mechanisms that had sustained property-led Type 3 programmes (Parkinson, 2009). The 2010 Coalition government then took a series of policy decisions that radically restructured the institutional architecture and reduced the remaining programme spend, trends that seem set to continue under the current government. At the time of writing, none of the major policy streams since 2000 are still operating, and overall funding has reduced by about two thirds (McGuinness et al, 2015).

As Matthews and O'Brien note in Chapter One, in important senses, this is a 'post-regeneration' era – although programmes like EZs and the RGF do survive, and have some continuities with previous waves of policy. As Lupton (2013: 66) puts it, in some ways, 'the Coalition ... picked up the baton laid down by Gordon Brown, not the one carried by Tony Blair'. In structural terms, there has been a major break, with Coalition and now Conservative Ministers pushing for localism at urban and city-regional scales, devolving limited powers and mainstream budgets from the centre to the urban level through City Deals (Cheshire et al, 2014).

The neighbourhood-level landscape is dramatically different. Holistic neighbourhood-level regeneration has essentially ceased as a state-led activity. Localism was also intended to involve devolution from the city to the community, through various community 'rights' to own and run local assets enacted in the Localism Act 2011 (DCLG, 2011) and through the 'Big Society' agenda. In practice, this community layer to localism has been underdeveloped and underfunded (Pugalis and McGuinness, 2012). Monitoring regimes are also minimal, making it hard to assess what activity, if any, is currently taking place.

'What happened?'

Making sense of these shocks and shifts is important as it moves us towards an understanding of the underlying effectiveness of urban regeneration policies. Superficial reasons for change are easy to identify. First, many Type 3 programmes – particularly property development – became literally unviable after 2007 (Parkinson, 2009). Second, the 2010 and 2015 elections led to changes in priorities and policy choices, towards deficit reduction and away from public spending.

Regeneration programmes are non-statutory and largely targeted at poorer communities and were therefore always at risk from cutbacks.

We can also highlight some deeper issues. As we have seen, the direction of regeneration thinking was already shifting before any macrostructural shocks occurred. The 2007 Sub-National Review highlighted that a decade of regeneration spending had resulted in very little change to regional economic disparities. As such, it put one of Labour's – and Gordon Brown's – principal goals at risk of failure. Further, despite narrowing gaps between conditions in the most deprived neighbourhoods and the rest, *local* spatial inequalities also remained (see later).

Existing regeneration initiatives also came under increasing attack from outside government. In part, this was political: notoriously, Leunig and Swaffield (2009) argued that urban regeneration as a whole had 'failed'. Spatial economists also began to question the premises of ABIs, especially economic initiatives (see, in particular, Glaeser and Gottlieb, 2008). Critics also noted the potential of neighbourhood renewal goals to be undermined by urban renaissance activities, particularly through mixed communities programmes and associated gentrification (Cheshire et al, 2008; Pugalis and McGuinness, 2012; Slater, 2013).

One reaction to these 'shocks' is to argue that effective urban regeneration programmes have been unfairly attacked. Pugalis and McGuinness (2012: 1), for example, describe a gradual 'ostracism and emasculation of regionalised policy frameworks and area-based regeneration initiatives'. They suggest that the shift in English regeneration is a part of a larger neoliberal moment. Localism is simply a wrapper for 'market-based reforms in the pursuit of economic growth' (McGuinness, 2012: 1); policymakers aim for city-regional gains and hope that these trickle down to poorer communities. More broadly, Hildreth and Bailey (2013) highlight that the city-regional focus prioritises some locations over others, and suggest that it has little to offer isolated and/or 'struggling' locations.

Certainly, the *explicit* aim of narrowing area-level economic disparities has gone; however, at the time of writing, it arguably remains *implicit* in the policy rhetoric. For instance, Coalition ministers have explained their desire to 'create a fairer and more balanced economy ... [with] new business opportunities across the country ... the Government is ... determined that all parts of the country benefit from sustainable economic growth' (Department for Business Innovation and Skills, 2010: 6). Whether this is *achievable* is highly debateable, however, especially given reduced resources and the current policy mix.

Rather clearer is the fate of community-focused state regeneration activity. It has essentially disappeared as a state-led activity, in part, because of austerity-driven constraints and, just as importantly, because of a shift in priorities from holistic towards economistic interventions. Lupton (2013) argues that governments have – consciously or not – overlooked the achievements of recent neighbourhood renewal programmes by retrospectively judging holistic initiatives on the basis of economic performance measures. As she puts it, after 2007, 'Labour changed its mind over the purpose of neighbourhood renewal – such that, seen through a new policy lens, its successes could be seen as failures' (Lupton, 2013: 67). At minimum, the Brown administration shifted its priorities: even if neighbourhood renewal was not seen as a failure, neighbourhood improvements were seen as simply less relevant compared to urban and regional economic growth. Furthermore, since 2010, Ministers have preferred to rely on 'Big Society' voluntarism to improve community-level outcomes, rather than put resources on the ground. Also, as Matthews and O'Brien emphasise in Chapter One, while the notion of 'Connected Communities' is strongly linked to 'Big Society' rhetoric, the research programme is not a substitute for actual policy.

So, what 'works' in urban regeneration?

Urban regeneration programmes aim to improve economic, social or physical conditions on the ground. To get a sense of their potential impact, we need to set these programmes in the context of the urban system as a whole. There is a growing body of evidence – from spatial economics and new economic geography, in particular – that casts doubt on the extent of economic impacts that regeneration initiatives can hope to achieve. This still leaves some space for action, however, particularly at the neighbourhood level.

A framework

As in most countries, economic activity in the UK is unevenly distributed across space. Moreover, large economic and social disparities exist within the urban system. As Cheshire et al (2014) put it, recent decades have seen 'resurgence, divergence and persistence' in population, wages and employment rates across and within British cities. These reflect some of the deeper macrostructural shifts that urban regeneration programmes hope to tackle. However, these features are also produced and reproduced by the urban system itself (Storper, 2013).

For instance, the UK's global comparative advantage has gradually shifted towards higher-value manufacturing and services. These changes have important distributional consequences. The UK has developed an edge in activities that disproportionately benefit skilled workers; returns to skill, in the form of higher wages for the best qualified, have been growing substantially. Entry-level employment opportunities have also expanded, but real wages are often low and competition for these jobs is high (Goos and Manning, 2007); labour market institutions have changed, with (*inter alia*) progressively weaker unions and the deregulation of entry-level occupations.

Cities are where many of these shifts play out on the ground. A post-industrial economy largely favours urban locations. Urban agglomeration economies around 'matching', 'sharing' and 'learning' help workers and firms become more productive (Duranton and Puga, 2004). Similarly, agglomeration of culture, retail and leisure provide 'economies of consumption' (Glaeser, 2011). Set against this are the costs of urban location, such as congestion, pollution and living costs, which rise as the urban population rises.

These factors help explain urban success on the average, but they also suggest why locations diverge. Agglomeration economies are self-reinforcing, so that cities with an advantage in certain industries or amenities tend to attract more of the same over time (Overman and Rice, 2008). Historic events and policy choices can lead to path-dependence, helping 'lock' neighbourhoods and cities into specific trajectories (Martin and Sunley, 2006). However, at the same time, technological change and sectoral differences also tend to produce 'production jumps' from higher- to lower-cost locations (Venables, 2006). As a whole, migration between and within cities is substantial, both in terms of daily commuting and moves over the lifecycle (Champion and Fisher, 2004). In practice, of course, ability and resources to move vary over households, with financial and family factors, among other, constraining mobility and helping cement disparities.

This means that processes of urban *resurgence*, as well as divergence, have helped generate new disparities. To put it very crudely, UK cities with an existing service base have tended to expand, while largely industrial cities have – until recently – declined. Resurgent post-industrial cities have seen growing populations, nominal wages and employment figures, alongside a rising cost of living. Global cities like London and New York are extreme cases characterised by substantial labour market polarisation (Sassen, 2001; Buck et al, 2002; Massey, 2007). In 'declining' cities, these processes are reversed: living costs are lower but so are economic opportunities.

If area disparities between and within cities are largely the result of spatial factors, this might suggest that conventional urban regeneration policies could help close them through ABIs. The interaction of individual, institutional and area factors is clearly important in generating spatial difference – not least through agglomeration processes (Storper, 2013). However, the empirical evidence for the UK and other countries suggests that disparities are *primarily* down to 'sorting' (or not) of individuals between locations (Moretti, 2012; Cheshire et al, 2014). Specifically, once area conditions are taken into account, individual characteristics, particularly human capital, directly explain a substantial part of area-level disparities.

All this has important consequences for urban regeneration programmes. First, urban systems are characterised by powerful market forces that generate spatial inequality, operate over the long term and are hard to halt or reverse. Area-level conditions matter in explaining outcomes, but individual characteristics, resources and opportunities appear much more salient. On the face of it, this implies that 'people-based' programmes often stand a greater chance of success than area-level initiatives (Glaeser and Gottlieb, 2008). Second, cities and urban systems are complex socio-economic systems, where effective policy is, in any case, hard to design, and where effectiveness may be limited. Third, for the same reasons, assessing the effects of urban initiatives is challenging, and in many instances, there are likely to be winners *and* losers. Fourth, the adjustment of urban systems is messy and uneven, and is characterised by multiple market and coordination failures.

Note that this leaves the *equity* rationale for regeneration intact but casts doubt on the optimal means for achieving it. An *efficiency* rationale for regeneration interventions remains but the analysis suggests that aggregate impacts will tend to be small and incremental. Put simply, most urban regeneration programmes are 'microsolutions for megaproblems': mitigating larger forces without rolling them back.

Economic regeneration initiatives

These structural constraints on urban regeneration are particularly evident for Type 3 growth initiatives in which a policy generally 'treats' one location and not another. Type 3 programmes can deliver valuable public goods. However, if economic disparities are largely driven by individual or firm-level differences, it follows that such area-based responses are likely to have a limited aggregate effect (Storper, 2011). Local gains from an ABI may also be offset by losses elsewhere: through firms moving into the 'treated' area from a non-treated location; through workers commuting in to take new jobs rather than residents winning work; or via gentrification-related impacts on the local housing market (Glaeser and Gottlieb, 2008; Moretti, 2010).

The limited evaluation evidence on Type 3 programmes tends to bear this out. For example, 1980s EZs in the UK largely shifted employment around rather than creating net new jobs (Office of the Deputy Prime Minister, 1995). The structurally similar LEGI programme appears to have done the same (Einio and Overman, 2013), and evaluations from similar initiatives in the US and France also show little or no net employment effects (Neumark and Kolko, 2010; Mayer et al, 2012). This also implies that the current crop of English EZs is unlikely to have much net employment impact. By contrast, the Regional Selective Assistance programme, which targeted firms, had some positive employment effects (Criscuolo et al, 2012). That suggests the similarly designed RGF should also have some net positive impact.

This still leaves space for programmes to tackle some of the within-city frictions outlined earlier. As Kline and Moretti (2013) point out, for instance, even in high-productivity resurgent cities, labour market dysfunction is common, and active labour market programmes (or hiring subsidies) can help matching. Similarly, area-based *delivery* may also be an effective way to target resources on key groups and individuals (Tunstall and Lupton, 2003). The US Empowerment Zone programme, which combined physical area improvements with firm-level job subsidies restricted to local workers, appears to have put this successfully into practice, improving local environments and raising the wages and employment of local people (Busso et al, 2013). Apart from the policy design, the programme also benefited from the lack of commuting into the target areas, which were seen as 'too dangerous' by many of those living outside.

Even urban-level ABIs that succeed on their own terms have not been able to do much to roll back wider patterns of spatial disparities. In theory, 'big push' programmes such as the Thames Gateway could achieve national rebalancing. Kline and Moretti (2014) provide one of the only evaluations of such an initiative, the New Deal-era Tennessee Valley Authority programme, which aimed to shift the region's economy from agriculture to manufacturing. The programme succeeded in structurally raising local incomes over a period of decades; however, at the national level, gains to the Tennessee Valley Authority region were offset by losses in neighbouring areas.

Neighbourhood renewal

How do these regeneration constraints shape outcomes for Type 1 and 2 programmes? Within cities, sorting arguably plays an even more important role than it does between cities (Cheshire et al, 2014). Where people live within cities partly reflects policy choices, for instance, through the planning system and through social housing allocation mechanisms. It also reflects individual and household preferences for those with the resources to choose. Crucially, though, neighbourhood composition and conditions also reflect the larger structural factors that shape the spatial economy in the first place. As Lupton (2013: 3) puts it: 'some places will always be poorer than others'. However, these spatial disparities are largely the area-level manifestations of *non-spatial* forces, in particular, those producing poverty and inequality at the macro-level (Slater, 2013).

This becomes clearer when we look at the empirical literature on neighbourhood effects (see Cheshire et al, 2008; Tunstall and Lupton, 2010). Broadly speaking, most high-quality studies find some evidence for area-level effects on social outcomes, notably, physical health and happiness. However, the bulk of the evidence finds little or no impact of neighbourhood effects on economic or educational outcomes (for one recent experimental evaluation, see Tunstall et al, 2014). (In the case of educational outcomes, peer effects within schools appear more important than interactions at the local area level (Gibbons and Telhaj, 2008)).

State-led neighbourhood renewal programmes in the UK have had an *individual* equity rationale, but have sought to raise outcomes through targeting *spatial* equity. The neighbourhood effects evidence suggests that this will be pretty difficult to achieve. By contrast, 'Connected Communities' activities, by being less bounded to administrative or physical geographies, might stand a greater chance of improving social outcomes for those taking part. In both cases, holistic neighbourhood renewal/community development programmes can deliver valuable public goods: improved environmental conditions; reduced crime and better public safety; more effective public services; or higher social capital. In the case of 'Connected Communities', the logic chains involved are diverse, distinct and complex: searching for and retrieving community-relevant information and memory; and co-producing activities that generate empathy and dissolve barriers between participants.

Unfortunately, the existing evidence at the time of writing is not readily able to convincingly demonstrate the *outcomes* of such programmes, state-led or otherwise. Lupton et al (2013) review the data for England. Official evaluations of the Decent Homes, NRF and NDC programmes show that between 1997 and 2010, 90% of social housing was brought up to a decent standard; there was a fall in vacant housing rates in unpopular estates; domestic burglary rates and worklessness fell in the 'worst' neighbourhoods; and user survey data suggested clear jumps in resident satisfaction (about cleaner streets and parks, lower crime, and better schools, crèche and day-care provision in the 'worst' areas). However, while gaps between the worst areas and the rest fell, they did not close. By 2007, there was still a 15 percentage point gap between the 'worst' 10% of areas and the national average on outcomes such as burglary, vandalism, litter and resident satisfaction. Furthermore, depressingly, there was no statistically significant closing of the gaps in life expectancy, overall crime rates or worklessness.

The preceding discussion suggests some reasons for these weak policy–outcome links. First, mainstream budgets in fields such as health and education dwarf even the largest neighbourhood renewal programmes: Lupton and colleagues show that the NRF was worth less than 1% of local authorities' total central budgets in 2007/08, and, at most, was worth between 1% and 2% of urban authorities' spend. Second, national macroeconomic conditions – notably, the long growth period from 1993 to 2007 – have had a major impact on neighbourhood-level outcomes such as crime and worklessness, and one that could have been bigger than any regeneration efforts. Third, sorting influences area-level outcomes: effective neighbourhood renewal programmes may lead to their beneficiaries leaving the area, with 'harder to help' groups moving in over time. As Cheshire et al (2008) find, this may lead to perverse results where the programme in question appears to become progressively less effective. Alarmingly, Lupton et al (2013) report that the national evaluation of the NDC finds an overall *negative* link between NDC participation and local education outcomes. It is implausible that the policy made things worse, so either the problems are bigger than the policy can deal with or other channels explain the result.

To be clear, such stylised facts and descriptive analyses are essential to help set the scene. However, as this discussion reveals, there are limits to this kind of evidence if we want to understand the effects of policy on outcomes we care about. In turn, this highlights the need for better evaluation of urban regeneration activity, state-led or otherwise, and the need to introduce new methods and bodies of evidence into regeneration debates. Lupton et al (2013) conclude that Labour's policies reversed the trend of increasing disparities in poor neighbourhoods but did not close them. In fact, it is not clear that we can even go this far. Social and economic life chances improved in 'poor neighbourhoods' under Labour, but we actually have very little idea as to how far Type 1 and 2 programmes contributed to these changes. For interventions that are process-oriented (rather than based on public service delivery), uncovering impacts is even harder to do. User surveys and natural feedback are valuable, but on their own, they tell us nothing concrete about the *causal* effects of the programmes involved. Time-series analysis is similarly limited without proper control groups and strategies to account for omitted variables (such as the national economic and policy regimes discussed in the previous paragraph). Most critically, we need to understand *how* areas were selected for 'treatment' in the first place, and what this implies for how they would have done without the policy.

This presents a challenge and an opportunity for the 'Connected Communities' approach. The focus on process and co-production creates difficulties in demonstrating impacts. Conversely, researchers can usefully deploy the qualitative evidence generated alongside more structured material in order to generate a rich, layered picture. The final section gives some pointers on how this layering approach might take place.

Evidence-making, experimentalism and 'what works'

Urban regeneration policy has gone through substantial shifts and shocks in recent years, reflecting both changing political moods and inherent constraints to what such initiatives can achieve given the real-world complexity of urban systems. Fundamentally, urban regeneration policies in isolation are likely to have incremental impacts, rather than the transformational effects sometimes claimed. The limited available evidence suggests that this is particularly true of city-level economic renewal programmes. *Neighbourhood* renewal programmes often have more holistic objectives and – crucially – provide public goods that are harder to 'capture'. However, it is very hard to assess the achievements of such programmes on the basis of existing stylised facts and evaluations.

The emerging experimentalist paradigm in British public policy, as encapsulated in the network of 'What Works Centres' (Haynes et al, 2013; Puttick and Mulgan, 2013), shows how structured techniques can start to get at the causal effects of urban regeneration initiatives. Existing systematic reviews of impact evaluations conducted by the What Works Centre for Local Economic Growth[3] typically shortlist less than 10% of the existing literature, and find that less than half of the policies evaluated have positive effects against their stated objectives. These evaluations typically deploy experimental or quasi-experimental techniques – tracking 'treatment' and 'control' groups over time – which could be used more widely in urban regeneration (Gibbons et al, 2014). Regeneration programmes often operate over long timescales, involve substantial capital spend and typically involve interventions where impacts are hard to reverse. For all these reasons, opportunities for randomisation are limited. However, randomised control trials could feasibly be used to test variations or 'arms' of a given policy, for instance, to test alternative versions of neighbourhood management or in-work training initiatives. Similarly, many programmes feature competitive bidding, which creates natural treatment and control groups from the successful and unsuccessful bidders. Such design elements also allow evaluation based on comparing people/places around an eligibility threshold (so-called 'discontinuity' designs).

On the other hand, there are limitations to the structured, experimentalist approach. Systematic reviews working across diverse bodies of evidence can be constrained in their ability to deliver clear 'lessons' to practitioners, even if they adopt rich, 'realist synthesis' approaches (Pawson, 2006). Quantitative impact evaluation is only part of the evaluation toolkit, especially for community development activities where outcome metrics are proxies. As noted earlier, opportunities for sensible randomisation are limited, valuations also typically provide estimates of 'average treatment effects', and techniques for breaking out the 'local' effect for a given milieu exist but are more challenging to implement. For any given community, then, these structured techniques are an input into policymaking, rather than providing precise answers. The rich qualitative material generated by initiatives such as 'Connected Communities' acts as another input. Local policymakers need to layer these bodies of evidence as they develop strategy.

As McGuinness et al (2015) point out, the current 'creative chaos' in English regeneration policy forces local policymakers to innovate, for better or worse. Certainly, the City Deals and Local Growth Deals processes are starting to shift (limited) powers and resources towards local government and LEPs. There is increasing political consensus on the need for further devolution to urban areas. The Scottish referendum result has further galvanised the urban devolution agenda. On the other hand, local government and its partners in England will be operating under severe financial constraints for years to come. This creates a strong incentive to do 'what works', but also places obstacles in the way of finding out. Localism also highlights the very variable capacity across the country to design and evaluate urban policy. The experience of other countries is that such capacity gaps can help widen future disparities rather than close them (Rodríguez-Pose and Ezcurra, 2011). A crucial task for future governments, then, is to help provide the conditions and resources to better understand what works in urban regeneration policy, as well as to help implement it.

Notes

[1] Author's personal views, not those of the What Works Centre for Local Economic Growth. Thanks to Ruth Lupton for useful comments and feedback.

[2] See: www.ahrc.ac.uk/Funding-Opportunities/Research-funding/Connected-Communities/Pages/Connected-Communities.aspx (accessed 30 October 2014).

[3] See the body of reviews available at: whatworksgrowth.org (accessed 30 October 2014).

References

Buck, N., Gordon, I., Hall, P., Harloe, M. and Kleinman, M. (2002) *Working capital: life and labour in contemporary London*, London: Routledge.

Busso, M., Gregory, J. and Kline, P. (2013) 'Assessing the incidence and efficiency of a prominent place based policy', *American Economic Review Papers and Proceedings* 103(2): 897–947.

Centre for Cities (2009) *Cities manifesto*, London: Centre for Cities.

Champion, T. and Fisher, T. (2004) 'Migration, residential preferences and the changing environment of cities', in M. Boddy and M. Parkinson (eds) *City matters*, Bristol: The Policy Press, pp 111–28.

Cheshire, P., Gibbons, S. and Gibson, I. (2008) *Policies for 'mixed communities': a critical evaluation*, SERC Policy Paper 2, London: London School of Economics.

Cheshire, P., Nathan, M. and Overman, H. (2014) *Urban economics and urban policy*, Cheltenham: Edward Elgar.

Criscuolo, C., Martin, R., Overman, H.G. and Van Reenen, J. (2012) *The causal effects of an industrial policy*, Spatial Economics Research Centre Discussion Paper SERCDP0098, London: SERC.

DCLG (Department of Communities and Local Government) (2009) *Transforming places, changing lives: taking forward the regeneration framework*, London: DCLG.

DCLG (2011) *A plain English guide to the Localism Bill*, London: DCLG.

Department for Business Innovation and Skills (2010) *Understanding local growth*, London: BIS.

Duranton, G. and Puga, D. (2004) 'Micro-foundations of urban agglomeration economies', in J.V. Henderson and J.-F. Thisse (eds) *Handbook of regional and urban economics 4*, The Hague: Elsevier, pp 2063–117.

Einio, E. and Overman, H.G. (2013) *The effects of spatially targeted enterprise initiatives: evidence from UK LEGI*, SERC Discussion Paper, London: SERC.

Gibbons, S. and Telhaj, S. (2008) *Peers and achievement in England's secondary schools*, London: SERC.

Gibbons, S., Nathan, M. and Overman, H. (2014) *Evaluating spatial policies*, SERC Policy Paper SERCPP12, London: LSE.

Glaeser, E. (2011) *The triumph of the city*, London: Pan Macmillan.

Glaeser, E. and Gottlieb, J.D. (2008) 'The economics of place-making policies', *Brookings Papers on Economic Activity* 2008(1): 155–239.

Goos, M. and Manning, A. (2007) 'Lousy and lovely jobs: the rising polarization of work in Britain', *Review of Economics and Statistics* 89(1): 118–33.

Haynes, L., Service, O., Goldacre, B. and Torgerson, D. (2013) *Test, learn, adapt: developing public policy with randomised controlled trials*, London: Cabinet Office.

Hildreth, P. and Bailey, D. (2013) 'The economics behind the move to "localism" in England', *Cambridge Journal of Regions, Economy and Society* 6(2): 233–49.

HM Treasury (2007) *Sub-national economic development and regeneration review*, London: HM Treasury.

Kline, P. and Moretti, E. (2013) 'Place based policies with unemployment', *The American Economic Review* 103(3): 238–43.

Kline, P. and Moretti, E. (2014) 'Local economic development, agglomeration economies and the big push: 100 years of evidence from the Tennessee Valley Authority', *The Quarterly Journal of Economics*, 129(1): 275–331.

Kluve, J. (2010) 'The effectiveness of European active labor market programs', *Labour Economics* 17(6): 904–18.

Leather, P. and Nevin, B. (2013) 'The Housing Market Renewal Programme: origins, outcomes and the effectiveness of public policy interventions in a volatile market', *Urban Studies* 50: 856–75.

Leunig, T. and Swaffield, J. (2009) *Cities unlimited*, London: Policy Exchange.

Lupton, R. (2013) 'What is neighbourhood renewal policy for?', *People, Place and Policy* 7(2): 66–72.

Lupton, R., Fenton, A. and Fitzgerald, A. (2013) *Labour's record on neighbourhood renewal in England: policy, spending and outcomes 1997–2010*, CASE Working Paper 6, London: LSE.

Martin, R. and Sunley, P. (2006) 'Path dependence and regional economic evolution', *Journal of Economic Geography* 6(4): 395–437.

Massey, D. (2007) *World city*, Bristol: Polity Press.

Mayer, T., Mayneris, F. and Py, L. (2012) *The impact of urban enterprise zones on establishments' location decisions: evidence from French ZFUs*, CEPR Discussion Paper 9074, London: CEPR.

McGuinness, D., Greenhalgh, P. and Pugalis, L. (2015) 'Is the grass always greener? Making sense of convergence and divergence in regeneration policies in England and Scotland', *The Geographical Journal* 181(1): 26–37.

Moretti, E. (2010) 'Local labor markets', in O. Ashenfelter and D. Card (eds) *Handbook of labor economics*, Amsterdam: Elsevier, pp 1237–313.

Moretti, E. (2012) *The new geography of jobs*, Boston, MA: Haughton Mifflin Harcourt.

Neumark, D. and Kolko, J. (2010) 'Do enterprise zones create jobs? Evidence from California's enterprise zone program', *Journal of Urban Economics* 68(1): 1–19.

Office of the Deputy Prime Minister (1995) *Final evaluation of Enterprise Zones*, Urban Research Summary No 4, London: ODPM.

Overman, H. and Rice, P. (2008) *Resurgent cities and regional economic performance*, SERC Policy Paper 1, London: London School of Economics.

Parkinson, M. (2009) *The credit crunch and regeneration: impact and implications*, London: Department of Communities and Local Government.

Pawson, R. (2006) *Evidence based policy: a realist perspective*, London: Sage.

Pugalis, L. and McGuinness, D. (2012) 'From a framework to a toolkit: regeneration in an age of austerity', *Journal of Urban Regeneration and Renewal* 6(4): 339–53.

Puttick, R. and Mulgan, G. (2013) *What should the 'What Works Network' do?*, London: NESTA.

Roberts, P. and Sykes, H. (2000) *Urban regeneration – a handbook*, London: Sage.

Rodríguez-Pose, A. and Ezcurra, R. (2011) 'Is fiscal decentralization harmful for economic growth? Evidence from the OECD countries', *Journal of Economic Geography* 11(4): 619–43.

Sassen, S. (2001) *The global city: New York, London, Tokyo*, Woodstock: Princeton University Press/Blackwell.

Slater, T. (2013) 'Your life chances affect where you live: a critique of the "cottage industry" of neighbourhood effects research', *International Journal of Urban and Regional Research* 37(2): 367–87.

Social Exclusion Unit (1998) *A national strategy for neighbourhood renewal*, London: SEU.

Storper, M. (2011) 'Justice, efficiency and economic geography: should places help one another to develop?', *European Urban and Regional Studies* 18(1): 3–21.

Storper, M. (2013) *Keys to the city: how economics, institutions, social interaction, and politics shape development*, Princeton, NJ: Princeton University Press.

Tunstall, R. and Lupton, R. (2003) *Is targeting deprived areas an effective means to reach people? An assessment of one rationale for area-based funding programmes*, CASEpaper 70, London: London School of Economics.

Tunstall, R. and Lupton, R. (2010) *Mixed communities: evidence review*, London: Department for Communities and Local Government.

Tunstall, R., Green, A., Lupton, R., Watmough, S. and Bates, K. (2014) 'Does poor neighbourhood reputation create a neighbourhood effect on employment? The results of a field experiment in the UK', *Urban Studies* 51(4): 763–80.

Tyler, P. (2011) 'Strategies for underperforming places', in P. Lawless, H.G. Overman and P. Tyler (eds) *What should be the long-term strategy for places with patterns of decline and underperformance?*, SERC Policy Paper No 6, London: London School of Economics.

Urban Task Force (1999) *Towards an urban renaissance*, London: Urban Task Force.

Venables, A. (2006) *Shifts in economic geography and their causes*, CEP Discussion Paper 767, London: LSE.

SIX

The work of art in the age of mechanical co-production

Steve Pool and Kate Pahl

We did not co-opt co-production, co-production co-opted us. (Blog, August 2014)[1]

Introduction

In this chapter, we draw on a collaborative practice that has developed through working with people in communities and in universities. We argue that the practice of co-production requires a mode of closeness to the everyday and a recognition of different ways of being. An important part of co-production is that it involves recognising and reacting to relationships of power. In community contexts, it might mean shifting attention away from preferred ways of knowing and being to unfamiliar ways of knowing and being for all involved. We consider the potential for spatially situated methodologies to surface different kinds of knowledge and the mechanisms for this knowledge to impact on policy decisions (Soja, 2010).

We provide as our example an experience of co-producing a film with the Youth Service and a group of young people in Rotherham in order to carry a message to the Department of Communities and Local Government (DCLG). The film encountered problems of interpretation when presented to the DCLG as part of a broader cross-disciplinary report (Connelly et al, 2013). Here, we argue that the opening up and surfacing of situated knowledge can be problematic when transferred to a national or academic discourse. We suggest that a more malleable perspective as to what constitutes evidence has the potential to inform policy debates, and that this involves working with ways of knowing from the arts and humanities. This can shape the field and respond to different needs while remaining rigorous, and can open up a space for discussion. A consequence of this might involve crossing imagined and real boundaries of representation and opening up different representational choices in the research process. In turn, this can then make space for different voices to come to the fore and can raise issues of power, meaning and ambiguity for research and practice.

Arts and humanities, co-production and ways of knowing

Arts and humanities approaches draw on historically situated traditions and methods. The humanities might include historical, literary and hermeneutic approaches, while the arts might include practice-based research, as well as forms of creative practice. Arts approaches encountered in this project include approaches from community and participatory arts, together with work in the field of symbolic creativity and improvisation (eg Willis, 2000; Hallam and Ingold, 2007). From the humanities, we drew on cultural studies, literary studies and narrative methodological approaches (eg Williams, 1961; Hull and Nelson, 2009). Our lens included the creative and visual arts, drawing on theoretical work both from relational arts practice (Kester, 2004, 2011) and the idea of practice as research (Barrett and Bolt, 2007). We also draw on literary and improvisatory ways of working with communities, with a focus on common cultures.

Policy discourse has tended to view social-scientific approaches as valid, useful and authoritative, with language and writing being the salient mode of communication. Our work in Rotherham engaged with a group of young people to make a film in order to send a message to government. When considering the value of our film, we were aware that the policymakers saw it as supplementary to the project report. Here, we unpack the process of making the film and consider how its context framed a discourse that structured value within a specific arena. The film presented an emergent, tacit, embodied, situated and aesthetic perspective that tended to be less powerfully present in arguments or reports at the end of the project. Feelings, emotions, hidden histories and ways of knowing were lost within the seemingly more robust and familiar genre of the research findings. An initial confidence in the potential to draw on multiple disciplinary approaches and methods to create a rich final report was lost within the complex feelings of ownership and what constituted authenticity from all members of the research team. One of our concerns was that the disciplinary bedrocks in social science could be displayed through citations and language while ways of knowing, understanding and representing from the arts and humanities might not include a citation, but might be embodied or represented differently. The foundations of knowledge production were different.

The project grew from a long-term working relationship and disciplinary experience through a series of encounters with the theory and practice of knowledge co-production. We (Kate Pahl and Steve Pool) have been working together for eight years. Kate has a background in ethnography: she engages particularly with the work of Lassiter and Campbell in thinking through the implications of collaboration within ethnographic practice (Lassiter, 2005; Campbell and Lassiter, 2010). This has involved a process of recording, through various means, as well as witnessing and trying to understand, by continuous engagement with one site, the cultures and literacy practices of a particular community: Rotherham. Drawing on the work of Barton and Hamilton (1998) in *Local literacies*, Kate has worked within Rotherham for a number of years, making sense of communities, practices, stories and ways of knowing (see Pahl and Pollard, 2010; Pahl and Allan, 2011; Pahl, 2014).

Steve balances his work within the academic community with a commitment to arts practice. Recent work includes the co-development of 'Poly-technic', an independent research-based arts organisation developing and delivering art projects. This includes a major Arts Council England-funded project, in partnership with Museums Sheffield, exploring the social thinking of John Ruskin. Steve is interested in the agentive potential of cultural practices and the role that artists play in informing and shaping change. His reflexive work with Kate Pahl explores the intersection between arts practice and ethnography.

Our work draws on multiple strategies and methodologies, including participatory arts practice (Kester, 2011) and collaborative ethnography (Lassiter, 2005). It also recognises the limitations of formal approaches and structures when attempting to build shared understanding among people with very different experiences and expectations. We describe our work as an entwinement: the slow process of growing a shared practice that reaches across relational arts practice, ethnography and participatory research. By building on the foundations of ethnography and arts practice, our joint work is characterised by an approach that privileges the fine-grained, small stories within the everyday over evidence that draws on large-scale data sets. We conceptualise this work as a set of encounters with place, people, theory, ideology and our respective disciplines as artist and ethnographer.

It was not initially our intention to co-produce research or knowledge, either together or with others. Our intention was, and the reason we continue to work together is, to destabilise our established ways of working, to subvert structures or hierarchies that exists within our own fields, and to build a space where new conversations and new objects can begin. Through drawing on arts-based methods, our ways of working became emergent and layered, contingent on practice and relationships, and with an attentiveness to different forms of knowing. Within the project, we recognised that policy often prefers a clear story, but that the murkiness of everyday life can also disrupt settled notions of what could be. Our work emerges from meetings, walks, encounters and long-term relationships that are situated and contingent on emerging issues within youth work, as well as university research priorities. We acknowledge how experience, practice and time are critical elements for promoting opportunities for change, yet there are no mechanical approaches to co-production. We bring no toolkits, codes of practice, top tips, idiot guides or basic steps. Rather, we suggest that a process of co-production has the potential to open up new opportunities to build new ideas of what it is to know, and we suggest that this approach has a definite and important contribution to make to current debates around active and informed participation.

In the following, we present an example of a project that, we feel, created moments of co-production, suggesting that co-production took place in this project through a set of moments. It is dangerous to see co-production as the joint manufacture of a product – we consider co-production as continually in process. We focus on one small part within a much larger project where we worked collaboratively, not always successfully, to make something together with a group of young people. We trace the journey that we took through to thinking about the relationship between co-production, power and ethics. Each encounter with co-production raises new ideas and concerns. The project is an example of 'working through' with people and acknowledging that project expectations cannot always conform to what is possible within the restrictions of time-based objective-focused projects. We offer this example as a way of thinking about the relationship between co-production and policy in a multidisciplinary space of practice that includes the arts and humanities.

The project

We discuss our work in the context of a policy review commissioned by the 'Connected Communities' programme to inform the DCLG. The brief was to consider '*Community governance in the context of* decentralisation: *Who should be taking decisions and for what? And how and to whom are they accountable?*'. Our proposal, called 'Making Meaning Differently' (September 2012), argued for the need to re-conceptualise the relationship between the state and citizens, with a focus on new forms of 'voice' and 'co-production' and with a particular interest in the role of representational processes and epistemologies from the arts and humanities in the making or informing of governance practices (Kester, 2004). In particular, we argued in the proposal that:

> Traditional forms of interaction do not work for many groups, and alternative spaces have emerged in which representation is staged. We will explore these 'other' spaces and modes of representation including symbolic creativity (Willis 2000) and film, theatre, visual arts and different kinds of digital and material textual practices (Kress 2010), and how they may articulate with traditional governance and power. (Quote from original bid, September 2012)

The final report we produced was accompanied by a series of films, which were also sent to the DCLG (Connelly et al, 2013). The intention of the films was to situate the document and to give a visual context, but we also wanted them to stand in their own right, to carry a message from the communities we were working with to inform the DCLG's perspective. Since the focus of the policy review was to consider alternative forms of representation outside traditional governance structures, this approach very much mirrored our perspective in the report, through enacting it in practice.

In the 'Making Meaning Differently' project, we were tasked with taking a message to the DCLG. This message was concerned with the ways in which people engaged (or not) with governance structures at a local level. The DCLG had clear concerns about disconnection, and this was surfacing issues of democratic representation within marginalised communities. We were keen to work in a hopeful way with communities in order to create opportunities for their voices to be heard. Much of our work develops locally. It is situated, involving small groups and organisations, for example, the Youth Service, schools, activist organisations and organisations supporting women, minority ethnic groups, specific interest groups or arts groups. These groups are directly and indirectly affected by policy yet rarely get a chance to influence it. For many of the people we work with, policy has an impact, for example, the layout of parks and streets, the closure of libraries and youth centres, and welfare decisions such as the bedroom tax. However, most people, particularly young people, do not feel in a position to inform or have any influence over policy decisions. Policy operates on a large scale, as Chapters Two, Three and Five of this book illustrate, while our work grows from numerous small-scale actions, small acts, small changes (Hamdi, 2004).

We intended to build on a long-standing relationship with the Youth Service in Rotherham, which was committed to high-quality work with disengaged young people. We approached the work optimistically, hoping to find a way to suggest that arts and humanities approaches could help to develop a new lens and make visible the impact of policy on people far removed from Westminster. Our task was to send a message to government in order to encourage a different kind of thinking about the ways in which people make sense of the world. In an interim report to the DCLG in February 2013, we started with a poem:

Tell all the truth but tell it slant,
Success in circuit lies,
Too bright for our infirm delight

The truth's superb surprise;
As lightning to the children eased
With explanation kind,
The truth must dazzle gradually
Or every man be blind. (Emily Dickinson)[2]

This poem suggests that ways of listening, hearing and recognising different representations might involve listening to something 'slant'. The message that 'the truth's superb surprise' is too bright for our eyes, is a point that we felt was key in trying to find a language that would cross between our work in the field and a policy document delivered to government. The arts and humanities broaden the range of material that may be important to understand something. For example, policymakers might characterise young people as 'hard to reach', but they will, nonetheless, expect communication to happen on their terms, in relation to written text, formal meetings and ways of displaying knowledge that are familiar to professionals. They might find artistic forms of expression opaque and difficult to read. Young people, likewise, might characterise those in power as 'hard to reach', and might use a range of creative expressions that may pass unnoticed by those in power. The arts and humanities widen the range of expression available to draw on in order to make sense of the world.

One of the issues for us is the way in which personal knowledge, stories and direct experience are often not recognised within academic discourse as they have not been collected via accepted methodological routes (Law, 2004). This has led to us recognising that ways of working that are multiple, situated and contingent on practice might be more useful than one approach and that creative approaches to enquiry can be productive (Rogers, 2012). Ingold (2013) suggests that personal knowledge grows from practitioners' awareness and ways of working. We wanted to foreground that knowledge, and are acutely aware of how important that process of listening is in the communities in which we work.

We considered how representation takes many complex forms and is sometimes not listened to (Back, 2007). Traditional formats, such as meetings and written reports, we argued, might not be the preferred way in which young people represented their ideas. We suggest that their modal choice, media and forms of representation might not match that of government (Rowsell, 2013). Instead, young people played with ideas, creating symbolic, creative spaces of representation where things might be represented not in language, but in other imaginative forms (Willis, 2000). The mix of modes was important in articulating the complex meanings that the young people wanted to articulate. Young people might inform government using aesthetic and moral schemas that lie outside the cultural framing of government officials (Hull and Nelson, 2009). Therefore, we wanted to uncover these ideas of representation through making. We hoped that our work with different communities would open a small window on people's lived experiences, and that by 'co-producing' a message to take to government, we would be able to also demonstrate a collective message that drew on the disciplinary strengths of a diverse team, and that would impact on policy. Co-production is seen here as a process, enacted in small moments, and deriving from a commitment to communities and to place. The process of co-production does not map easily onto academic ways of doing things and knowing things; rather, it is a wide-open process of engagement in which meanings are contested and research intent is framed by wider purposes and structures, resting on broader logics and ways of knowing.

'Making Meaning Differently'

In November 2012, we began working with a group of about 15 young people, who came from an estate in Rawmarsh, in Rotherham. This group of young people were identified by the Youth Service as needing support, but as having interesting and useful things to say. The estate where they lived had been characterised in the media as low-income, with people eating an inadequate diet. Sociological accounts of Rotherham have been equally negative (see Charlesworth, 2000).

We wanted to focus on the lived experience of the young people, and on what it was like to live on an estate and have only the street as a meeting place. This experience was both important to value and articulate and one that is hard to define just within sociological analysis (Reay and Lucey, 2000; Mathews, 2003; Hanley, 2012).

In order to deliver a clear message to the DCLG, we asked the young people on the estate to come to a community centre near to them to meet with us and discuss what they felt about local and national governance. What was clear to us was the dissonance that the young people felt in relation to any kind of government structures. The young people also felt demonised by the press and wanted to emphasise that they were not bad people. One young man suggested that we use shadow puppets as a form of representation, while a young woman suggested drama.

We gathered a series of observations from the young people about the nature of their lives on the estate. They described feeling cold and having nowhere to meet. We also walked with the young people around the estate and developed a feel for the area. Meeting weekly, we recorded stories by the young people about their lives, together with the dance they liked to dance together, and through this process, built up a picture of key themes. One key story that emerged was of being at knifepoint and finding this scary. Marcus, the youth worker, managed to encourage the young people to tell this story using flip charts and drawing. Through this process, a number of themes emerged, including the stories and the need to feel safe. The story of being at knifepoint became something of a focal point that signified a lot of feelings that the group wanted to share.

One evening, Steve, who often explores stories through the making of shadow puppets, came in with a camera and some materials to do a shadow puppet film. He brought in cardboard and the young people cut this up and made models of a police car and the person who scared them. They dramatised the incident with the knife and this was filmed. The resulting film was powerful but could be regarded as incoherent; the team felt that we could distil the key political ideas that had surfaced through conversation and inscribe a series of slogans onto the film. One evening, Kate and the youth workers worked with the young people to do this. As a result, the final film was a mix of messages, 'We want to feel safe', and stories, 'Being at knifepoint is scary', plus an overall message that, while scribed by the youth workers, was the message we sent to government (see Figure 6.1).

Figure 6.1: Shadow film

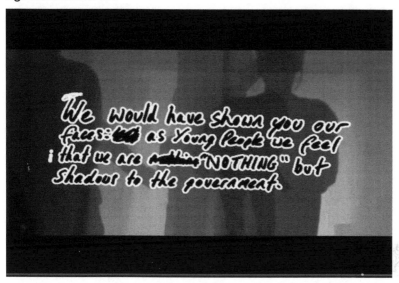

What is complex about this film is that it represents a bricolage of meaning across a number of disparate spaces. It does not have a particular single message; rather, personal and conflicting messages emerge in the context of where the film is shown. Within the film, the young people's knowledge swirls around, and some of what they know is obscured. The young people remained anonymous, they had conflicted ideas about politics and representation and this is contained within the disjointed form of the film. The unsettled nature of the video footage mirrors the unsettled nature of the young people's lived experience. The film had an urgent, edgy and yet contained feel, with strong messages surfacing strong bonding between girls. The young people were in control of both the space and the level of engagement. The film and work around it made space for their modal choices to find strong representation.

We continue to see the film as a form that held some of the tensions of working within communities, drawing on different methodologies (ethnography, art practice), which was changed by having to present it as part of the broader report to government while remaining close to the feelings that we encountered in that community centre. We are concerned that the very thing that we were trying to do – to initiate a discussion about the way in which young people make meaning in contexts that are not heard by adults – was reflected in the reaction to the film. The film, while uneven in quality and imperfect, did reflect some of what went on in that community centre, and did have some of the raw and vulnerable feelings that the young people had about being ignored, demonised and misunderstood. By removing this film from its context and taking it to government, we did not pay enough attention to mediating how its complex messages could weave with other elements of our report, which meant that we were limited in our ability to convey the intended relevant meaning. We suggest that the complexities of working through the practice will generate new ways of knowing and inform future collaborative interdisciplinary projects.

Implications for practice

We have used the concept of research as 'bricolage' to highlight ways in which our work was connected to other cultural forms and ways of knowing, including the young people's experience of music, dance and story (Rogers, 2012). We also recognise, with Ingold (2013), how personal knowledge swirls around more formal ways of knowing, but can be enshrined within different kinds of stuff. The process of making together can become a site where these tensions are played out. We suggest that this work is concerned with space (Soja, 2010) and a set of spatial relationships that is in a simultaneous state of collapse and reconstruction. In many cases, our work was framed by a site, whether a park, a community centre or a school, which became the 'holding form' for a set of relationships to unfold (Witkin, 1974). This process can be generative and has an emergent quality. For example, the 'Making Meaning Differently' project grew from a story that Marcus, the youth worker, told us about his concern about a family who came from the estate, and his desire to work there grew after a series of walks we did with him in the area. From these walks, grew the project. This echoes a point made by Steve Pool in an earlier publication: 'Co-produced knowledge is not about finding consensus it recognizes the vast potential that lies beneath the surface of things. Rather than cultivating fruit, it identifies and promotes the conditions for growth' (Pool, 2012). We argue here that our approach to co-production is embedded in a set of relationships and is situated within the everyday.

Others, however, have argued that co-production as an approach does bring with it risk and danger. In a recent conference paper, Flinders, Cunningham and Wood (2014) described co-production as 'high-risk, time consuming, ethically complex, emotionally demanding, inherently unstable, vulnerable to external shocks, subject to competing demands and expectations and other scholars (journals, funders, etc.) may not even recognise its outputs as representing "real" research'. To us, this description also seems to contain quite a powerful message about the dangers of co-production, which is reinforced by their use of the concept of 'social pollution' from Mary Douglas to describe how co-production methodologies can damage academic careers. The concept of 'social pollution' can, they argue, be used to describe marginal, transgressive and risky behaviour. Douglas's own words make sense of this concept: 'A person accused of pollution is always in the wrong. He has developed some wrong condition or simply crossed some line which should not have been crossed and this displacement unleashes danger for someone' (Douglas, 1991 [1966]: 113). This idea of 'crossing the line' could potentially be applied to those who attempt to engage in such research. Co-production, they argued, offered these challenges.

Co-production as an approach is also, we think, an opportunity to do things differently. The 'Connected Communities' programme has opened up different ways of knowing and doing things, the implications of which are still not fully known (see Chapter One). We think that co-production opens out possibilities that create intersections between disciplines that can lead to enabling conversations (Kester, 2004). We recognise that in situations where we are co-producing together with the youth services, young people, artists and ethnographers, roles may be unclear and outputs may be unfamiliar to an academic audience. It may also be the case that timelines will be muddled and people will feel lost and out of control. However, we also think that this process of muddle and chaos can create the conditions for growth and for new things to happen. More importantly, we think that co-production offers a process for recovering hope for new and situated ways of working and listening to each other. In order to recover hope within communities such as the one in which we worked, we need to value and recognise this process of listening to stories and experiences and the potential truths they hold (Vasudevan, 2011; Bright, 2012).

We need to consider how to represent co-production both in terms of how it is enacted, that is, in its messy, emergent way, and also in terms of what it can potentially offer regarding the production of knowledge with community partners. Models of co-production across university and community contexts have included many different approaches. Some of the approaches relevant to community projects include dialogic co-inquiry spaces (Armstrong and Banks, 2011) in which community groups have shared experience with academics in equitable spaces. Hart et al (2013) and Hart and Wolff (2006), drawing on the work of Etienne Wenger, have developed what they describe as a 'communities of practice' approach, and have worked to reposition knowledge creation with community partners. Campbell and Lassiter (2015) offer a model of collaborative ethnography whereby people in communities themselves, together with academics, frame and construct an agenda for future research that draws on historically and socially situated research. However, we want to broaden this approach to include the history of participatory and community arts (Bishop, 2012) in a way that recognises approaches from practice as research (Barrett and Bolt, 2007). We also acknowledge the importance of unknowing (Vasudevan, 2011) and stories. Drawing on philosophy, we have found it helpful to consider Bloch's conceptualisation of stories as a space to think; as Bloch (2006 [1969] p 6) argued, 'It is good to think in stories too'. Stories are potentially important sites of knowledge in community projects (Pahl, 2014). This conceptual framework creates a structure for a shared epistemological space of practice to unfold in which participants can co-create stories and make aesthetic decisions about how these stories are told.

What we were seeing with 'Shadow Dance' was a playful space in which improvisation and learning to be together, to script together and to dance together were unevenly experienced across the lifetime of a three-month project. However, this was also characterised by cooperation and ways of sharing experience, a process that Hull et al (2010) called 'engaged cosmopolitanism'. This was not perfect, but it opened out a different kind of space, one that could be missed through the frame of social science. Over time, our work has captured such complex moments, which might have been lost in traditional sociological work. Through the initial period of the project, we had many conversations with the young adults, some of which took the form of recorded and filmed interviews. Many of the issues that were raised by young people were political, for example, one person talked about the impact on his life of recent changes in social care provision. This more traditional approach did have the potential to harvest a useful data set, and in a more traditionally constructed research programme, provided potentially useful data. However, the form of data collection did not present opportunities to co-produce knowledge; rather, it provided raw material for the professional researcher to take information from. We recognise the value of multiple research strategies and the importance of established methods, but we suggest that co-produced knowledge production requires a more nuanced relationship to these methods. Traditional social science methods (interviews, focus groups) are not necessarily appropriate in settings such as these, where young people are meeting to create stuff together and to dance. An attempt to interview the young people might have ended up not capturing some of the complex emotions about not being listened to, the dance, the need to feel safe, but also the feelings of anger that the young people had. While traditional social science methodologies still appeal to concepts of validity and reliability, we would rather privilege a mode of research that is about becoming, emergent practice and embodied, situated ways of knowing. We suggest that through the 'making' of something new, and developing a lens that privileges stories, lived experience and spatial considerations, new knowledge can surface, as illustrated by the example of our film. To imagine co-production as continually in process, to see all outcomes as stages along the way to a shared destination we will never reach, allows for research to draw on multiple ways of knowing. This approach enables a relationship to the field site that is both situated and contingent. Therefore, we have to work to adapt and shape this process to people, place and time, to make it necessary and relevant to the people who we encourage to get involved in it. There are different ways of seeing this process, but we wanted to highlight the complexity of how things are seen within moments rather than after the event.

We began this chapter by suggesting that we would not provide a toolkit for co-production. We can, however, share our key learning points from this specific project and our reflections through looking back with hindsight. We do not suggest that we have abandoned our respective disciplines, but, rather, that co-production can offer the potential to flatten spatial, epistemological and historical power relations that are often problematic in other forms of research. In a co-produced space, the lines around disciplinary knowledge, so visible within the university, can lose their relevance. However, for many, letting go of the safety net that a disciplinary framework provides can be difficult. Developing enquiry teams requires us to consider what is useful, with each situation requiring a different set of skills and approaches. For example, a particular role and identifiable set of skills that we can label as 'expert' can provide useful starting points. It is essential, however, to question the impact that the expert person, whether 'ethnographer', 'artist' or 'social scientist', has on emerging co-produced knowledge. We argue that consensus is not co-production. By 'tracing the epistemological unconscious' (Bourdieu and Wacquant, 1992), the researchers can make sense of the disciplines she or he is in, but can also acknowledge the limitations of that discipline. What counts as knowledge is being questioned through this process, and the new knowledge can grow and evolve spatially rather than being fixed and contained.

Acknowledgements

Thanks to Matt Collins and Ansgar Allen for reading drafts of this chapter. Also thanks to the Arts and Humanities Research Council (AHRC) 'Connected Communities' programme for funding 'Community Governance in an Age of Decentralisation', or 'Making Meaning Differently'.

Notes

[1] The Big Bid: Volume 1.

[2] Emily Dickinson, "Tell all the truth but tell it slant", from *The Poems of Emily Dickinson: Reading Edition*, ed by Ralph W. Franklin. Copyright © 1998 by Emily Dickinson. Reprinted by permission of The Belknap Press of Harvard University Press.

References

Armstrong, A. and Banks, S. (2011) *Community–university participatory research partnerships: co-inquiry and related approaches*, Newcastle: Beacon NE.

Back, L. (2007) *The art of listening*, London: Berg.

Barrett, E. and Bolt, B. (2007) *Practice as research*, Chippenham: I.B. Tauris and Co.

Barton, D. and Hamilton, M. (1998) *Local literacies: reading and writing in one community*, London and New York, NY: Routledge.

Bishop, C. (2012) *Artificial hells: participatory art and the politics of spectatorship*, London: Verso.

Bloch, E. (2006 [1969]) *Traces* (translated from German by A.A. Nassar), Stanford, CA: Stanford University Press.

Bourdieu, P. and Wacquant, L. (1992) *An invitation to reflexive sociology*, Oxford: Polity Press.

Bright, G. (2012) 'A practice of concrete utopia? Informal youth support and the possibility of "redemptive remembering" in a UK coal-mining area', *Power and Education* 4(3): 314–26.

Campbell, E. and Lassiter, L.E. (2010) 'From collaborative ethnography to collaborative pedagogy: reflections on the Other Side of Middletown Project and community–university research partnerships', *Anthropology and Education Quarterly* 41(4): 370–85.

Campbell, E. and Lassiter, L.E. (2015) *Doing ethnography today: theoretical issues and pragmatic concerns*, Oxford: Wiley-Blackwell.

Charlesworth, S.J. (2000) *A phenomenology of working class experience*, Cambridge: CUP.

Connelly, S., Dabinett, G., Muirhead, G., Pahl, K. and Vanderhoven, D. (2013) 'Making meaning differently: community governance in an age of decentralisation', unpublished report.

Douglas, M. (1991 [1966]) *Purity and danger*, London: Routledge.

Flinders, M., Cunningham, M. and Wood, M. (2014) 'The politics of co-production: risks and limits, pollution and witchcraft', unpublished conference paper, Sir Bernard Crick Centre for the Public Understanding of Politics, University of Sheffield.

Hallam, E. and Ingold, T. (eds) (2007) *Creativity and cultural improvisation*, Oxford: Berg.

Hamdi, N. (2004) *Small change: the art of practice and the limits of planning in cities*, London: Earthscan.

Hanley, L. (2012) *Estates: an intimate history* (2nd edn), London: Granta Books.

Hart, A. and Wolff, D. (2006) 'Developing communities of practice through community–university partnerships', *Planning, Practice and Research* 21(1): 121–38.

Hart, A., Davies, C., Aumann, K., Wenger, E., Aranda, K., Heaver, B. and Wolff, D. (2013) 'Mobilising knowledge in community–university partnerships: what does a community of practice approach contribute?', *Contemporary Social Science: Journal of the Academy of Social Sciences* 8(3): 278–91.

Hull, G. and Nelson, M.E. (2009) 'Literacy, media and morality: making the case for an aesthetic turn', in M. Baynham and M. Prinsloo (eds) *The future of literacy studies*, Basingstoke: Palgrave Macmillan, pp 199–227.

Hull, G., Stornaiuolo, A. and Sahni, U. (2010) 'Cultural citizenship and cosmopolitan practice: global youth communicate online', *English Education* 42(4): 331–67.

Ingold, T. (2013) *Making: anthropology, archaeology, art and architecture*, London: Routledge.

Kester, G.H. (2004) *Conversation pieces: community and communication in modern art*, Berkeley, CA: University of California Press.

Kester, G.H. (2011) *The one and the many: contemporary collaborative art in a global context*, California, CA: Duke University Press.

Kress, G. (2010) *Multimodality: the modes and media of contemporary communication*, London: Routledge.

Lassiter, E.L. (2005) *The Chicago guide to collaborative ethnography*, Chicago, IL: Chicago University Press.

Law, J. (2004) *After Method: Mess in Social Science Research*, London: Routledge.

Mathews, H. (2003) 'The street as liminal space: the barbed spaces of childhood', in P. Christiansen and M. O'Brien (eds) *Children in the city: home, neighbourhood and community*, London: Routledge/Falmer, pp 101–17.

Pahl, K. (2014) *Materializing literacies in communities: the uses of literacy revisited*, London: Bloomsbury.

Pahl, K. and Allan, C. (2011) 'I don't know what literacy is: uncovering hidden literacies in a community library using ecological and participatory methodologies with children', *Journal of Early Childhood Literacy* 11(2): 190–213.

Pahl, K. and Pollard, A. (2010) 'The case of the disappearing object: narratives and artefacts in homes and a museum exhibition from Pakistani heritage families in South Yorkshire', *Museum and Society* 8(1): 1–17.

Pool, S. (2012) 'Co-production', in the 'Imagine Project' brochure, unpublished.

Reay, D. and Lucey, H. (2000) '"I don't really like it here but I don't want to be anywhere else": children and inner city council estates', *Antipode* 32(4): 410–28.

Rogers, M. (2012) 'Conceptualising theories and practices of bricolage research', *The Qualitative Report* 17: 1–17.

Rowsell, J. (2013) *Working with multimodality: rethinking literacy in a digital age*, London: Routledge.

Soja, E. (2010) *Seeking spatial justice*, Minneapolis, MN: University of Minnesota Press.

Vasudevan, L. (2011) 'An invitation to unknowing', *Teachers College Record* 113(6): 1154–74.

Williams, R. (1961) *The long revolution*, London: Chatto and Windus.

Willis, P. (2000) *The ethnographic imagination*, Cambridge: Polity Press.

Witkin, R. (1974) *The intelligence of feeling*, London: Heinemann.

SEVEN

"There is no local here, love"[1]

Rebecca Bernstein, Antonia Layard, Martin Maudsley and Hilary Ramsden

Introduction

"There is no local here, love." These were the evocative words said by an elderly participant at an arts-led research intervention at Patchway Community Centre at a monthly, volunteer-facilitated older person's tea party. Responding to arts-led research methods (in this instance, storytelling), the participant was evoking an absence of 'the local' in her locality. Pointing out the lack of cafes, pubs, amenable parks or community centres that did not have to cover their costs ("it costs money to be local"), she explained how 'the local' needs physical space in order to exist.

While we might bristle at the singularity of the description of 'the local', in our research, we found participants referring to 'the local' over and over again. In this sense, the local, the keystone concept in the current policy landscape of local*ism*, was confirmed when interrogated through arts-based methods. In addition, however, participants also stated repeatedly that feeling local, or recognition of the local, is dependent upon whether or not there are spaces in which to get together to 'be' local. Specifically, this research found that the local can be both present and absent, even though the assumption with the Localism Act 2011 and related policy initiatives is that there are 'locals' all across England.

Certainly, research is consistently illustrating that local*ism* is geographically, socially and politically uneven (Featherstone et al, 2012; Clarke and Cochrane, 2013; see also Chapter Three, this volume). This chapter, however, goes further to illustrate that the very existence of 'the local' is also uneven. Being local is not a private activity; it is one that is performed in spaces that are, to some extent, public. In English culture, the pub is the iconic 'local', but local shops, parks, cafes or community centres are also thought of as providing a space for people to get together and 'be' local. Without space in which to meet, there is no local. There is a very real connection between both the built environment *and* community: we cannot disaggregate the two (see Chapters Two and Three, this volume).

Investigating the local in this way was possible through using arts-based research methodologies, and this chapter explores the potential of these techniques and approaches. Of course, 'the local', like 'place' or 'home', could be investigated through interviews or surveys. These are all methods to show 'what works'. Yet, arts-led research methodologies let us investigate feelings, sometimes ultimately captured as text. These methods attempt to capture the sensations, emotions and reactions to performances and representations of 'the local', encompassing a broader set of responses. The suggestion here is that the diversity of responses elicited through arts-led research can increase opportunities for exchange and communication.

In this way, arts-led research can raise research questions just as for the political strategy of localism that more conventional social science methods might not reveal, for how can you take localism forward if there is no local? Certainly, this was a question that without these responses on one wet Sunday afternoon, we, as researchers on localism, would not have thought to ask.

Methodology and method

In order to interrogate what is 'local' for this research, creative participants (a storyteller, photographers, a writer and a filmmaker) developed articulations of a, the or their local. Their articulations were within their creative discretion and the performances, photographs, writing and films revealed a diverse array of real, imagined or remembered locals. When these artistic interventions on the local were publicly performed, we asked audiences for their responses. The aim was to use diverse entry points into the research process in order to see whether the arts-led interventions revealed a response that produced any consistency or, instead, consistent plurality.

The working assumption behind the research was one of plurality. We presumed that the rather unitary construction of 'the local' in the Localism Act 2011 and policy debates would sit uneasily with empirical evidence, which social science research suggested to us would be relational, multiple and dynamic. We assumed that there would be multiplicity, and, consequently, we methodologically followed Crang and Cook (2007: 149), taking the position that '[t]he process of analysis is not a matter of developing a definitive account, but of trying to find a means to understand the inter-relations of multiple versions of reality'. In the storytelling-led investigations, we used the stories as the intervention to which responses were gathered from audience members in response.

The iterative methodology we used to investigate these research questions was designed to reflect the tension we saw between the unitary and overlapping understandings of the local. Drawing on the narratives of the local, both oral and visual, and the comments from audience members, as well as the analysis of semi-structured interviews with the creative participants, we sought to determine whether these representations of 'the local' were different and/or better conceptions of the local than those routinely employed in policy and media debates.

This piece of research was not designed to prove a hypothesis, but, rather, to reveal responses to identify lines of enquiry. There is great potential in these methods to tap into emotional and lived understandings of complex issues.

Arts-based methods of inquiry and ways of knowing

Emerging during the Renaissance and prevalent in Western culture, there has long been a distinction made between science and arts, or the 'outer' and 'inner' worlds. From this perspective, 'the "arts" are seen primarily as exploring the "inner" world in a gestalt, intuitive way', letting the external world intrude on it, while 'science' has the 'task of depicting and exploring the "external" world in an objective way, unimpaired by the "inner" world of the scientists' (Inns, 2002: 307).

A number of assertions support the use of the arts for inquiry: that words are proxies for direct experience; that we know more than we can say; and that the arts access the range of human emotion and make a more holistic contribution to our understanding (Polanyi, 1983 [1966]). Karen Estrella and Michele Forinash (2007: 377) suggest that arts-based inquiry allows us to retrieve and explore the 'marginalized, controversial, and disruptive perspectives that have often been lost in more traditional research methodologies'. Through these methods, research 'becomes a process of overcoming distance rather than creating it' (Estrella and Forinash, 2007: 381–2).

This working assumption – that arts-led methods can retrieve perspectives and sensations that otherwise might be ignored – is particularly useful when investigating both a unit of governance and a felt place. Arts-led inquiry enables researchers to tap into some of the emotional resonance of 'the local' in order to get beyond a more familiar understanding of the local as local government (the local authority, local schools, local police beats). As Estrella and Forinash

(2007) suggest, arts create a sense of knowing through the creative process and the experiencing of it.

Using arts-led methods allows researchers to draw on 'tacit' knowledge (Tsoukas, 2002), which opens up 'undiscovered avenues of understanding' (Estrella and Forinash, 2007: 381). This can make the invisible visible, and bring into the foreground that which has been suppressed and silenced (Taylor, 2002). This appears to support Taylor and Ladkin's (2009) argument that arts-based methods can enable those involved to apprehend the 'essence' of a concept, situation or tacit knowledge in a particular way, revealing depths and connections that more propositional and linear developmental orientations cannot. Accessing tacit knowledge would, we hoped, enable participants to communicate the 'unthought known'.

A further reason for using arts-based interventions was that these methods allowed us to give voice to those not heard through traditional mechanisms. Vaara, Tienari and Säntti (2003) have suggested that such methods elicit different kinds of thinking from people who have not found voices through traditional mechanisms. This is because such methods enable us to explore the places that we do not usually go to comfortably, releasing what Taylor (2002: 827) describes as 'aesthetic muteness', where 'discourse about the aesthetic aspect of day-to-day experience is not legitimate'. Arts-based methods are a participatory process that invites and validates people's personal narratives, enabling individuals to feel empowered to take 'constructive action'. Empathy for the other also becomes possible through the multiple perspectives that 'allow for recognition of the otherness of the other' (Estrella and Forinash, 2007: 381–2).

There is also a very practical way in which arts-based methods can give voice to participants whose views and understandings might not otherwise be captured through conventional research. Arts-based researchers can enable creative participants to lead academic researchers, follow creative networks and, consequently, research in locations that are different from those localities that academics conventionally focus on. This certainly led us in our research to a very rich series of comparisons between more privileged (in terms of public and green spaces and community facilities, as well as income) 'locals' and places where both financial and other resources are in much shorter supply.

We were led to research in the locations we did through artistic, rather than academic, connections. St Werburghs in Bristol was a clear choice of our storyteller and photographer, who explained the site as follows:

"The local in St Werburghs, there isn't a prissiness that you might get in a small town or a village or in the suburbs – these people in the choir live all around Bristol – some might live in St Werburghs – and they're completely willing to do this thing in the street – people are walking past smoking joints or whatever – they aren't precious. They are representative of this area."

Similarly, in Bridport and Patchway, we followed artistic connections, which was incredibly productive given the frequent overemphasis of some locations in social science (eg, Stokes Croft in Bristol) and the subsequent *under*emphasis on research on less familiar locations. We also worked with colleagues at Durham in the North East and at the Durham Book Festival, again mixing academic and creative connections.

Third, arts-based methods of inquiry ask participants to suspend their habitual patterns of mind or understandings of the world, their cynicism, their indifference, their negativity, in order to find new ways of imagining, perceiving, creating and analysing (Mainemelis and Ronson, 2006; Estrella and Forinash, 2007). New understandings may begin and emerge from an interruption in or a questioning of the 'accepted ways of understanding the world' (Estrella and Forinash, 2007: 379).

Storytelling and narrative

There are specific reasons to use storytelling as a form of artistic intervention. As Gabriel and Connell (2010: 508) suggest, poetry and fiction can 'reach beyond literal truth for deeper truths'. This is an insight that has been increasingly accepted in the social sciences over the last 30 years, particularly in ethnography, geography, medicine and sociology, where scholars have suggested that storytelling can elicit, unpack and disclose material and information that might not be revealed through other, more traditional methods, such as surveys, questionnaires and interviews (Pye, 1995).

Certainly, while storytelling and narrative are frequently conflated, which can contribute to a confusion within research methodology discussions, they are distinct. Narrative inquiry is a social science-based research method that analyses the narrative of a particular event, organisation or process in order to reveal or address specific or hidden issues. Itself once a non-traditional research method, narrative inquiry has joined the ranks of established social science methodologies to investigate themes and propositions in a variety of disciplines, from medicine and psychotherapy to visual and performing arts.

Storytelling, on the other hand, is particularly useful for participatory projects that draw on the voices of diverse publics, not necessarily involved in the political processes of central government. Stories and the telling of stories are open to multiple interpretations. These 'leaps of faith' can provide researchers with potential opportunities to question the complexities and nuances that make up public opinion and perception but that are not possible to elicit through simple questionnaires or surveys. Moreover, in this opportunity for complexity, nuance and multiple interpretation, they also provide an oppositional element to the governmental unitary notion of what constitutes the local.

In this sense, storytelling-led research can be more of an investigation of the complexities and nuances of subjectivities and the creative interpretation of data by both participants and researchers than 'finding' objective discoveries or building theory. This is particularly important in projects that investigate human perceptions, measuring them against party-political concepts that appear to be put forward by governments as if from a positivist, natural world of science-based fact. From this perspective, arts-led inquiry might also be seen as creating a potential connective tissue between macro-political governance and micro-political processes and perceptions. It provides alternative perspectives from which to understand – or feel – units of governance that are presumed by politicians, without any confirmatory empirical research on their part.

In particular, the 'seduction' of storytelling, where 'stories ... draw us in and at times, fix us under their spell' (Day Sclater, 2003: 621), is incredibly powerful. Storytelling is an embodied practice not just for the storyteller, but also for the audience. Audiences sense-take from stories and narratives by taking 'snippets' (Sims et al, 2009), which they reframe and re-contextualise for making sense of their own situations. Gabriel and Connell (2010: 507) have suggested that storytelling is located between lived experience and fantasy, thus allowing the storyteller to 'sacrifice factual accuracy in the interest of making and "sharing" a point'. This is particularly useful in projects where researchers are interested not so much in every last factual detail, but in how people feel, understand and perceive something like 'the local'.

In our research, what we were really interested in was listening to people 'tell' the local, be they the creative participants or members of the audience or local communities. This focus on 'telling', rather than more discursive understandings of narrative, became even more relevant as the project developed and we realised that our intention was, in fact, more to understand the audiences perceptions as articulated by themselves rather than just through the stories told.

This is useful in localism research as storytelling, film and photographs are media that can help researchers explore the different ways in which the local is understood and experienced in communities. Stories may be told, and photographs and films may be taken, from multiple perspectives, the variety of which has the potential to spark a corresponding multiplicity of responses from audiences and participants. Diverse, even contradicting, responses offer increased opportunities for exchange and communication, with the potential for creating more nuanced understandings of complex issues instead of simple broad generalisations. Conversely, diverse opinions that chime (eg on the absence, as much as the presence, of the local) also appear to us to be significant.

Throughout the project, these arts interventions were co-produced between academics and creative practitioners. The storytelling, photography and films were facilitated by an outline specification but rested primarily on the creative talents of the storytellers, filmmakers and photographers, respectively. These creative researchers engaged with the participants directly, without academic mediators. Between ourselves, as researchers, there were equal and reciprocal relationships; in this sense, the research was genuinely co-produced.

Of course, power is never absent from research processes (see Chapter Four, this volume). The project was funded and so had to broadly comply with the initial research proposal. There were institutions involved with their own requirements. Further, and more significantly, the relationships with participants – the respondents who gave us these incredibly valuable findings – were not so reciprocal. Participants in St Werburghs, Patchway and Bridport, for example, were not involved in designing the form of the artistic intervention. Nevertheless, in the broadest sense, the resulting 'data', including the stories themselves, the interviews with creative participants and the responses on index cards, were co-produced. They came from the relationships between all the participants and researchers, evolving over time and shaped by performances and interventions in particular localities.

There are also still questions of translation and uptake (see Chapter Six and Twelve, this volume). Using index cards, which encouraged immediate and short responses, means that findings could be more easily disseminated than a lengthy report. "There is no local here, love" is one such instantly telling response.

The local and (no) local

Can a story resonate with participants' daily lives? In our research, we found that it did, in both positive and negative ways. 'Telling the local' in this way proved incredibly powerful, at times, leading to confirmation by audience members that, yes, they had understood a local and were part of it.

Conversely, the figurative presentations of an (imagined) local sometimes also had a very unexpected effect. It enabled different audiences, in both Bristol and Durham, to reflect that they had no local or that they were no longer local, and that they missed this. Respondents understood the idea of a local perfectly well, but it represented for them a place where they had been born and grew up, and not where they now lived.

As Michael Smith (2012) wrote:

> I'm not local anymore, but I used to be, and I miss it.... Breathing in a town's worth of memories: everything I look at I'd forgotten, everything I look at I already know, all these thousand things evoking this particular terroir with all the subtle nuance of a fine rare Burgundy: my long lost home, The Town.

In this sense, our findings illustrated that, to a very large extent, you find what you look for when you look in places that you might expect it. That is, in St Werburgh's in Bristol – a residential area with four pubs, a city farm, a community cafe with a playground attached, self-build eco-housing and shared open space – we found many expressions of 'the local'. Responding to storytelling, including at a 'Tasty Tales' event, where local food was matched with local stories in the iconic community cafe, residents expressed their understanding that there was a local 'there' and that they were often part of it. Asked 'What is local?', they said: "Next door. Nearby, in the vicinity. Neighbours. Local Shop. Friends round the corner"; "Food, energy, culture produced locally, controlled locally and shared"; "Are you local? Yes I have an allotment just up the hill". The following are responses of a local singing group rehearsing in a local tunnel: "Local is where I live"; "Local is where I've raised my family"; "Local is where my allotment is"; "Local is where I get rested – refreshed"; "Local is where my best friends live". Again, at the Arts Centre in Bridport in Dorset, we found similar understandings:

"Living locally is about getting to know people, overlapping circles, young and old."

"Localism: for generations, families would live in the same place, grow their own food and vegetables in the land and eat them, and, in effect, become one with the land."

This finding of the local, and such strong assertions of it, indicated that perhaps our initial hypothesis was misplaced: that 'the local' is understood and lived, in an embodied sense. (Although it is worth noting that when two of us presented this material to a culturally and ethnically diverse group at the Balsall Heath Arts Biennale in 2013, [white] respondents were concerned about this focus on previous generations. There is a widespread concern that the local can still be created.)

Certainly, however, for most people, the local is small in scale. In Dorset, two respondents mentioned cycling, one stating "Knowing people whenever I'm in town. The community orchard. The Meeting House. Happy Island. Cycling everywhere", while another evocatively delimited the extent of the local: "*The local is as far as I can cycle before breakfast*". For other participants, however, there was a clear sense that there was a 'local' but that it was elsewhere, behind them. This was well expressed in a piece of writing commissioned from Michael Smith (2012) at the Durham Book Festival: 'I'm not local anymore, but I used to be, and I miss it'. When Micheal Smith's piece was performed, this sense of a 'local' being elsewhere was also felt by an audience member:

"I'm very neighbourly but I don't feel remotely local to where I live. I phone the neighbours, I couldn't go into their houses, but I don't feel like I belong. But I sort of hanker towards what Mike was saying when I go back to Portsmouth, where I'm from, I walk down through the streets and I don't have to speak to anyone, there's just this intrinsic sense of belonging that kind of makes me feel as if it's just something that's maybe in the genes or something like that."

This point about absence was also strongly made in Patchway, where a very elderly woman, who had lived there for 45 years, still did not feel local. She was local in Devon, where she was born: "*Once a Devonian, always a Devonian*". Land use decisions about that part of Bristol where she lived now were "up to the people of Filton, it's their place", although she might contribute to some consultations given that she was a council tax-payer.

So, the project found that people could identify with the idea of 'the' or 'a' local, even if they were not presently there. For some, this may have been a result of travelling around, not settling in a neighbourhood (Michael Smith). For the resident of North Bristol, however, there was a pragmatic concern. As she put it, "there is no local here". It was her view that there were no local shops (except Tescos), the last remaining pub had closed down and the community centre had to charge for its activities in order to remain solvent. The Older Person's Tea Party, run by a charity, was an 'oasis' in this landscape: a place for conviviality and connection, but it was not 'local'.

Subsequent (social science) analysis of shops, pubs and public spaces in this area confirmed her feeling in empirical terms. South Gloucestershire Council, the local authority for Patchway, confirmed that there is a serious lack of public space in the locality. Based on a population of 262,800 residents (2011 Census), it identified a deficiency of some 68 hectares in informal recreation space, 78 hectares in outdoor sports facilities, 50 hectares in provision for children and young people, and 19 hectares of allotments against these new standards.

South Gloucestershire Council acknowledged, however, that these deficits are not simple to fix: 'At current prices it is estimated that it would cost in the region of £135 m (excluding the cost of land and fees) to deliver the existing quantitative shortfall'. Furthermore, it is not just the amount of public and open space that is missing in Patchway, 'qualitative shortfalls are also known to exist' (South Gloucestershire Council, 2012: 4).

Implications for policymaking

For Lucy Lippard (1997, p 7), who famously used artistic practices to deepen understanding of engagement between people and place, the local has a 'lure', which is:

> the pull of place that operates on each of us, exposing our politics and our spiritual legacies. It is the geographical component of the psychological need to belong somewhere, one antidote to a prevailing alienation. The lure of the local is that undertone to modern life that connects it to the past we know so little and the future we are aimlessly concocting.

For Prime Minister David Cameron, introducing a programme of 'localism' (an ideology that governance should be both of and by the local) in 2010, 'the' local can also be identified. It is not as personal and subjective, or multiple or dynamic, as critics suggest. 'The local' is capable of being spatially delineated (drawing a line around it on a map) and becoming, for governance purposes, an entity similar to 'the neighbourhood' or 'the community' in both long-standing and ongoing administrative initiatives.

Yet, even if both these views of 'the local' draw on a shared understanding of 'the' local, the move to local*ism*, a political ideology that mandates that 'locals' should make local decisions or be responsible for their own needs, is a step beyond. Perhaps this is a distinction between social science (particularly in political theory) and arts and humanities understandings of the local. We might broadly agree that the local is a place, a coming together, a practice, without necessarily agreeing that this place has political implications simply by being. Should the 'lure of the local' be translated into governing in an administrative or legal sense?

This is a normative question. Should the desire (which we found) and acceptance of 'the local' lead to a political ideology of local*ism*, that local areas should be responsible for themselves? Cameron's view that the government should be 'giving more power to local government, to drive it out to the lowest level, so they can help build those strong economies of the future' (http://news.bbc.co.uk/1/hi/programmes/politics_show/7877564.stm) is well known. Yet, for many, 'austerity localism' is seen as a smokescreen, a trope, to justify reductions in public spending. The fact that we seemed to find 'locals' does not lead to an inevitable or desirable consequence that 'locals can develop local solutions to major social problems', thereby 'reducing the distance between the Government and the governed' (HM Government, 2010). This is the basis of the 'local trap' according to (Purcell, 2006).

Certainly, there has been great scepticism about the localism agenda. This relates not only to the political project, but also to the very idea of 'a' or 'the' local. As Adrian Barritt, Chief Officer of Adur Voluntary Action, wrote in the Trade Union Congress's response to the Localism Act cited earlier, the word 'local' doesn't mean anything, and 'localism' is consequently meaningless:

> The word 'local' doesn't mean anything. It is defined by the context and intention of its use. Unpacked, it is loaded with spatial, social and cultural assumptions, and not a few emotional undertones. My 'local' is probably not

yours.... Anyone can understand 'localism' – because it is meaningless. The government understands that, but knows that this is a robust lie, eel-like in its ability to slip out of criticism, and turn attackers back upon themselves. It's no surprise that it has picked up on a term custom-made to appeal to fox hunters, community activists, UKIP [United Kingdom Independence Party] members, MPs and local councillors, trade unionists, village public bar regulars, and the small shop keeper. (TUC, 2012: 2)

From a legal point of view, neither localism nor the local have been defined in legislation and in the lead-up to the passing of the Localism Act, the government was criticised by the House of Commons Committee for an understanding of 'localism' that was 'extremely elastic', marked by inconsistency and incoherence (House of Commons, 2009). In their response, the government pointed to an article by David Cameron in *The Observer* as grounding their justification of the term (HM Government, 2010), implicitly suggesting, once again, that 'local' and 'localism' do not require detailed consideration, they are 'common sense', everyday expressions. Cameron assumes that there is 'a local', as if this is different from established forms of local government. There can be 'local solutions' to social problems.

Given this political and academic scepticism, it is striking how vibrant the idea of 'the local' has remained. In our research, this was true even in those locations where respondents felt that they were no longer local, but that they had been. In these instances, understandings of 'the local' often harked back to an earlier time and place, where people felt connected and 'a lure'. This was evidenced in Patchway, as well as in responses to the Durham Book Festival (outlined earlier) and in a film commissioned for the project. For participants who see the emptying out of local shops and places to be local, with a drift towards the city centre, 'there is no local here'. It was not (just) the absence of lyricism or nostalgia that was striking, but a very practical concern about the lack of public space.

It was argued above, and we would agree, that 'spatial disparities are largely the area-level manifestations of *non-spatial* forces, in particular, those producing poverty and inequality at the macro-level' (Nathan, Chapter Five, this volume, emphasis in original). This is undoubtedly true, the lack of public spaces in Patchway and other similarly spatially deprived neighbourhoods is the result of rapid house-building without provision for convivial spaces and the decline of local shops in favour of a single large superstore. Yet, as this research illustrates, the spatial is still deeply implicated here. Spatial disparities are largely manifestations of social, political and economic conditions, but not exclusively so. As Soja (2010a), has argued in his debate on this point with Marcuse, it is important to emphasise 'urban spatial causality and how society and space are mutually formative, with neither the social nor the spatial privileged over the other'. Spatiality is more than simply a causal effect here (Soja, 2010b). If the local looked and felt different, there might be very different social, economic and political effects. This is an important implication in understanding localism as a political strategy.

Conclusions

Ultimately, this project found 'the local', albeit one mediated by access to property and public space. This then raised a key policy question for our project: how could there be localism in places where people did not feel local? This is not always a difficulty, as Jones et al make equally clear in Chapter Eleven of this volume. Frequently, participants are both concerned and proud of their locality. Yet, the lack of public space in which to meet on a day-to-day basis, talking in local shops, the pub and the street, clearly impacts in other locations. The older participants in North Bristol talked of acts of neighbourliness; these still occurred on an intimate, next-door scale. Expanded out, this might form a sense of the Big Society, of a contribution to help each other, but it did not seem to provide a basis for localism.

What, then, of the arts-based methods. Did this project innovate as it had hoped? As with Lippard's work on the local, then, arts-based interventions have allowed us to gather data that initially appeared to stand in stark contrast to the kind of material and data that are required by policymakers. The two different worlds of policymaking and qualitative research often appear to be oppositional: policymakers require researchers to provide them with simplified portrayals of social and political life so that they can create policy that can be carried out at a broad, national macro-level.

Qualitative researchers, on the other hand, 'normally have a diametrically opposed view of simplification' (Donmoyer, 2012: 798). According to Donmoyer (2012: 798), the aim is, then, to try to influence policymakers without 'losing ... [one's] methodological soul' as a qualitative researcher. Koro-Ljunberg and Mazzei (2010: 1) argue that trying to simplify can lead to 'over-generalizations of findings' and can even 'disempower those whom research purports to benefit'.

There is unlikely to be a neat solution to these different approaches (and ontologies). Geertz (2000 [1973]: 23) suggests that 'cultural analysis is intrinsically incomplete', making clear that there can be no point where ends are neatly tied up into policies that reflect and benefit everyone. Social action is created through human interaction, which constantly constructs and reconstructs meaning. Quantitative or qualitative methods that rely on surveys, questionnaires or interviews are not capable of conveying these complexities. Other, non-traditional methods (including arts-based methods) can more effectively help us in gathering and interpreting such messy, complex and diverse material.

Perhaps the most important aspect that we found was that the interventions generated a whole new research question. Rather than examining a unitary conception, or multiple conceptions, of the local, we needed to look at spatial and social variability. We found the idea of 'the local' more robust than we had assumed. In some localities, it was socially incorporated and spatialised. We believe that these methods enabled us to tap into something that conventional social science surveys or interview questionnaires might not have found, asking 'Where is the local?'. An embodied, phenomenological experience triggered different responses.

It is not just that localism, despite being uniformly legislated in England, is uneven. This is well established. What this research has demonstrated is that the very existence of 'the local' is socially, spatially and culturally uneven. Without arts-led research, this is not a question that we would have thought to ask.

Note

[1] This chapter explores the methodology and methods underpinning a project, 'Localism, Storytelling and Myth', funded by the Arts and Humanities Research Council in 2012/13. The project was inadvertently in two parts as a consequence of logistics and geography. Joe Painter and Raksha Pande worked on delivering arts-based research in the North East, in Durham and South Shields, while we worked in the South West, in Bristol and Dorset, collaborating also with the team at the Beyond the Borders festival, connected by Hamish Fyfe. This chapter tells the story of our investigations into 'what is local' and who feels local in the South West. The creative interventions and illustrations, as well as the final project report, is available at: http://localismnarrativemyth.weebly.com

References

Clarke, N. and Cochrane, A. (2013) 'Geographies and politics of localism: the localism of the United Kingdom's Coalition government', *Political Geography* 34: 10–23.

Crang, M. and Cook, I. (2007) *Doing ethnographies*, London: Sage.

Day Sclater, S. (2003) 'The arts and narrative research – arts as inquiry: an epilogue', *Qualitative Inquiry* 9(4): 621–4.

Donmoyer, R. (2012) 'Two (very) different worlds: the cultures of policymaking and qualitative reesarch', *Qualitative Inquiry* 9(18): 798–807.

Estrella, K. and Forinash, M. (2007) 'Narrative inquiry and arts-based inquiry: multinarrative perspectives', *Journal of Humanistic Psychology* 47: 376–83.

Featherstone, D., Ince, A., Mackinnon, D., Strauss, K. and Cumbers, A. (2012) 'Progressive localism and the construction of political alternatives', *Transactions of the Institute of British Geographers* 37(2): 177–82.

Gabriel, Y. and Connell, N.A.D. (2010) 'Co-creating stories: collaborative experiments in storytelling', *Management Learning* 41(5): 507–23.

Geertz, C. (2000 [1973]) *The interpretation of cultures*, New York, NY: Basic Books.

Georges, R.A. (1969) 'Toward an understanding of storytelling', *Journal of American Folklore* 82: 313–28.

HM Government (2010) *Decentralisation and the Localism Bill: An essential guide*, London: DCLG, p 4.

House of Commons Communities and Local Government Committee (2009) *The balance of power: central and local government: Sixth Report of Session 2008–09*, London: The Stationery Office.

Inns, D. (2002) 'Metaphor in the literature of organizational analysis: a preliminary taxonomy and a glimpse at a humanities-based perspective', *Organization* 9(2): 305–30.

Koro-Ljunberg, M. and Mazzei, L.A. (2010) 'Problematizing methodological simplicity in qualitative research: editor's introduction', *Qualitative Inquiry* 18(9): 728–31.

Lippard, L. (1997) *The lure of the local: senses of place in a multicentered society*, New York, NY: New Press.

Mainemelis, C. and Ronson, S. (2006) 'Ideas are born in fields of play: towards a theory of play and creativity in organizational settings', *Research in Organizational Behavior: An Annual Series of Analytical Essays and Critical Reviews* 27(0): 81–131.

Polanyi, M. (1983 [1966]) *The tacit dimension*, Gloucester, MA: Peter Smith Publisher.

Purcell, M. (2006) 'Urban democracy and the local trap', *Urban studies* 43(11): 1921–41.

Pye, A. (1995) 'Strategy through dialogue and doing: a game of "Mornington Crescent"?', *Management Learning* 26(4): 445–62.

Sims, D., Huxham, C. and Beech, N. (2009) 'On telling stories but hearing snippets: sense-taking from presentation of practice', *Organization* 16(3): 371–88.

Soja, E. (2010a) 'Spatializing the urban, Part I', *City* 14(6): 629–35.

Soja, E. (2010b) 'Spatializing the urban, Part II', *City*, 15(1): 96–102.

Smith, M. (2012) 'Are you local', commissioned for the project and on file with the authors.

South Gloucestershire Council (2012) 'Community infrastructure levy funding gap paper'. Available at: https://consultations.southglos.gov.uk/gf2.ti/f/328930/8272581.1/PDF/-/Draft_Funding_Gap_paper.pdf

Taylor, S.S. (2002) 'Overcoming aesthetic muteness: researching organizational members' aesthetic experience', *Human Relations* 55: 821–40.

Taylor, S.S. and Ladkin, D. (2009) 'Understanding arts-based methods in managerial development', *Academy of Management Learning & Education* 8(1): 55–69.

Tsoukas, H. (2002) 'Introduction', *Management Learning* 33(4): 419–26.

TUC (Trades Union Congress) (2012) *Localism: threat or opportunity? Perspectives on the Localism Act for union and community organisers and activists*, London: TUC.

Vaara, E., Tienari, J. and Säntti, R. (2003) 'The international match: metaphors as vehicles of social identity building in cross-border mergers', *Human Relations* 56(4): 419–51.

Part Three
New places for communities

EIGHT

Forging communities: the Caerau and Ely Rediscovering Heritage project and the dynamics of co-production

Clyde Ancarno, Oliver Davis and David Wyatt

Introduction

Cardiff is Europe's youngest capital city and its history is dominated by its maritime and industrial heritage. However, nestled deep in one of its suburbs, surrounded by houses, is one of the most important, yet little known and understood, prehistoric monuments in the region: Caerau Hillfort. Enclosing an area of more than five hectares, Caerau Hillfort is by far the largest Iron Age hillfort in South Glamorgan. The housing estates that surround the hillfort are home to more than 25,000 people – the largest social housing estates in Wales. Despite strong community ties, the people who live there are burdened by significant social and economic deprivation, particularly high unemployment. Its large population once fed major manufacturing employers, such as Ely Paper Mill and Ely Brewery, but since these closed down in the 1980s, employment in the area has never recovered. This is partly due to poor educational attainment – almost 50% of 16- and 17-year-olds have no qualifications and only 2% of school leavers go on to university (compared with 95% in other areas of Cardiff). Moreover, a disturbance in the summer of 1991 was publicised in the media as a 'riot' and led to a deluge of long-lasting bad publicity that has given these communities a real stigma, particularly in the minds of residents of wider Cardiff.

As modern political and economic power have become concentrated in the centre of Cardiff and at Cardiff Bay, Caerau and Ely have become increasingly marginalised. Whereas this challenging environment has deterred archaeologists in the past, this was the very reason why the Caerau and Ely Rediscovering Heritage (CAER) project was established. However, CAER is not a straightforward community archaeology research project; it is underpinned by objectives forged during a series of initial meetings involving local residents, local school representatives, the local community development agency, local heritage institutions and a small team of academics. Importantly, these objectives are focused not upon archaeological or historical research, but, rather, on how such research might be employed to transform negative views associated with these local communities and the broader challenges that they face. From its outset, the project sought to utilise the community's rich and untapped heritage assets and local expertise to develop educational and life opportunities for its inhabitants: building confidence, challenging negative stereotypes and realising the positive potential of the process of research co-production. To date, the project has involved community members (including school pupils, young people facing exclusion, people experiencing long-term unemployment and retired people) in a variety of co-produced initiatives, including: geophysical surveys, museum exhibitions, adult learner's courses, art installations, creative writing, dance performances, banner processions, history projects, film-making and the creation of heritage trails. At the heart of these heritage-themed initiatives have been two major community excavations at Caerau's magnificent Iron Age hillfort; these have involved a wide range of local community members and schoolchildren in the co-production of archaeological research.

This chapter will begin by providing a summary of key aspects of the literature surrounding participation and co-production in Wales. It will move on to provide an overview of CAER's approach to co-production, summarising the co-produced archaeological research activities to date. The concluding section will focus on the evaluation data gathered during these co-produced activities, that is, the reflections of a small group of community members on their involvement in CAER, particularly its community excavations carried out in June–July 2013 and 2014. These reflections, captured in the form of interviews, are used: first, to think about the potential benefits and problems of utilising co-production in relation to community heritage assets within the broader 'post-regeneration' policy context; and, second, to explore the challenges of evaluation in the community co-production of research.

CAER therefore provides an interesting case study for exploring the implications pertaining to the evaluation of community co-produced heritage projects. Evaluation, a crucial exercise in terms of gauging the impact of such projects, formed an important focus of CAER, which implemented a strategy of evaluation that is participatory in nature. In other words, community members, whenever possible, were involved in the evaluation process (see Jackson and Kassam, 1998). It is our premise that despite increasing interest in the implications of evaluating engagement in relation to co-produced research in recent years, a lot of work still remains to be done to get unorthodox approaches to evaluation more widely recognised and accepted. This is echoed by Elliot et al (2012), who provide examples of reasons 'why community-strengthening interventions do not have strong evidence base' (this is in relation to health and well-being). The qualitative analysis of the evaluative interviews incorporated in this chapter is therefore presented with these challenges and deficits in mind.

The Caerau and Ely Rediscovering Heritage project and co-production

The term 'co-production' was developed in the US during the 1970s in response to urban fiscal cutbacks in public services. It advocates the involvement of citizens in 'producing public services as well as consuming or otherwise benefitting from them' (Alford, 1998: 128). In the UK, co-production was initially associated with the public service reforms of the successive Labour governments since 1997. It has more recently, and somewhat conversely, been taken up by the Conservative leadership's 'Big Society' agenda in opposition to the perceived 'big state' policies associated with the previous Labour government (Needham, 2008: 221; Durose et al, 2012a). In theory, co-production is concerned with realising the potential of a thriving civil society through transformative, democratic, inclusive participation in public services, incorporating mutually beneficial reciprocal partnerships centred upon community activism, involvement and empowerment (Boyle and Harris, 2009). Several key 'ingredients' for successful and transformative co-production have been identified by a number of authors. These include: a focus on community assets rather than deficits; valuing equally the contribution of all participants (whether trained professionals or community volunteers); project sustainability and continued or long-term involvement; the development of social networks through face-to-face contact; reciprocal and mutually beneficial partnerships (both organisational and individual); and gaining skills and enrichment through the processes of co-production (Cornwall, 2008; Needham, 2008; Boyle and Harris, 2009; Durose et al, 2012b).

In Wales, values of community activism have long been the rallying cry of Welsh politicians (Rees, 1997). Indeed, active citizenship and community participation were effectively hardwired into the 'Yes' campaign for devolution (Dicks, 2014). Following the success of the devolution campaign, the Welsh Assembly government placed a statutory obligation on local partnerships that was intended to ensure the inclusion of previously excluded groups in their decision-making processes – with equal representation for the public, private and voluntary sectors – 'the so called "three-thirds" principle' (Bristow et al, 2009: 905). They also instigated a radical 'non-prescriptive' regeneration programme, Communities First (C1), within the 'most disadvantaged communities' across Wales (Dicks, 2014: 960). From the outset, the C1 programme was steeped in the co-production principles of active citizenship, community activation and 'radical aims of empowering communities' (Dicks, 2014: 960). Yet, as recently highlighted by Dicks, there is a significant gulf between rhetoric and practice in relation to this drive for participatory regeneration in Wales. Dicks contends that since the programme's inception in 2001, C1's radical co-production objectives have been inhibited, over time, by a range of factors, including: 'top-down' political agendas; rigid systems of financial accountability; target-driven monitoring procedures; and a culture of 'risk-averse' management at both local authority and national levels (Dicks, 2014; for a practitioner's perspective on these issues, see Horton, 2012). Bristow et al (2009: 917) have similarly noted that significant tensions have arisen 'between the inherent focus of policy programmes on governance efficiency and the desire for greater inclusion' in relation to the implementation of the Welsh government's 'three-thirds' principle.

The work of Dicks and Bristow et al reveal the problematic and politically charged nature of co-production in relation to community development initiatives in Wales. Yet, while discussions concerning co-production are frequently framed around the highly politicised arena of public service provision, there has been far less emphasis on the significance of the co-production of research. At first glance, this would appear to be an avenue of discussion liberated from the heavy political 'baggage' surrounding public service co-production. However, as Matthews and O'Brien (Chapter Three, this volume) point out, in the face of cuts in services to community development, community heritage and participatory arts, the 'Connected Communities' programme, a cross-Council programme funding co-produced research projects, has been criticised for being a 'very expensive community development project' that has 'merely stepped into a funding void left by others'. Moreover, Durose et al (2012b: 7) have highlighted the parallels between the perceived 'democratic deficit' of public institutions and the challenge of the 'relevance gap' in research – both of which have 'prompted attempts to increase participation from citizens and communities'. While employing the rhetoric of equality and reciprocity, research co-production projects, especially with marginal communities, can easily fall into the trap of top-down leadership, which can intentionally or unintentionally reproduce unequal power relations (Durose et al, 2012b: 4–5; Hart et al, 2012).

So, while the CAER team was not directly influenced by policy agendas pertaining to public service provision and austerity cuts, they were, inevitably, influenced by similarly framed agendas pertaining to funding directives, university strategy and the Research Excellence Framework. The aspiration of co-production was therefore not approached uncritically; the team was well aware of the potential issues around power, politics and participation. In synergy with the practices of its partner community development organisation, Action in Caerau and Ely (ACE), and with the recent literature produced by a range of 'Connected Communities' scoping studies (e.g. Durose et al, 2012b; Hale, 2012; Hart et al, 2012), the CAER team was committed to actively involving community members in the co-production of research; valuing the contribution of all participants and partners in a mutually beneficial and reciprocal relationship.

To date, the project has involved a myriad of non-higher education partners (e.g. primary and secondary schools, community groups, youth workers, community development workers, local residents, the National Museum of Wales, Cardiff Story Museum, Glamorgan Archives, Cardiff Council) alongside academics, undergraduates and postgraduates from a range of disciplines at Cardiff University (history, archaeology, social sciences). A range of key strategies have been employed by CAER to ensure meaningful co-production and mutual benefit between the wide range of academic, heritage sector and community partners involved. These include: community consultation and involvement in funding bids; the embedding of an academic member of staff (Oliver Davis) within ACE; the development of a close partnership with local secondary schools; the establishment of community-based adult learner's courses; the creation of partnerships with a local youth centre and the National Museum of Wales to involve young people facing exclusion in creating heritage-themed art; and community outreach opportunities for university students working closely alongside community participants. The wide-ranging nature of the project's impacts and partnerships, and the embedding of academics and a professional artist within a community context, resulted in multifarious, often 'organically' nurtured, forms of engagement and co-production. This included the embedding of research co-production within the curricula of participating secondary schools, with pupils undertaking geophysical surveys and archaeological excavation, creating museum exhibitions, performances, artwork and heritage trails, and participating in a *Time Team* programme in April 2012. The involvement of a professional artist, Paul Evans, in all stages of the project proved a particularly successful strategy in this respect. Paul designed and facilitated creative forms of engagement with local heritage themes, including large eco-graffiti art installations, puppet shows, the design of a heritage trail and the creation of an Iron Age-themed mural with both local pupils in mainstream secondary education and young people excluded from school. Furthermore, the embedding of research within a series of free, accredited adult education courses in practical archaeology, in association with the Cardiff Centre for Lifelong Learning, proved successful in engaging long-term unemployed males in co-production – with undeniable benefits in terms of progression and confidence-building for a number of these individuals (Davis and Sharples, 2014: 59–60).

CAER also sought to establish new social and professional partnerships, thereby creating a new 'community of practice' (CoP) (Hart et al, 2012). A crucial ingredient in this creation was the equal value placed on the contributions and 'knowledge bases' of all partners, whether trained professionals or community volunteers (Hart et al, 2012: 6). From the outset, community members, secondary schools and community development agencies were integrated in the project's development. This included the establishment of a 'Friends of Caerau' community group, which continues to meet bimonthly and organises litter picks, trail clearances and heritage events. It also included the establishment of a special partnership with the management team at two local secondary schools, Glyn Derw and Michaelston Community College, who have embedded aspects of local heritage into the curriculum. Moreover, CAER has grown from relatively humble beginnings in 2011 to become one of the key community projects of partner organisation ACE. ACE is a community-based organisation that aims to support the social, economic and environmental regeneration of Ely and Caerau. ACE staff worked with the university staff every step of the way to plan the development of CAER, providing access to a network of local community groups that enabled the involvement of local residents in project activities. ACE also facilitated further funding grant successes (e.g. the Heritage Lottery Fund's 'All Our

Stories') and ensured that CAER was integrated into, and benefited from, 'Timeplace' (Ely and Caerau's timebank). ACE therefore brought undeniable assets to the project, most notably, the trust and networks that they had built up over years with local people and community groups, but it also brought a deep knowledge of the area and an insightful understanding of the challenges faced by these communities. Over time, it is fair to say that the mutual respect that grew between the academic team and ACE staff moved beyond partnership and is now akin to friendship.

The 'Digging Caerau' excavations

Of all CAER's varied co-production activities, the visceral and practical nature of archaeological research has arguably proved extremely effective in addressing the project's social objectives. This brief overview of the community excavations is therefore intended to provide context for the qualitative evaluative analysis that follows. Both excavations were funded under the 'Connected Communities' programme and involved hundreds of community members as active research participants.

Caerau Hillfort occupies the western tip of an extensive plateau, now cut through by the A4232 link road, and is surrounded by the housing estates of Caerau and Ely. The now-ruinous and heavily vandalised parish church, St Mary's (c 13th century), and a small Medieval ringwork, are located in the north-eastern corner of the hillfort. The entire area is a Scheduled Ancient Monument, a legacy stretching back to the early 20th century when its significance as an archaeological site of national importance was first recognised. Despite this, the ramparts of the hillfort are now obscured beneath thick woodland cover, which means that the obvious physical remains of prehistoric activity are hidden from view and hence difficult to understand. As a result, many local people, even those who live in the shadow of the monument, are unaware of the site's importance.

Although the site was subject to a topographical survey by the Royal Commission on the Ancient and Historical Monuments of Wales in the 1970s, it has otherwise been largely ignored by archaeologists. This is partly explained by the paucity of archaeological research on Iron Age sites in South Glamorgan – no hillforts in the region have seen large-area excavations for instance – but the lack of previous work at Caerau may, to some extent, be due to external perceptions and unwarranted stereotypes concerning the hillfort's location within the estates.

At the outset of the project, knowledge of the Iron Age in South-East Wales, and of hillforts like Caerau in particular, was extremely limited

– even basic chronological frameworks were poorly understood and questions about later prehistoric agricultural and economic systems, which could place South Glamorgan in a regional and national context, were unaddressed. Therefore, the CAER team realised early on that archaeological excavations at Caerau could provide the opportunity to explore these issues through co-produced research with the community.

In December 2012, a grant was secured from the Arts and Humanities Research Council's (AHRC's) 'Connected Communities' Heritage Development Awards to undertake large-scale excavations of the hillfort in the summer of 2013. This phase of the project, known as 'Digging Caerau', was designed to provide opportunities for a range of local people to be involved in all stages of the archaeological process, from survey to excavation to post-excavation analysis. It built upon our obvious appetite for the co-production of archaeological research that had been demonstrated by the engagement between academic researchers, local community members and schools in the planning, delivery and interpretation of a geophysical survey of the hillfort interior and the *Time Team* programme early in 2012.

Co-production was embedded into the project's DNA. Local schools, community groups and local residents, together with academics, were part of the project planning from the start, helping to identify research questions to be explored through excavation and the target groups for engagement in the archaeological work. 'Digging Caerau' started with a training excavation for local people at St Fagans National History Museum in May 2013. St Fagans is only a mile away from the hillfort and recent redevelopment of the museum meant that the museum's 'Celtic Village' (made up of three reconstructed Iron Age roundhouses) was due to be demolished. This provided an opportunity for local people to learn basic excavation skills on a 'replica' Iron Age site before encountering the real thing as part of an accredited adult learner's course.

This was one of three adult learners' courses delivered by Cardiff University's Centre for Lifelong Learning that were embedded into the project. Each course, in archaeological skills, excavation and post-excavation analysis, was designed to provide local adults from a range of educational backgrounds with experience of archaeological research processes and to facilitate progression – the courses were free. Other, more general, objectives included confidence-building, the development of transferable skills and breaking down barriers to higher education. In total, there were 42 enrolments on the courses, with 11 individuals enrolling on more than one. One of the students went on to enrol in a module on Cardiff University's Exploring the Past progression route to a degree.

Following the dig at St Fagans were four weeks of excavation at Caerau Hillfort in June and July 2013. This 'community dig' was combined with a Cardiff University training excavation for more than 20 undergraduate students. More than 1,000 local people visited the excavations while they were in progress and 120 more were directly involved in the archaeological work, many coming back every day. The visitors and volunteers represented a diverse cross-section of the local community, with all ages and genders represented, from primary and secondary schoolchildren, sixth formers, and young people excluded from education, to long-term unemployed people, people with physical and mental health issues, retired people, and working parents.

Three local secondary schools, Glyn Derw, Mary Immaculate and Fitzalan, were directly involved in the excavations, with several classes from each school taking part. More than 80 pupils, varying in age group from Year 7 to Year 13, visited the site and worked in small groups alongside professional archaeologists and undergraduate students. They were actively involved with various on-site activities, including excavation, sieving and finds processing, and more creative activities, such as making Iron Age pots.

An important aspect of the project was to maintain participation in the research process by non-academics beyond the end of the excavation. Indeed, studies on co-production and community partnership have identified the need for 'continuing involvement' and 'the sustained pursuit of a shared enterprise' (Boyle and Harris, 2009: 16; see also Hart et al, 2012: 4). For the Digging Caerau excavations, this was achieved through the ongoing involvement in the analysis of the finds recovered – for example, an adult learners' course entitled 'Conserving Caerau's Finds' provided the opportunity for community members to conduct their own guided research into the artefacts derived from the excavation. They then produced posters that were displayed at CAER events and were incorporated into a published booklet on the excavations.

In late summer 2014, a second year of excavation at Caerau was completed. Almost all of the local participants from 2013 returned, along with a large number of new visitors and volunteers. As the project gathered momentum and visibility, interest significantly increased. This was amply demonstrated by a media story run by the BBC in June 2014 in which a misquoted headline stated that CAER were looking for 2,000 volunteers for the 2014 excavations (It had meant to say visitors!). Needless to say, this resulted in several hundred offers, which had to be carefully managed but that demonstrated the power of archaeological research to engage and enthuse the local communities.

The educational benefits of the excavations have been various, ranging from heightening awareness of the area to developing skills and raising aspirations to go to university. Most important of all, the process of Digging Caerau and the new friendships and social and professional connections that it has forged are as valuable as the archaeology being uncovered. However, some of the most significant impacts have been at a very personal level. It is these qualitative experiences and the evaluation techniques employed to capture them which form the focus of the closing sections of this chapter.

The Caerau and Ely Rediscovering Heritage project and the dynamics of evaluation and co-production

Despite the importance of evaluation in co-produced research, there appears to be little agreement over what evaluation of community co-production looks like, little debate over the fact that evaluation 'outcomes and outputs' are often aimed at very different people/ organisations (e.g. funding bodies, community members/partners, academic institutions), and little recognition that there are many types of evaluation (e.g. quantitative, qualitative and participatory evaluation methods).

In many respects, CAER's evaluation approach evolved 'organically', like the project, from an ad hoc and widespread 'separate approach' to an 'integrated' approach in which an evaluation plan was built into project activities and co-produced with project participants. It is contended here that the latter approach was the most worthwhile, both for community members/partners and academics, with evaluation activities being tailored to clearly identified evaluation aims. Evaluation therefore came to be regarded as an ongoing process. Adopting this integrated approach led the CAER team to develop and employ an evaluation plan that addressed the following key factors: aims, objectives, people involved, indicators and methodology. From this standpoint, evaluation was not seen as a feedback-gathering activity, but, rather, as suggested by Jackson and Kassam (1998), as a 'reflection on action'. The CAER evaluation strategy was therefore framed around the three following questions:

1. What is the purpose of the evaluation (e.g. who is the recipient of the evaluation)?
2. Who is evaluating whom?

3. What is the transformative potential of the evaluation (e.g. to what extent can it contribute to changing power relations)?

As alluded to earlier, the CAER evaluation approach was (and continues to be) participatory, i.e. we consider that evaluation must emerge primarily from 'within' to be authentic. For reasons of space, focus here is on evaluation data concerning local residents' experiences, although CAER equally valued the experiences of other parties, for example, undergraduates, community partners and academics (see Davis and Sharples, 2014: 57–60). The interviews used to explore the impacts of the excavations and evaluation-related issues are derived from video and audio recordings (on average, two to five minutes long) obtained, respectively, by a community member and trained film-maker, Vivian Thomas, and one of the three authors, Clyde Ancarno, both of whom worked in close collaboration. Conveying here the full extent and significance of Vivian Thomas's involvement – as a community member who interviewees could 'open up to' – is impossible. But as suggested during an interview where Viv was himself interviewed, when Viv was himself interviewed, Viv's continued involvement and dedication to the project have equally impacted on his life in a range of transformative ways, particularly in terms of expanding his social network in a manner that he had not foreseen and that he acknowledged had resulted in an improvement in the depression he suffers.

Responses from four community members have been selected for this brief analysis. All have been involved in CAER since the start of the project and all participated in both excavations. They are Mary, Sam, George and Tom (all local residents' names have been changed apart from that of Viv). Their ages range from 35 to 55 and they are all facing challenges relating to long-term unemployment.

Working on the premise that insights into negative impacts are potentially more valuable for evaluation than those of positive impacts (Elliot et al, 2012), the community members were encouraged to be truthful and to contribute negative/critical/questioning views on the project should they wish to. What ensues is a summary of the qualitative analysis of the discourse of these interviews (based on transcripts of relevant sections).

Insofar as they were explicitly probed for critical perspectives on the project, the interviewees expressed clear views that the project had been largely beneficial for both themselves and for the communities of Caerau and Ely more broadly. The few criticisms voiced were directly related to issues concerning the continuity of involvement and project sustainability. For example, a key issue that was raised on a number of occasions by several interviewees related to funding. Concerns were raised about financial constraints that, in the past, have significantly restricted the scope and longevity of community projects in the area. Within this context, one of the local residents' frustration about the periods of time when things were not moving fast enough is particularly relevant: "Things from my point of view could be moving quicker but I think that's more on the lines of the fundraising and getting the politicians to pull their fingers out if they can but I think we're getting there" (George, 2014).

These concerns appear to highlight an important tension facing academics involved in the community co-production of research, namely, the collusion between the financial and capacity-related constraints that they work under and the need for continuity from the perspective of communities. Indeed, it is interesting that George's comment emerged during the 2014 excavation, following an unsuccessful application for a large three-year grant and at a time when Oliver Davis had ceased to be embedded in ACE because the 'Connected Communities' grant that supported his position there had come to an end. The desire for project continuity (and thereby implicit concerns that it would not continue) were also evident from a number of interviewees, both in 2013 and 2014: "Hopefully, the same thing will happen next year because there's lots to be done up here, it's obvious" (Mary, 2013). The desire for continuity, beyond the 2013 and 2014 excavations, was also made clear:

> "I'm already hoping that next year they'll be coming back to do it again, get involved again." (Tom, 2014)

> "I was up here all last year and again this year and hopefully next year [laughter]. I hope so, I really keep my fingers crossed." (Mary, 2014)

The interviews also indicated that the project allowed for a new or revived sense of 'ownership' to emerge in relation to both local heritage and the project itself. Indeed, the community members' sense of ownership of the project repeatedly permeated the interviews – a factor that, it has been argued, is critical for the success of co-produced community research projects (Needham, 2008: 223; Durose et al, 2012b: 5–6; Hale, 2012: 5; Hart et al, 2012: 5–6):

> "I happened to help get the whole thing off the ground I suppose. The initial meeting with Olly Davis and the

Friends of St Mary's and I popped up to have a go with the Time Team." (George, 2014)

"To be actually involved myself and get out and sort myself out. I can say it's such a privilege to me. You'd have never think you'd be sort of trusted or allowed to do such things like you know. It's been excellent, really good." (Tom, 2013)

Views regarding improved attitudes towards local heritage and community cohesion also emerged, alongside stories of personal transformation:

"It's a lot more looked after since they've started…. It does definitely look a lot better up here. It was going to decline. It was quite bad up here at one stage so, yes, it's definitely helping what they're doing, for sure." (Sam, 2013)

"I don't usually sort of interact with many people so it's been great really to meet different people, good people, you know, and have a focused interest, you know, so it's been, for myself it's been excellent so." (Tom, 2013)

All the interviewees also stressed the ways in which CAER allowed for alternative and positive narratives about the community to emerge, hence offering a much-needed counter-discourse to the systematic negative framing of the area (e.g. in the media). This was best summed up by Tom: "Yes, we've sort of been as an area we're pushed to the back a lot and have been for years so all of us we're at the forefront for something you know which is pretty amazing really" (Tom, 2013).

The interviews also provided unforeseen insights into the way in which the project has benefited the health and well-being of some of the community members interviewed. This included Tom's ongoing fight against long-term depression (which also reflects Viv's experience alluded to earlier):

"I suffer quite a bit from depression so it's given me drive to get out of the house, get involved, become part of a team. You know, I sort of stick to myself a lot so, I've talked to more people here in the last two weeks than I have in a long time so it's pretty, for me it's cool like you know. It's given me a bit of drive you know and picked myself up, given me a boost, which I'm really grateful for." (Tom, 2013)

Interestingly, these stories of significant personal transformation echo academic claims regarding the therapeutic nature of co-produced research (Needham, 2008: 223). All interviewees also commented on how the project allowed them to gain new skills, including practical excavation skills, teamwork and confidence-building, and a better understanding of archaeological research. Indeed, archaeology is a recurrent theme in the interviews (and other sources of evaluation too). Community members expressed an avid interest in finding out about archaeology, particularly the archaeology of a 'historic environment' that means something to them. Their deep sense of enjoyment (despite also frequent allusions to how much physical hard work it was) while digging physical remains of the past in their own community was clearly evident.

Hart et al (2012: 9) have noted that there is a significant lack of empirical data on how community–university partnerships work in practice. Others have highlighted that there is 'little evidence or evaluation of impact in participatory research' (Durose et al, 2012b: 4). It is contended that CAER provides a fruitful avenue for future research in this respect; the first few tentative steps towards this have been taken here. Insofar as a CoP can be defined as 'a collection of people who engage on an ongoing basis in some common endeavour' (Eckert, 2006), this concept offers a compelling perspective for examining the new and multifaceted 'community' that the CAER excavations have brought into being. The interviews build a picture of this new CoP as perceived and experienced from within. Notably, they emphasise the social nature of the excavations, the possibility to share/acquire knowledge and transcend apparently unequal power relations (including those pertaining to archaeological knowledge-related hierarchies). This new CoP, framed by the historic environment in which it is embedded, therefore contributes interesting insights into the mechanisms underpinning 'the challenge of working across and between organisations and sectors' in co-produced research (Hart et al, 2012: 5) and provides a potent physical metaphor for digging down into the heart of the community to acquire knowledge. It also gives way to a re-energised sense of confidence and identity among the community members involved, founded upon a distinct and unique past.

The data presented also illustrates the challenges of evaluating impact within the context of co-produced arts and humanities research, particularly in relation to complex heritage projects such as CAER. The qualitative analysis of this small sample of evaluative interviews therefore allows for critical reflection on such evaluation concerns. The sample of interviews – conducted with and by community members

– provides insights into the impacts of the project that quantitative methods could not have revealed, hence highlighting that new ways of thinking about evaluation are timely. There seems to be an urgent need for a broader range of 'forms of evidence' to be more widely accepted within academic circles, including 'creative' methods that some contexts (e.g. community festivals) or project characteristics (e.g. complexity of engagement in CAER) sometimes demand. This echoes Elliot et al (2012), who argue that mixed-methods evaluation should be favoured. Yet, the need for innovation in evaluation methods should clearly go beyond this dichotomous view and requires methods 'sensitive enough to pick up whatever individual stories are hidden behind the numbers' (Evaluating Your HLF Project, 2008).

Conclusion

The analysis of the small sample of evaluative interview data presented in this chapter suggests that the impacts of CAER on the communities of Caerau and Ely and their local residents have been multifarious. As might be expected, some directly reflect the aims and objectives outlined in the co-produced project design, namely, to create educational opportunities and to address negative stereotypes. However, unexpected stories of personal transformation, sometimes involving long-lasting changes in individuals' life trajectories, have also emerged. Arguably, these transformational stories have only been possible because of the CAER team's commitment to the core principles of co-production, as outlined by Boyle and Harris (2009), Needham (2008), Durose et al (2012b) and others.

Although the CAER team has adopted reflexivity in their approach to co-production, they would be the first to admit that their aspiration to full co-production has not been fully achieved. Funding criteria parameters and short-term timescales, together with career-based academic commitments and capacity issues within schools and other community partner organisations, are just some of the factors that continue to inhibit that goal. It is true that all key project development and funding decisions have involved ACE and the local schools. Yet, the clamour for funding to ensure 'the sustained pursuit of shared enterprise' (Hart et al, 2012: 4) has resulted, at times, in prescriptive funding applications that could only involve community members from a consultative perspective. This, perhaps, helps to explain some of the frustrations about the project 'not moving fast enough' expressed by the community members earlier. Moreover, while CAER does involve community members in the research process and, indeed, values all contributors, project events and activities continue to be instigated largely by the academic team in conjunction with ACE's development workers. As such, CAER is best regarded as what Hale has termed a 'middle-way' heritage project – amalgamating both 'top-down' and 'bottom-up' approaches to develop 'a collaborative model between funders, participants, engagement organisations and other community members' (Hale, 2012: 6). Full co-production is, without any doubt, a hard objective to achieve. Yet, the small sample of evaluative data provided here provides some indication that it is nonetheless an objective worth striving for.

References

Alford, J. (1998) 'A public management road less travelled: clients as co-producers of public services', *Australian Journal of Public Administration* 57(4): 128–37.

Boyle, D. and Harris, M. (2009) *The challenge of co-production*, London: NESTA.

Bristow, G., Entwistle, T., Hines, F. and Martin, S. (2009) 'New spaces for inclusion? Lessons from the "three-thirds" partnerships in Wales', *International Journal of Urban and Regional Research* 32(4): 903–21.

Cornwall, A. (2008) 'Unpacking "participation": models, meanings and practices', *Community Development Journal* 43(3): 269–83.

Davis, O. and Sharples, N. (2014) 'Excavations at Caerau hillfort, Cardiff, South Wales 2013 – an interim report', Cardiff Studies in Archaeology Specialist Report 34. Available at: https://caerheritageprojectdotcom1.files.wordpress.com/2013/02/caerau-interim-web.pdf (accessed 21 April 2015).

Dicks, B. (2014) 'Participatory community regeneration: a discussion of risks, accountability and crisis in devolved Wales', *Urban Studies* 51(5): 959–77.

Durose, C., Beebeejaun, Y., Rees, Rees, J. and Richardson, L. (2012a) *Illuminating the evolution of community participation*, Swindon: AHRC Connected Communities.

Durose, C., Beebeejaun, Y., Rees, J., Richardson, J., & Richardson, L. (2012b) *Towards co-production in research with communities*, Swindon: AHRC Connected Communities.

Eckert, P. (2006) 'Communities of practice', *Encyclopedia of Language and Linguistics* 2: 683–5.

Elliott, E., Byrne, E. Shirani, F. Gong, Y., Henwood, K., Morgan, H., Shepherd, M., Palmer, S., Williams, G. (2012) *Connected Communities: a review of theories, concepts and interventions relating to community-level strengths and their impact on health and well being*, Swindon: AHRC Connected Communities.

Heritage Lottery Fund (2008) *Evaluating your HLF project*, London: HLF.

Hale, A. (2012) *Linking communities to historic environments: a research review summary*, Swindon: AHRC Connected Communities.

Hart, A., Ntung, A., Millican, J., Davies, C., Wenger, E., Rosing, R. and Pearce, J. (2012) Community–university partnerships through communities of practice, Swindon: AHRC Connected Communities.

Horton, D. (2012) 'Is there a place for community development in Wales? Reflecting on 6 years of Communities First in Caerau and Ely', in *Creating co-op councils and empowering communities*, Cardiff: Ideas Wales, pp 7–13.

Jackson, E.T., and Kassam, Y. (eds) (1998) *Knowledge shared: participatory evaluation in development cooperation*, Canada: International Research Development Centre.

Needham, C. (2008) 'Realising the potential of co-production: negotiating improvements in public service', *Social Policy & Society* 7(2): 221–31.

Rees, G. (1997) 'The politics of regional development strategy: the programme for the valleys', in R. Macdonald and H. Thomas (eds) *Nationality and planning in Scotland and Wales*, Cardiff: University of Wales Press, pp 98–110.

NINE

Lessons from 'The Vale' – the role of hyperlocal media in shaping reputational geographies

David Harte and Jerome Turner

Introduction

This chapter focuses on the tensions around the media representation of a city suburb that has undergone a major urban renewal process. The Castle Vale estate at the edge of North East Birmingham, referred to locally as 'The Vale', has been through significant physical and social changes since the 1960s: from high-rise council estate to low-rise social housing, and from being an area seen as having significant social problems to one where the potential of community-led localism might be enacted with a degree of success. Throughout these changes, community media have played a role in both representing the process of change and being a vehicle through which such change is made palatable to residents. Yet, assumptions about the democratising, empowering function of community media inevitably come up against the tensions over representation that exist between readers and producers of media texts. Given the historic reputational issues of the estate, what stories do citizens now expect to be told about the area? What role could citizen journalists play in the digital age in countering what David Parker and Christian Karner (2011: 309) have described as externally imposed 'negative reputational geographies'?

As part of a strand in a major 'Connected Communities' project focused on the notion of 'Creative Citizenship', the research presented here has looked closely at the role that community media play in Castle Vale, drawing upon a range of primary research: workshops with residents; interviews with the estate's community media organisation; and reflections on the undertaking of a participatory journalism project.

Urban policy and the role of the citizen in 'The Vale'

Following major post-war inner-city slum clearances in Birmingham, Castle Vale was one of a series of edge-of-city estates that became home to families whose previous inner-city dwellings had been declared unfit to live in. Although the new estate had a large proportion of low-rise maisonettes, it was the 34 high-rise flats that dominated the landscape when built throughout the 1960s. When the nearby M6 was later completed, it was these tower blocks that greeted visitors to the city, a symbol perhaps of Birmingham's famously brutal approach to city regeneration that brought radical change to its city centre as much as to its edges. If it can be said that Castle Vale ever had a reputation as a 'nice' place to live, by the 1970s, it was clear that this reputation had suffered as crime rose and living conditions deteriorated. Ali Madanipour's (2005: 51) account of Castle Vale's reputation is stark: 'the neighbourhood suffered from poor quality infrastructure and buildings, lack of services, fear of crime and vandalism, poor health, unemployment, low educational standards, and a poor image'. Veronica Coatham and Lisa Martinali (2010: 91) outline how by the early 1990s – the point at which the estate began its journey from being a high-rise estate to a less imposing mix of suburban houses and low-rise flats – there was 'an identified need to develop a long-term strategy for Castle Vale encompassing the key priorities of a regeneration initiative'.

The Housing Action Trust (HAT) set up in 1993 was tasked with initiating a radical transformation of the urban realm, emphasising the 'redevelopment of the social infrastructure and combating social exclusion from the outset' (Evans and Long, 2000: 309). Their 1995 master plan for the area makes clear that the future for the estate would mark a move away from state control and towards a more significant role for citizens:

> A revitalised Castle Vale, its grey monotony replaced by buildings and places with interest and vitality, must engender a greater pride of place and community spirit than at present. In turn this may lead to the residents assuming greater responsibility for setting standards and taking wider responsibility and authority for the future management and maintenance of the new Castle Vale. (Castle Vale Housing Action Trust, 1995: 2)

As Jones et al make clear in Chapter Eleven, the trajectory towards urban renewal policies at that time were very much focused on citizen involvement, with 'the community' articulated as a partner in the process of change, as well as being its beneficiary. Evans and Long (2000) go into some detail on how HATs across the UK (Castle Vale was one of six) shared an understanding that their remit would need to move beyond simply refreshing housing stock and would need to situate citizens as stakeholders. Further, it was clear that activities that would contribute to the well-being of residents needed to be initiated, although these were not always adequately funded (Evans and Long, 2000: 311). In Castle Vale, a community fund was established that would eventually prove important in sustaining community media provision in the area.

The potential of hyperlocal media and citizen journalism

The owners of the by-now well-established community newspaper *Tyburn Mail* and its associated website were partners in the 'Creative Citizens' research project discussed in this chapter. The project has primarily been interested in exploring the tensions between amateur and professional creativity, which are particularly stark in the area of journalism, where the rise of the citizen journalist is seen by some to inevitably bring significant democratic benefits as a result of us all being 'active users of news, not mere consumers' (Gillmor, 2004: 238). Not only is 'everyone a journalist' (Hartley, 2009: 154), but they also have the potential to be a proprietor, digital publisher and digitally networked news-gatherer as well. The counter-position is expressed by Gary Hudson and Mick Temple (2010: 66), who offer an acerbic critique in their essay 'We are not all journalists', arguing that many academics are 'stretching the concept of journalism to extremes' by claiming that any 'user' that generates news content is therefore a journalist. However, the 'Creative Citizens' project shared Nick Couldry's (2004: 25) concern that 'websites or portals that collect information for consumption and civic activism on a relatively local scale' should be the focus of empirical research for those seeking to understand the role of 'new networks of trust'.

At face value, such a network might be seen to exist in the over-600 'hyperlocal' websites (see analysis in Harte, 2013) covering small geographic areas, from rural villages to urban housing estates such as Castle Vale. Their emergence should be seen in the context of the UK newspaper industry's trend towards the closure and retrenchment of their local and regional press titles[1] and the subsequent concerns about the impact that this may have on the public sphere (Siles and Boczkowski, 2012). While some of the commentary around hyperlocal media has focused on its potential to fill this gap left by the decline of the local press (Beckett and Herve-Azevedo, 2010: 10–13), a more common claim is made for it as an authentic outlet for community concerns. Mark Glaser (2010: 585) claims that 'the motivation of starting independent hyper-local sites is often to tell the previously untold stories of communities', while Metzgar et al (2011: 774), in attempting to define hyperlocal, see value in it being 'community-oriented' and promoting 'civic engagement'. In a comprehensive report into the use of the internet by communities in London, Flouch and Harris (2010: 6) argue that hyperlocal websites can 'make a distinctive contribution to local social capital, cohesion and civic involvement'. Even the UK media regulator's interest in hyperlocal media is focused not just on their role as providers of news: 'the value and role of this type of community media may go beyond the provision of content, with the potential for specific value in the social capital generated through the production of hyperlocal websites' (Ofcom, 2012: 111).

This narrative around hyperlocal media has a tendency to echo the technological optimism of journalism scholars writing about the emerging importance of the internet to journalism in the 1990s and early 2000s. Borger et al (2012: 125) have noted that scholars tended to display a 'strong faith in the democratic potential of digital technologies'. Such technological optimism 'can be traced back to internet enthusiasts of the 1990s who voiced great expectations regarding the reinvigoration of the public sphere' (Borger et al, 2012: 125). Borger et al offer a critique of the normative values of journalism studies and, in particular, its positioning of 'public journalism' – now recognised as a short-lived phase of journalism practice in the mid-1990s (for examples, see Rosen, 1999) that saw a concerted attempt by some newspapers in the US to 'actively nurture the conversation that healthy public life requires' (Merritt, 2009: 21). Scholarly positions on public journalism played a key role in shaping the utopian technological discourse around participatory journalism, offering 'a renewed chance to realize public journalism's goal.... In the theoretical ideal underlying participatory journalism, the audience is explicitly approached as citizenry' (Borger et al, 2012: 126).

Irene Costera Meijer (2012) has noted the decline in enthusiasm of scholars in the potential of participatory approaches to journalism and instead makes the case for participatory 'storytelling' as a way for 'problem neighbourhoods' to 'ease the pain caused by mainstream news' (Costera Meijer, 2012: 14). Her detailed content and audience analysis showed the adverse effects on people of living in suburbs of Utrecht that had press coverage focusing on the 'undesirable' aspects of living in these areas. The development of a community media project aimed at giving greater voice to residents resulted in a different set of stories emerging: 'everyday stories about everyday life by ordinary people living or working in the neighbourhoods' (Costera Meijer, 2012: 25). The intention was not to exclude the more problematic nature of these environments, but to ensure that the 'ordinary' was also covered: 'residents valued items that visualized everyday personal, social and geographical landmarks' (Costera Meijer, 2012: 22). John Postill (2008: 422), in his study of the 'vibrant internet scene' in a suburb of Kuala Lumpur, Malaysia, has likewise noted the value of this focus on the everyday. He argues that this represents a kind 'banal activism' that academics too often ignore at the expense of a focus on the '"serious" cyberactivism of the intelligentsia' (Postill, 2008: 420). Rather, the focus should be on the ways in which 'people, technologies and other cultural artefacts are co-producing new forms of residential sociality in unpredictable ways' (Postill, 2008: 426). It was clear that such 'banal', everyday issues were the focus of concerns in Castle Vale as we undertook our research.

Local media in 'The Vale'

Although the development of community media within Castle Vale is directly attributable to funding interventions from the HAT, it was very much a resident-led project. A radio station, Vale FM, set up in 1995, might have initially been developed out of concerns to address wider public perceptions of the 'Vale' but it soon settled into being a vehicle for the training and development of individuals who might then go on to fulfil educational or creative ambitions. Its manager at the time, Neil Hollins, describes its early development:

> "Vale FM was borne out of an idea by local residents who were maybe involved in pirate radio or who were maybe mobile DJs and believed that a community radio station would be good for Castle Vale.... We then began running training courses under franchise. Contract radio courses for unemployed people to use it as a way of developing skills, confidence, employability. But of course those with talent and real dedication would be able to use this as a great opportunity to potentially get into the industry."

Although subsequently organised through a single charitable organisation at arm's length from the housing association, the ongoing development of the station and the later hyperlocal newspaper and website are bound up in the changing reputation of the estate itself. Like others trying to pitch for funds for community activities, Hollins had to become adept at expressing the value of Castle Vale as a place where funders could see the potential for interventions to transform lives: "this is about putting out an image of Castle Vale as a vibrant creative place, where things are happening. It might not be the best place in the world, but things are happening" (Hollins). Different funders might require different articulations of place but the desired outcomes were always the same: "the primary benefits were very much about the personal outcomes for beneficiaries. The secondary ones … were about reputational aspects and challenging negative stigmas" (Hollins).

In 2001, a community newspaper was developed (with just eight pages at that stage) as an adjunct to the radio station, which could at that time only operate for 28-day periods under a Restricted Service Licence. Yet, there was initial distrust about the impartiality of the newspaper: "it was still under the control of the HAT so wasn't particularly trusted, it was seen a bit of a propaganda sheet, and it was rather disorganised and didn't look very nice really" (Hollins). However, problems with the radio station as it attempted to transfer from an occasional to a more permanent operation having secured a broadcast licence worked in the newspaper's favour as it went "from strength to strength" (Hollins). Hollins makes the claim that it became "the predominant form of communication in Castle Vale at the time". From 2011, the newspaper broadened the area it covered to surrounding suburbs. *Tyburn Mail*, as it is now called, is a monthly, 24-page free newspaper, delivered directly to a population of 24,000 in the Castle Vale, Pype Hayes, Erdington Hall and Birches Green areas of Birmingham. It employs just one journalist, Clive Edwards, who also runs the associated news blog, Facebook page and Twitter account. This results in a constraint argues Edwards:

> "the size of the organisation limits the extent to which we can do proper investigative journalism that would be helpful to the community in revealing to them what is actually happening, as opposed to what the organisations say are happening."

Edwards points out that the newspaper's initial content was very much focused on the area's regeneration: "all the work that the HAT did to regenerate Castle Vale in terms of its buildings and its organisations, they thought would be well served by a monthly newspaper". However, since the separation of the community media operation and the HAT in 2005, the newspaper now acts more in the mode of traditional, local journalism. Indeed, at one point, Edwards articulates his pride in one of his stories having "a real *Sunday Mercury*[2] stance". The shift to a more formalised journalistic tone was not a comfortable change to make by any means:

> "[We] took the view that we would include bad news as well as good news. We still hold true to that for all of the downside that that creates. It creates an uncomfortable relationship sometimes within what is a fairly small community. We can, and we have, alienated some organisations and some individuals as a result." (Edwards)

Although *Tyburn Mail*'s digital outlets prove useful both for news-gathering and for gaining a sense of which content its audience is most interested in, it is the newspaper that remains the focus of its operation: "there are some stories that we leave out of the web because we want the print version to have impact when it comes out ... I think the newspaper has got more status than the web output" (Edwards). Edwards points out that his contacts are largely formal in nature (school, police, council, local politicians), although he recognises that digital has a role to play in allowing citizens to express civic pride: "if you look at social media sites, such as people's Facebook pages, they are always referencing the community ethos around Castle Vale".

Edwards's narrative suggests a maturing role for *Tyburn Mail* just at the time that Castle Vale itself was moving into a 'post-regeneration' phase (as outlined by Matthews and O'Brien in Chapter Three, this volume). The formal organisation of the media operation echoes this as it moved from direct control by the HAT to charitable status and now a small media company. As portrayed by Hollins and Edwards, their various media outputs now play a role not dissimilar to other local media in holding power to account and being a powerful advocate for citizen concerns: "they turn to us because they want us to apply pressure. That's a great credit to us and the work we've done to engineer that position" (Hollins).

Who is represented in the hyperlocal?

However, in our discussions with citizens (in two workshops) about how they felt towards *Tyburn Mail*, we noted a degree of suspicion and distrust about its 'voice'. There were still concerns that it was too closely linked to the HAT: "lot of people's negative articles or opinions are being filtered out, especially if it's against the housing and social" (local resident). Likewise, in our interviews, residents cited concerns that coverage of the city council tended to shy away from controversy: "there's always something about what the council are doing. They print all the good things, of course. It's very, very rare you get failings, unless it comes from the locals". Although there was a general awareness of the digital output of *Tyburn Mail* across its website and Facebook page, there was a tendency to favour reading the newspaper despite a recognition that the infrequency of its publications means that "there are major things that are missed in the *Tyburn Mail*".

As part of the research approach, one of the workshops afforded residents the chance to mock up their own newspaper with the intention of revealing what their own concerns about Castle Vale might be. In doing this, we saw some potential for citizens to become 'produsers' (Bruns, 2008). Alex Bruns (2008: 339) has described the importance of the 'produser' function: 'the capacity to be an active produser ... equates increasingly with the capacity for active, participatory citizenship'. He cites citizen journalism as a key example of how produsage behaviour 'can be seen to help build the capacities for active forms of cultural and democratic citizenship' (Bruns, 2008: 398). What the exercise revealed were examples of citizens as both active community members (one person talked about their attempt to tackle local traffic speeding) and potential chroniclers of the everyday (another talked about wanting to write about a local homeless person who had not been seen for a while), often mixing fact and fiction to create alternative narratives about life on the estate.

As Jones et al note in Chapter Eleven's discussion of the MapLocal project, there is a danger in situating responses like these as examples of ground-up, 'authentic' knowledge that sit in opposition to professional expertise. Indeed, the danger here in focusing on the minutiae of estate life is that the more significant impacts of localism (outlined in detail by Matthews and O'Brien in Chapter Three, this volume) might be less discussed. In one sense, the professional norms of journalism might be better able to tie these 'everyday' stories of Castle Vale into a larger narrative of the impact of significant cuts to public services in the area.

Hyperlocal media and its audience

To further explore the nature of the relationship between the *Tyburn Mail* and its audience, it was decided to develop a co-creation activity that would offer citizens a greater chance for participation in the newspaper. As researchers, we were keen to see if the potential for individuals on the Castle Vale estate to act as 'creative citizens' could be realised and, in turn, allow Edwards to see where in the cycle of story development the citizen can play a role. The first element in our project was to create a blank space in the newspaper for citizens to write in their own news. Chris Atton (2002: 24) describes a similar project in a New York underground paper of the 1960s: 'Other Scenes once offered an entirely blank set of pages for readers as a do-it-yourself publishing project'.

In our experiment, readers were asked to bring this filled-in blank page to a News Cafe event organised in a local supermarket. The cafe was intended to bring reader into contact with journalist and enable them to discuss and co-create stories based on the sheets that they had filled in. Just a small number of readers brought back completed blank pages but their content drew attention to the ways in which they felt Castle Vale's image is contested. Respondents implored the journalist to "tell it like it is" and worry about problems being "swept under the carpet". By contrast, another voiced concern that there was "too much focus on individual crime". The issue of crime and how much of it gets covered was a recurring issues in our research. One resident argued that the coverage of crime on the estate was disproportionate: "the problem is it's no worse than others, but it gets reported more, so it makes it look worse.... It's reported more, giving a worse opinion of Castle Vale". Although considered essential by the *Tyburn Mail* journalist, coverage of crime can be problematic in creating an informed citizenship: 'the focus on the spectacular rather than the typical – endemic in news coverage of crime, for example – rarely implicates citizenship in useful or informative ways' (Lewis, 2006: 315). As with Irene Costera's Meijer's research in Utrecht, we found that the people of Castle Vale were acutely aware of the mediatisation of their locality. Limited as it was by its one-off experimental nature, the blank space in the *Tyburn Mail* did at least offer readers a modest role in countering the 'problem neighbourhood frame' (Costera Meijer, 2012: 18).

To a degree, the implementation of the cafe idea helped to place the organisation more centrally in people's gaze. The concrete outcome of the intervention was that the News Cafe continued on a monthly basis and that some stories mentioned in the filled-in sheets were followed up. This resulted in Edwards establishing a regular feature in the paper of 'news from the cafe' and he continued to appear monthly in the supermarket cafe awaiting input from local people and often finding new stories as a result. In the subsequent interview with Edwards, he was clear not only that citizens can play a role in news-gathering, but that the initiative had changed perceptions of the *Tyburn Mail*:

> "clearly the News Cafe is a good idea. We feel that it has worked for us in terms of opening us out and saying we are after domestic stories.... It may well be that we are now being perceived as a voice of the people, as opposed to a voice of the council, or a voice of the councillor."

Edwards is cautious in his optimism for the continuation of the cafe but recognises that there is now a shift towards more 'human interest' in the newspaper: "I think we have got to be realistic about what we expect from the News Cafe, but it terms of it breaking the paradigm, it certainly has done that".

Although *Tyburn Mail*'s journey towards a more participatory approach in its journalism is at an early stage, the co-creation exercise offered it a route into seeing the value of developing closer relationships with readers and potentially converting some of them into contributors. Indeed, two recent approaches from school pupils to write for the paper have been so unexpected that they left Edwards puzzling: "Why has that happened?" His explanation is that, in part, it is due to a perceived shift in the newspaper's image, away from a voice of officialdom and towards more human interest.

The limits of digital media

Despite the potential shown in the workshops and the News Cafe, it must be said that, in general, our research revealed that the citizens in Castle Vale were not by and large active players when it comes to contributing to their community media. Mechanisms for input (comments on the blog or Facebook) were never used by any of our workshop participants. One interviewee demonstrated their resistance to digital participation over privacy concerns: "it [the *Tyburn Mail* website] links into Facebook and stuff like that; it can trace you back in terms of your personal identity. I don't know what they do with that." Yet, as an artefact, the newspaper was very much part of people's lives, with everyone having knowledge of it and expressing clear views about its worth, and with some people even involved in its distribution (it relies on a large network of residents who are paid to deliver the papers).

There had also been a change in the use of digital media, with Edwards now noting that story ideas from individuals are coming in via

Facebook. However, there is still a sense that his use of digital platforms is not developed in terms of a participatory approach:

> "Facebook is a means of feedback to us. So, for example, if we put an article on our website, some people might comment upon the website, but on the whole the majority of people will comment on the Facebook site. I am not sure why that is.... So, Facebook is a very good means of asking for feedback for our stories. Are our stories interesting? We will find out via Facebook."

Edwards goes on to describe how controversial stories about crime are more likely to receive anonymous comments on the blog rather than personal comments on Facebook. Indeed, the Facebook page, with about a thousand likes, is relatively quiet in comparison to some hyperlocal news websites, but Edwards recognises that "we are slow on the uptake with it, but it has become important to us, yes. As a news source, particularly Twitter, and as a feedback mechanism, particularly Facebook."

Conclusion: telling it like it is in The Vale

The research discussed here was an attempt to intervene in the well-established, professionally prescribed routine of making news about place, and for that intervention to allow reflection on what a 'sense of place' means for those living and working in 'The Vale'. The relationship between *Tyburn Mail* and its audience might be described as 'tetchy' at best. While there is a shared desire to "tell it like it is", the residents of Castle Vale seem to contest the idea of what 'it' is. During the workshops, residents were asked to react to example stories from the *Tyburn Mail* news blog as points for discussion; again, there was a genuine bristling when the first story was about local crime: "It gives a bad name to Castle Vale.... Someone from Castle Vale is always getting arrested for doing something, always." In contrast, another wanted the newspaper to "never flinch from reporting truths about the area". While our research did not find a vigorous alternative media scene acting as a counter to *Tyburn Mail*'s dominance, there clearly exists the desire to push against the journalistic norms it operates within. One resident, in filling in the blank space we created, came up with a whole list of story and content ideas that could be taken up: "maybe have a panel of moms review baby groups.... The children's centre is going through major cuts and changes and this needs covering....

More coverage on what's on for under fives.... Advice on how to pick nurseries and schools." Such a rich, detailed response reveals much about the everyday lived experience of life in suburban housing estates, creating the potential for an effective counter-narrative at odds with Castle Vale's dominant reputation.

In their examination of a nearby area of East Birmingham, David Parker and Christian Karner (2011: 308) reflected on the notion that 'localities contain multiple "subjugated knowledges" [to use Foucault's phrase] and previously largely private, rarely heard memories of social struggle, exclusion and self-assertion. Such subjugated knowledges need to be excavated, captured and articulated'. They claim that such an excavation needs to take place online via the social web as much as offline through located local cultural expressions such as graffiti. The point is to counter the partial accounts of communities that narrowly position places such as Castle Vale in the public gaze. Instead, richer 'spatial biographies' might have a counter-hegemonic role in working against dominant external myths and instead 'recognise the intertwined histories of places and people, roads and their residents' (Parker and Karner, 2011: 309). However, as Kirsty Hess has pointed out, despite the proliferation of the digital, newspapers can play a significant role in shaping such reputational geographies. Small local newspapers act as nodes, she claims, holding 'a degree of symbolic power in constructing the idea of "community" and the "local"' (Hess, 2012: 56). In particular, she makes the case that news media contributes to the 'sense of place' felt by local residents and that we need to rethink the role of such media as being 'geo-social'. That is, to recognise their 'solid link to geographic territory while acknowledging the wider social space in which these publications play a role' (Hess, 2012: 49).

More than 20 years after the beginning of the regeneration process, Castle Vale's former reputation still looms large in the minds of those who live and work there: "you live 'on' The Vale, as though it's a ship.... As though you have to take a step up to get towards it" (Edwards). The visitor to Castle Vale is often struck by the way it feels slightly cut off from the city, surrounded as it is by fast main roads on all sides, and to an extent, its media feels a little cut-off too. In being imitative of existing local media and dealing with bread-and-butter concerns such as crime, it comes up against the contested notions of how The Vale should present itself to the outside world. The opportunity for *Tyburn Mail* is to build on the experiment in participatory journalism that it has undergone and reflect on the importance of its role as one of the vehicle's through which a collective understanding of Castle Vale is articulated. With the citizen – digitally 'tooled up' as they inevitably are – as co-contributor, co-editor, perhaps even co-publisher, the opportunity is there for it to play a more confident role in expressing the fullness of the everyday, lived culture of the estate.

Acknowledgements

Thank you to all of the participants in this research (carried out in 2012/13), both the residents of Castle Vale and Topcliffe Media, publishers of *Tyburn Mail*. Jerome Turner designed and led the workshop activities described herein and John Coster from *Citizens' Eye* helped with the development of the News Cafe. The 'Media, Community and the Creative Citizen' project has received funding from the Arts and Humanities Research Council's 'Connected Communities' scheme and the Engineering and Physical Sciences Research Council's 'Digital Economy' scheme, grant number AH/J005290/1.

Notes

[1] See: http://www.journalism.co.uk/news/third-of-local-newspapers-to-have-disappeared-between-2002-and-2013-says-enders-chief/s2/a533054/

[2] The *Sunday Mercury* is a tabloid-format newspaper published weekly by Trinity Mirror group in the West Midlands area.

References

Atton, C. (2002) *Alternative media*, London: SAGE.

Beckett, C. and Herve-Azevedo, J. (2010) *The value of networked journalism*, The Value of Networked Journalism Series, London: London School of Economics and Political Science.

Borger, M., Van Hoof, A., Costera Meijer, I. and Sanders, J. (2012) 'Constructing participatory journalism as a scholarly object', *Digital Journalism* 1(1): 117–34.

Bruns, A. (2008) *Blogs, Wikipedia, Second Life, and beyond: from production to produsage*, New York: Peter Lang.

Castle Vale Housing Action Trust (1995) *Castle Vale master plan*, Birmingham: Hunt Thompson Associates.

Coatham, V. and Martinali, L. (2010) 'The role of community-based organisations in sustaining community regeneration: an evaluation of the development and contribution of Castle Vale Community Regeneration Services (CVCRS)', *International Journal of Sociology and Social Policy* 30(1/2): 84–101.

Costera Meijer, I. (2012) 'When news hurts', *Journalism Studies* 14(1): 13–28.

Couldry, N. (2004) 'The productive "consumer" and the dispersed "citizen"', *International Journal of Cultural Studies* 7(1): 21–32.

Evans, R. and Long, D. (2000) 'Policy review. Estate-based regeneration in England: lessons from Housing Action Trusts', *Housing Studies* 15(2): 301–17.

Flouch, H. and Harris, K. (2010) *The Online Neighbourhood Networks study – the future for citizen-run neighbourhood websites*, London: Capital Ambition.

Gillmor, D. (2004) *We the media*, Sebastapol: O'Reilly Media, Inc.

Glaser, M. (2010) 'Citizen journalism', in S. Allan (ed) *The Routledge companion to news and journalism*, London and New York, NY: Routledge, pp 578–90.

Harte, D. (2013) '"One every two minutes": assessing the scale of hyperlocal publishing in the UK', *JOMEC Journal*. Available at: http://www.cardiff.ac.uk/jomec/research/journalsandpublications/jomecjournal/3-june2013/index.html

Hartley, J. (2009) *The uses of digital literacy*, St Lucia, Qld: University of Queensland Press.

Hess, K. (2012) 'Breaking boundaries', *Digital Journalism* 1(1): 48–63.

Hudson, G. and Temple, M. (2010) 'We are not all journalists now', in G. Monaghan and S. Tunney (eds) *Web journalism: a new form of citizenship?*, Eastbourne: Sussex Academic Press, pp 63–76.

Lewis, J. (2006) 'News and the empowerment of citizens', *European Journal of Cultural Studies* 9(3): 303–19.

Madanipour, A. (2005) 'Value of place: can physical capital be a driver for urban change? The experience of Castle Vale, Birmingham', in: Commission for Architecture and the Built Environment (ed) *Physical capital: how great places boost public value*, London: CABE.

Merritt, D.B. (2009) 'What citizen journalism can learn from public journalism', in J. Rosenberry and B.S. John (eds) *Public journalism 2.0: the promise and reality of a citizen engaged press*, New York, NY: Taylor & Francis.

Metzgar, E.T., Kurpius, D.D. and Rowley, K.M. (2011) 'Defining hyperlocal media: proposing a framework for discussion', *New Media & Society* 13(5): 772–87.

Ofcom (2012) *The communications market report: United Kingdom*, London: Ofcom.

Parker, D. and Karner, C. (2011) 'Remembering the Alum Rock Road: reputational geographies and spatial biographies', *Midland History* 36(2): 292–309.

Postill, J. (2008) 'Localizing the Internet beyond communities and networks', *New Media & Society* 10(3): 413–31.

Rosen, J. (1999) *What are journalists for?*, New Haven: Yale University Press.

Siles, I. and Boczkowski, P.J. (2012) 'Making sense of the newspaper crisis: a critical assessment of existing research and an agenda for future work', *New Media & Society* 14(8): 1375–94.

TEN

Contemporary governance discourse and digital media: convergences, prospects and problems for the 'Big Society' agenda

Chris Speed, Amadu Wurie Khan and Martin Phillips

Introduction

This chapter looks at how concepts and vocabularies emerging in relation to the internet (online) could usefully be applied to understandings of offline contemporary community life and practices. It is an account of this exploratory enterprise into the linkage between the discursive practices of the internet and contemporary governance. The chapter has four sections.

The first considers the discursive resonances between the internet (as a form of digital media) and contemporary governance as articulated in the 'Big Society' agenda of the former Conservative–Liberal Democrat Coalition government (henceforth referred to as 'the UK Coalition government'). The second considers how such discourses are embodied in digital media practices of 'hacking' and 'read–writing', which provided the conceptual framework for the development of an innovative public artwork in Wester Hailes, Edinburgh, Scotland.

The third section is an account of the practical application of 'hacking' through the design and functionality of the 'totem pole' as a public digital artwork. The section explains the context from which digital technology was 'hacked' into by local residents to create public art, the research team's role in it and how the created physical digital platform was, in turn, used to 'hack' into images and memories that enabled individuals to engage in collective conversations and to share a sense of community.

The fourth section offers insights into how an embedded 'read–write' facility in public art presented possibilities for community engagement and regeneration. It also highlights that this form of 'hacking' into technology through community-generated public art was possible through co-production. While we acknowledge the varied conceptions of this term, by 'co-production', we mean a research approach that emanated from and is informed by the community. It is about working with communities in an empowering way that offers them greater control of the research and opportunities for learning. Such control implies involving communities in all stages of the research process, from design through implementation to the dissemination of research outcomes and outputs (Pohl et al, 2010: 271). Co-production is also about striving to maintain respect and openness in negotiating terms of engagement between researchers and the communities in order to reflect their lived experiences (Robinson and Tansey, 2006: 159). Given that our use of the 'hacking' concept is heuristic and metaphorical, the fourth section highlights the utility and risks of employing discourses derived from digital media culture to inform and inspire new models of governance, social reality and community regeneration.

Exploring discursive resonance in digital media and the 'Big Society'

The Coalition government's 'Big Society' policy was seemingly inspired by new media technology. For instance, a key characteristic of the 'Big Society' is 'open source planning' and 'localism' as a means of encouraging individuals and communities to participate in civic engagement and collaborative work in order to find imaginative and sustainable solutions to the everyday social, political and economic challenges they face (see Lesley, 2010; Conservative Party, 2010 [2009]).

The Coalition government suggested that 'open source planning' was inspired by the digital media industry, where the aim is to make computer programming accessible or open to all in a flexible and adaptable way (Conservative Party, 2010 [2009]). The discursive logic of the Coalition is that through 'open source planning', citizens would be encouraged to participate collectively and collaboratively in local initiatives and the inherent decision-making processes (see Lesley, 2010). As Jones et al (Chapter Eleven) and Cohen and McDermont (Chapter Four) have enunciated in this volume, the aim is to influence and shape all aspects of initiatives, and to make policymaking transparent and accountable to citizens who are the recipients of such service provision.

The figurehead of the 'Big Society' agenda, UK Prime Minister David Cameron, claimed that 'open source planning', among other initiatives, will enable people to feel empowered enough to help themselves and is the 'biggest, most dramatic redistribution of power from elites to the man in the street' (Conservative Party, 2010 [2009]). By so doing, 'open source planning' becomes a bottom–up process that transforms policymaking and service delivery from a centralised bureaucratic control system to one that is grassroots-led, decentralised and localised. As others in this volume have suggested (see Chapters Two, Four, Five and Eleven), such 'localism' would make citizens active or even proactive social actors in the development and regeneration of their neighbourhoods and communities, hitherto the exclusive terrain of bureaucrats and elected representatives (see Lesley, 2010; see also the Localism Act 2010). Services are more likely to be tailor-made to the needs and specifications of local people and, at the same time, with greater quality. This transforms service users into stakeholders in the design and delivery of local services.

In order to reduce structural inequalities in delivering, accessing and benefiting from welfare services by citizens, the Coalition government created the 'Big Society Bank' (see Chadwick, 2009). The bank is tasked with financing social enterprises, charities and voluntary groups to widen participation in service delivery. Proponents of the bank claimed that this would promote diversity in the markets, innovation and entrepreneurship by opening up local service provision to market competition (Conservative Party, 2010 [2009]). Here, it is worth noting the discursive parallel with the digital media software industry: the 'Big Society' proponents claimed that market access would promote transparency, lower costs and quality improvement as service users become part of the collaborative design and delivery of services. Policymaking and service provision therefore moves from a one-size-fits-all design approach to one that gives service users the freedom to shape and choose services (see Chadwick, 2009).

Another digital media feature that has stimulated contemporary governance is Web 2.0. The latter marked a departure from a top-down or elite-led dimension of Web 1.0 'read-only' to a bottom–up or grassroots-led approach with a 'read–write' facility for users. It has been argued that Web 2.0 has improved and widened public access to knowledge and information, which was hitherto restricted and available only to political elites (see Mayo and Stenberg, 2007). Through 'tweeting', 'blogging', 'Facebook' and other social media, individuals can formulate, disseminate, access and share their own and others' news and information much more easily and at lower cost than before. These digital media platforms are avenues for networking, sharing and mobilising resources among individuals towards social, political and economic ends.

The practice by politicians of sounding out public opinion and consulting in an ad hoc basis on their policies and actions through 'tweeting' and 'blogging' is an attempt to be part of the network society that is a common characteristic of contemporary governance (see Chadwick, 2009). It is also an indication that attempts are being made by elected representatives to elicit the views of the electorate and to engage them in collaborative democracy, as advocated by the 'Big Society'. Individuals can also probe, query or seek information from their elected representatives through such media.

New media's role in widening collaborative democracy and access to public knowledge underpins the Coalition government's 'open data' and 'public government data' programmes. These facilitate an individual's right to access some government-held data sets, including the publication of local crime statistics on a monthly basis. This mimics the 'network society' and 'file-sharing' practices of Web 2.0 by which the public can learn about developments and initiatives elsewhere and link up with other citizens and communities (see Margetts, 2011). The potential to influence the redesigning or copying of initiatives that have been successful elsewhere and to enable citizens to compare performance among public officials and service provision is also central to the 'Big Society'.

At this juncture, it is worth noting a key criticism of the 'Big Society' policy: that it is a ploy by the Coalition government to 'upload' social problems onto citizens. It is another reminder of the propensity by political elites to evoke the vernacular of digital media in order to highlight the policy as another tool to deflect the harsh consequences of the current economic austerity programme when welfare services are 'cut' or 'downsized'. What the preceding discussion suggests, however, is that the characteristics, rhetoric and logic deployed to articulate the UK government 'Big Society' agenda seemingly mimics and is aided by digital media culture. It is therefore not surprising that proponents of the 'Big Society' have argued that when individuals use digital technology to access information and knowledge, participate in the formulation and delivery of policies and services, make choices among welfare services, and hold public officials to account, they become empowered social actors and responsible 'active' citizens. As Jones et al's MapLocal project in Chapter Eleven reminds us, digital media are crucial to the 'Big Society' in achieving 'localism', 'open source planning' and citizens' 'sense of community', access to information, networking and sharing and mobilising resources (Conservative Party, 2010 [2009]).

Political elites also claim that the 'Big Society' agenda subsists on 'reciprocity' and the 'resilience' of community ethos given that residents, either individually or collectively, harness social capital within their neighbourhoods to respond to and cope with the social problems that they encounter in their everyday lives (see Crabtree, 2003). This is because individuals and communities can share their experiences, skills and resources with others in other parts of the polity who are faced with similar social challenges in order to help them cope. They, in turn, would expect others to reciprocate in a similar manner. Such reciprocity and resilience among users to solve societal challenges is parallel to the 'file-sharing' of Web 2.0, where individuals depend on each other to pull skills and resources together for mutual benefit. In addition, there is also a reciprocal benefit for individuals of feeling part of a community or belonging and identifying with their community (virtual and actual), and a sense of sharing a common purpose with others (Tonnies, 1957). It is worth noting here that other contributors to this edition, including Matthews and O'Brien (Chapter Three) and Jones et al (Chapter Eleven), have cautioned about the elusiveness of such claims by the Coalition government (see also Chapters Four, Five and Seven). We have only singled out the 'Big Society' as a facade for 'uploading' social problems onto society insofar as this criticism is relevant to consideration of the discursive linkages with digital media culture.

The preceding discursive parallels provided the context from which digital technology was hacked into through a process of co-production between the research team and the Wester Hailes community to create the 'digital totem pole'. We were interested in the consideration of the hypothesis that concepts and vocabularies emerging in relation to digital culture could usefully be applied to understandings of offline contemporary practices. Our assumption was that community-generated public art that is contingent upon the internet (Web2.0) activity of connecting individuals and communities is akin to 'hacking', as the next section explains.

The 'hacking' metaphor: relevance to community and the 'Big Society'

The concept of 'hacking' is drawn from the techno-scientific domain and is widely perceived to derive from student pranksters who 'hacked' a car on the Massachusetts Institute of Technology (MIT) university campus to make it look like a police patrol car (Burnham, 2009; see also Levey, 2002; Lapsley, 2011). Internet 'hacking' can be

The digital totem pole

understood to involve individuals and communities who are interested in modifying aspects of the web in ways that challenge messages and the representation of circumstances. They do so through creative ways that could be perceived as proactive social action, which can be positive deviance and/or transgressive. Kulikauska (2004) argues that individuals actively engage in groups (online and offline) to help each other remake and restructure their lives and their world, as well as to challenge social norms (laws and morals). By 'challenge', we refer to both breaking and not breaking social norms to facilitate action by linking and bringing together different individuals, groups and communities.

The process of 'hacking' encourages other social actors or agents to create and link up with other worlds, communities and networks through the internet. This is not to say that 'hacking' activities are exclusive to the internet. However, individuals who 'hack', either inadvertently or deliberately, might not perceive or conceptualise such activities as 'hacking'. Kulikauska therefore argues that 'hacking' becomes a metaphor for the practices and actions that exploit (or explore) weaknesses or deficiencies in a system that behave or function in a certain way (see also Ariely, 2011). 'Hacking', in this sense, connotes simple approaches deployed by online users that are fluid, constantly evolving and responsive to specific social circumstances. 'Hacking' is also associated with digital media to connote simple approaches deployed by online users that are deviant or resourceful.

'Hacking', therefore, has both positive and negative connotations, is transactional in nature, and is part of network culture.

Given these conceptions and practices of 'hacking' and the onset of cuts to government support to families and individuals with low incomes, the concept has utility in exploring how communities dealt with government cuts within the 'Big Society'. In addition, given the methods of user-generated content that defined Web 2.0 and now constitute social media processes, the contemporary internet could provide spaces for 'hacking' by communities of everyday social processes and relations. Our use of the term is therefore metaphorical and heuristic. Consequently, we went on to use the term to frame a cooperative community-designed artwork through the development of an innovative public artwork and the use of local historical images to 'hack' local perceptions of a deprived area of Edinburgh, Scotland. We assumed that, as other digital interventions featured in this edition, with the appropriate design intervention in a community, related activities could potentially facilitate 'hacking' and the attendant co-production of social engagement, social connectivity and social interaction, which are the focus of the 'Big Society' agenda. As suggested by others in this volume, such social networking has transformative potential to connect citizens with policymaking, foment a shared digital culture and nurture communities (see Chapters Six and Ten; see also Mayo and Steinberg, 2007). Our exploratory work is significant because it will shed significant light on the relationship between community-generated public art, digital media culture and design practice. In addition, by developing a system for networking, our project moves beyond a 'read-only' dimension to creating an opportunity for 'writing back' into a community-generated digital platform. In the main, digital media platforms tended to focus on read-only social media components as an instrument for empowering communities (Moulder et al, 2011). Much of the interactive component of community-based digital art occurs on internet web sites through which individuals contribute text (Bowie and Fels, 2009; Andreyev, 2010; Moulder et al, 2011).

The rest of the chapter will demonstrate how a 'read–write' component was embedded in a public artwork – the 'digital totem pole' – which has possibilities for community engagement and regeneration. We further demonstrate that this form of 'hacking' into technology through community-generated public art is possible when the design intervention is shaped by and among the community.

Wester Hailes and the design process

The 'digital totem pole' was a significant social design output of 'The Community Web 2.0: Creative Control Through Hacking' project funded by 'Connected Communities'. Wester Hailes is a large housing estate constructed in the 1970s in West Edinburgh, Scotland. It has been characterised by urban regeneration, and is generally perceived as afflicted with social and economic deprivation, crime, and unemployment. These problems have provided the impulse for residents to organise community development and service delivery initiatives, as observed in the similar geographies of Birmingham and Bristol (see Chapters Four, Seven and Eleven). In addition, Wester Hailes has historically deployed community art towards community development, regeneration and empowerment. Community art has also been central to projecting a positive image of the community to contrast a mainly negative media representation of its residents.

At the outset of the research project, two local service providers, Prospect Community Housing Association (Prospect) and Wester Hailes Arts for Leisure and Education (WHALE Arts), became very interested in how social media offers a platform to exchange ideas. Interested in exploring this aspect to recover, circulate and comment on past images within Wester Hailes and its diaspora, Prospect set up a Facebook page to post images of the area that were originally published in the community newspaper, the *Wester Hailes Sentinel*, latterly the *West Edinburgh Times*, which ran from 1989 to 2008. The page quickly became popular, with photographs attracting many comments about whom, when and where they were taken (see: http://on.fb.me/mOPPwp). This 'write-back' facility began to enable residents to recover memories of the past and drew out many connections beyond the image itself. By the summer of 2010, the project had found a design method that encapsulated 'hacking', simply the development of platforms that facilitated the community 'writing back' on to representations of Wester-Hailes. While the Facebook page offered a globally accessible online platform for information exchange, the residents were interested in offering a hyperlocal and physical access point to make visible the development of a digital community network. Consequently, the community, in collaboration with the authors, developed what became known as a 'digital totem pole'.

The production of the four-metre pole was coordinated by WHALE Arts, who were involved its design and carving. A steering group of community members and project partners was created to ensure that clear targets were set and achieved. The steering group also facilitated the networking, engagement and capacity-building that underpinned the five participatory workshops within the community. The workshops were held during local civic events, including the tenth anniversary celebration of the Union Canal, the annual general meeting (AGM) of service providers and the annual community Road Show in the Westside Plaza shopping centre. Participants to the workshops include local residents, the staff of services and community activists.

A central element of the workshop was the display of a portable banner with embedded 'Quick Response' (QR) codes (as proof of concept) and historical photographs depicting people, events and places of Wester Hailes on the outer wall of a portable shed. The portable banner and photographs were used in combination to introduce residents with different levels of technological expertise and interest to the technology used in the project. Participants were asked to look at the photographs to trigger their memories or any other associations that they might have with the people, event or place depicted. They were then encouraged to share their stories/memories about these, which were captured through a voice and film recorder. Participants were also encouraged to scan the QR codes embedded on the photographs and to record and upload their stories to the Tales of Things website (see: www.talesofthings.com) directly from their smartphones. They were then asked to scan and listen to the replay. This exercise gave them experience of the opportunities that the technology would offer, which is the ability to read and write into the codes. The workshops were also opportunities for participants to ask questions and provide any suggestions or views about the project and how best to improve it, and to get their sustained involvement in its future development. The overall ethos of the workshops was one that promoted engagement with residents and their exposure to new developments in web-based technology in a way that was empowering, collaborative, non-threatening and meaningful. The workshops were therefore central to community participation in all aspects of the digital totem pole project, including the design, timescales and location of the pole.

A professional artist led a group of five to 10 people to carve the wooden totem pole. The final product was installed within Wester Hailes. The wooden totem pole had carvings and five QR codes that give access to a variety of services, residents' stories and memories of the area. The QR codes offered the network dimension to the pole from which it gained the name 'digital totem pole'. A significant practical dimension of the totem pole was that it provided a physical platform for 'hacking' images (through the ability of people being able to comment and create new meanings for the images) and sharing conversations about the area. People could scan one of the labelled tags and access and contribute to historical photographs, stories and video and audio clips. The intention was that pole would act as a social resource to help build connections between the people and the place, as well as drawing upon online resources (see Margetts, 2011).

Connecting Communities: prospects and risks for the 'Big Society'

What, then, can we infer from the design and practicality of the totem pole that is relevant to developing our understanding of the implications for using discourses derived from digital media to inform new models of governance, community engagement, regeneration and actual practices within communities? The 'digital totem pole' was perceived by local residents and those beyond it, including the press, as a public artwork that added to the aesthetic beauty of the locality. It was also celebrated for being a networked museum or repository for audio, written and visual recordings of the current and past memories, narratives, works and ideas of local residents and others in the diaspora. While these benefits of community-generated digital art have been observed elsewhere (Moulder et al, 2011), the totem pole moved beyond its aesthetic and archival value to have a symbolic relevance to Wester Hailes as a community with historic problems of marginalisation. The general feeling among residents was that the totem pole served a symbolic function: that of community resilience and regeneration. In addition, it symbolised the community's resilience in contesting negative depictions of their community as afflicted with social delinquencies and deprivation.

The 'digital totem pole' also suggests that co-production of a public artwork is a process that incorporates a mix of approaches to enable social connections, human interactions and networking (Tacchi et al, 2003; Moulder et al, 2011: 4). The community/human agency was also possible because the process of designing and producing the digital totem pole depended on the input of residents. As Moulder et al (2011: 2) observed during their 'Talking Poles' project, most public artwork that incorporated digital technology and was produced by non-professional artists tended to exclude people from the final stages of the creative process. Our work, as with Moulder et al (2011) and others in this volume, facilitated community participation at every stage – from the design process of the pole and the QR codes, the web content and themes therein contained, to the installation of the finished product. This involvement of residents as co-creators of the artwork cemented an ownership of the project.

We were also mindful of the need for the project to contribute to the skills of locals for it to be a successful participatory community art project in ways similar to those employed by other projects featured in this volume (see also Ackoff, 1974; Moulder et al, 2011: 8). The lack of digital technology skills, therefore, did not preclude anyone from participating. As explained earlier, the workshops were aimed at building such skills among those that lacked them. Overall, the process of design nurtured an engagement between professional and non-professional artists, academics and non-academics, and digital media technologists and non-technologists. This process and the functionality of the pole, as a network museum of the services, works, ideas, histories and narratives of individuals and service providers, made this digital art platform connect to different communities. It connected Wester Hailes and the academy, local residents and service providers, residents in different neighbourhoods of Wester Hailes, those outside Wester Hailes, and the diaspora. The social connectedness and networked communities was also possible by the in-built 'read-write' component of the digital totem pole. In this way, we generated significant social capital by engaging with the diverse ages, backgrounds and interests present in the Wester Hailes community to explore and capture their memories of the area and also to articulate a collective future ambition for the community. This, therefore, demonstrates how community-generated public art could draw from or be informed by online practices associated with everyday social media platforms.

What the preceding highlights is that 'hacking' is not restricted to online activities, but also applies to everyday life situations and challenges. It is about the capacity of individuals and communities to deploy digital media spaces to develop or organise innovative social solutions, whether transgressive or conformist to established protocols (norms, laws), for the improvement of their lives and neighbourhoods. The co-production in the design and delivery of 'hacking' is characterised by reciprocity, resilience, intentionality, functionality, imaginativeness and creativity. These characteristics are crucial for mobilising social capital and practices by and among marginalised communities. These have the potential to enable citizens to collaboratively take control over their welfare and cope with everyday challenges. The actions constitute a kind of social responsibility, community empowerment and 'active' citizenship that is consistent with localism and the 'Big Society'.

We anticipated the totem pole to have relevance and potential for achieving the 'Big Society' agenda. As already stated, the government had expected service users, through 'open source planning', to become part of the collaborative design of services through public consultations, among other channels. The 'digital totem pole' provided opportunities for this by enabling local residents, service providers and politicians to share opinions, information and knowledge. This had a potential to influence the design and delivery of services to meet local needs and tastes and in reducing structural inequalities to access and benefit from such services. It facilitated a network community and we anticipated residents would be able to use its 'read–write' facility to hold local service providers and politicians to account. Service providers and politicians would also use this as an avenue for generating feedback and views from residents. It had the potential to influence the redesigning or copying of experiences of services within the locality. More importantly, as residents shared memories through uploading photographs and stories of the community, they would have a feeling of belonging and identification with Wester Hailes.

However, any digital media intervention in marginalised communities like Wester Hailes is bound to be fraught with risks, which constitute a hindrance to realising the 'Big Society'. First, in a networked community of participants, reciprocity may not be spontaneous and symmetrical. While policymakers would expect appreciable and equal levels of participation, it is likely that these will be asynchronous. This is because individuals will choose when and where to participate in online spaces, and their level of participation is based on their abilities and the resources at their disposal. This is a potential risk to achieving the 'Big Society' agenda: not all individuals and communities will participate either in all services or activities, or in equal measure. There are structural inequalities that are bound to affect, in different ways, individual and community participation, an issue also raised by Matthews and O'Brien in Chapter Three. There might be varying access to and use of digital technology due to prohibitive costs and the lack of skills in using them. We anticipated that the asynchronicity in the way networked individuals contribute might be caused by the differences in abilities/capabilities and the availability of resources (internet) among them. It is likely that those who can afford Web facilities are likely to be empowered middle-class citizens, which could lead to a widening of inequality and the social divide, as other contributors to this volume have observed.

Second, a potentially contentious issue relates to the extent and form of participation by individuals in service delivery and other 'Big Society' initiatives. It is not clear how policymakers will respond to activities of individuals that are outside the stipulations or rules of engagement of a policy or service. Will the government tolerate such transgressive behaviour by individuals and communities, albeit it in their own interest and benefit? If tolerated by policymakers, will they provide the facilitative base for other grassroots or community-inspired services that can be shared with or disseminated to others within the polity? Such opportunities to develop independent community action should be accorded prominence by the government. As Matthews and O'Brien stated in Chapter Three, policymakers should direct their energies to creating the legal and funding framework to enable communities to achieve their preferred activities. If this was to be the case, then localism will be a radical and real prospect. This kind of service provision will empower residents in driving forward the 'Big Society' agenda.

Given the heuristic nature of our work and speculations regarding risks, we propose that research energies ought to be devoted towards an empirical project to investigate the intersections between online practices (virtual communities) and offline practices, or the daily experiences of individuals and actual communities. As highlighted in Chapter Nine, Harte and Turner, following Parker and Karner (2011), argued that such empirical research is urgently needed to enrich current debates about the exclusion and "everyday activism" that citizens undertake in online and offline spaces with a view to counter 'hegemonic' accounts of communities. Adding to this, we should also seek to understand how the intersections between online and offline practices by citizens could influence political culture and governance. We believe that the metaphor of 'hacking' offers an understanding of community processes that anticipates how people are likely to turn to 'creative' processes to sustain their lifestyles. The nature of the investigation will offer radical insights into how digital media culture can inform new forms of community engagement and regeneration. Of the many problematic strategies that such empirical studies are likely to record, there will be an equal number of completely new processes that will challenge traditional models of community support and governance. These new constructive processes will offer new approaches with which to facilitate aspects of the 'Big Society'. We can anticipate that, by definition, these methods will be best understood through the use of cross-disciplinary research: social science, arts and humanities, and models of co-production. These will provide insight into the implications of using an extended metaphor derived from the contemporary internet to inform new models of governance and social responsibility (Margetts, 2011).

Conclusion

The chapter has argued that community-generated public art that is contingent upon the internet (Web 2.0) activity of connecting individuals and communities is akin to 'hacking'. It has explored how Wester Hailes residents have used the digital totem pole to derive maximum benefit from their use of virtual and public spaces. It considers that through a collaborative partnership with our research team, the Wester Hailes community 'hacked' into images and memories that would enable individuals to engage in collective conversations and to share a sense of community. This case study offers unique insights into how a 'read–write' facility in public art enabled community engagement, regeneration and digital inclusion. The latter is made possible because through workshops, individuals learn digital media skills. It has been highlighted that this form of 'hacking' into technology through community-generated public art was possible when residents informed the design process.

We have considered that community participation in 'hacking' embodies the resilience of individuals and communities to address everyday challenges in society through online and offline practices. The 'hacking' metaphor is therefore relevant insofar as the 'Big Society' agenda of the current UK Coalition government expects both local communities and service users to become part of the collaborative design of services through public consultations in a way that is empowering. It has also been explored that 'hacking' into digital media has the potential for community regeneration. We hope that this will demonstrate how concepts and vocabularies emerging in relation to the Internet could usefully be applied to understandings of offline contemporary relations and practices, and vice versa.

Acknowledgements

The 'Community Web 2.0: Creative Control Through Hacking' project was funded by the UK Arts and Humanities Research Council under the 'Connected Communities' theme. Many thanks to residents of Wester Hailes, particularly Eoghan Howard and staff at WHALE Arts, and Prospect Community Housing Association.

References

Ackoff, R.L. (1974) *Redesigning the future*, New York, NY: Wiley.
Andreyev, J. (2010). *glisten) HIVE. Retrieved Jan. 20, 2010 from http://julieandreyev.wordpress.com/

Ariely, D. (2011) 'Social hacking'. Available at: http://danariely. com/2011/01/20/social-hacking/

Bowie, F. and Fels, S. (2009). Flow. Retrieved Jan. 20, 2011 from http://fionabowie.org/

Burnham, S. (2009) 'Finding the truth in systems: in praise of design-hacking', RSA Design& Society orwww.scottburnham.com/files/ScottBurnham-Hacking-Design-2009.pdf

Chadwick, A. (2009) 'Web2.0: new challenges for the study of e-democracy in an era of information exuberance', *I.S.: A Journal of Law and Policy for the Information Society* 10(5.1): 9–41.

Conservative Party (2010 [2009]) *Open source planning*, Policy Green Paper No 14, London: Conservative Party.

Cramer, F. (2003) 'Social Hacking, Revisited'. Retrieved Jan. 20, 2011 from http://cramer.pleintekst.nl:70/all/social_hacking_revisited_sollfrank/social_hacking_revisited_sollfrank.pdf

Kulikauskas, A. (2004) 'Social hacking: the need for an ethics'. Available at: http://www.freeebay.net/site/index.php?option=com_content& task=view&id=289&Itemid=99999999

Lapsley, P. (2011) 'Phone phreakers'. Available at: http://voicegal. wordpress.com/2011/04/10/phone-phreakers/

Lesley, C. (2010) 'Localism & the Coalition – A neglected aspiration', http://idea.gov.uk/Idk/core/page.Id=24346328, 2010

Levey, S. (2002) *Hackers: heroes of the computer revolution*, Penguin Books Ltd.

Margetts, H. (2011) 'The internet and political science: re-examining collective action, governance and citizen–government interactions in the digital era'. Available at: http://www.oii.ox.ac.uk/research/projects/?id=71

Mayo, E. and Steinberg, T. (2007) 'The Power of Information: An Independent Review by Ed Mayo and Tom Steinberg', June 2007. Retrieved Jan. 20, 2010 from http://www.opsi.gov.uk/advice/poi/power-of-information-review.pdf

Moulder, V., Boschman, L.R. and Wakkary, R. (2011) 'The Talking Poles – public art based in social design', CHI 2011, May 7–12, Vancouver, BC, Canada, ACM 978-1-4503-0268-5/11/05.

Parker, D. and Karner, C. (2011) 'Remembering the Alum Rock Road: reputational geographies and spatial biographies', *Midland History* 36(2): 292–309.

Pohl, C., Rist, R., Zimmerman, A., Fry, P., Gurung, G.S., Schneider, F., Speranza, C.I., Kiteme, B., Boillat, S., Serrano, E., Hirsch Hadorn, G. and Weismann, U. (2010) 'Researchers' roles in knowledge co-production: experience from sustainability research in Kenya, Switzerland, Bolivia and Nepal', *Science and Public Policy* 37(4): 267–81.

Robinson, J. and Tansey, J. (2006) 'Co-production, emergent properties and strong interactive social research: the Georgia Basin Futures project', *Science and Public Policy* 33(2): 151–60.

Tacchi, J., Slater, D. and Hearn, G. (2003) *Ethnographic action research: a user's handbook developed to innovate and research ICT applications for poverty eradication*, New Delhi: UNESCO.

Tonnies, F. (1957) *Community and society* (trans C.P. Looms), East Lansing, MI: Michigan State University Press.

Part Four
New spaces for policy

ELEVEN

Localism, neighbourhood planning and community control: the MapLocal pilot

Phil Jones, Antonia Layard, Colin Lorne and Chris Speed

Introduction

In this chapter, we examine a contradiction in contemporary regeneration between a discourse of putting communities in control and creating policy instruments that disempower the poorest. Our focus is the Neighbourhood Plan, introduced as part of the Localism Act 2011, which epitomises this contradiction. The localism agenda apparently offers greater choice to communities, but, in practice, this new approach to the redevelopment of neighbourhoods requires expertise, organisational capacity and finance in a way that favours already well-resourced communities. Thus, the rhetoric of community empowerment within this new policy landscape has done little to overcome the mechanisms by which the middle classes have historically taken disproportionate benefit from public services (Matthews and Hastings, 2013).

MapLocal, the project described here, was an attempt to tip the scales back slightly by providing a tool for communities to begin the process of neighbourhood planning. The tool was limited to tackling the first stage of a plan-making process: gathering community intelligence about issues facing the neighbourhood and making suggestions for change. In doing so, we placed community knowledges at the forefront of a plan-making process, though with the important caveat that such knowledges and aspirations need to be analysed and mediated, both within a community and with expert knowledges from outside. This, arguably, requires a much greater degree of state involvement than is permitted within the current neoliberal discourse that dominates planning policy.

After assessing the potential that MapLocal offers to improve the neighbourhood planning process, we critically assess the issues with devolving decision-making to neighbourhoods. We conclude that neighbourhood planning does offer some real opportunities for developing democratic discourse at the neighbourhood scale. Nonetheless, this potential is unrealised and the policy offers a sop to middle-class NIMBYism while doing little to enable more deprived communities to shape changes and see improvements to the areas in which they live.

The 'failure' of community regeneration and the rise of localism

The New Labour period (1997–2010) saw a return to building in city centres at a scale not seen since the post-war reconstruction, characterised by shiny, high-density complexes of well-appointed, if rather small, apartments. Distinct from flagship projects in city cores, however, a plethora of policies were focused on community renewal, attempting to help struggling neighbourhoods via a combination of social, economic and infrastructure investments. By dint of their greater visibility, over time, it tends to be the infrastructure projects that are remembered, rather than, say, grassroots-driven attempts at social renewal through building confidence and skills. As such, perhaps the clearest legacy of New Labour community renewal was in large neglected areas of housing undergoing major programmes of demolition/refurbishment, radically altering the tenure mix through bringing in third sector providers of social housing and a higher proportion of owner-occupiers (Jones and Evans, 2013).

These kinds of New Labour community renewal schemes followed the general drift of policy established by the previous Conservative government: bringing in private and third sector partners to deliver projects. Within these approaches, the idea of 'community' took on a particular importance as another partner within the process, giving these schemes a veneer of democratic accountability, although communities were, in practice, rather sketchily defined and always the 'partner' with the least resources to bring to any negotiation over priorities (Imrie and Raco, 2003). It should come as no surprise, therefore, that many of these policies, particularly the Housing Market Renewal Pathfinders (Cameron, 2006), proved controversial, not least for the way in which market mechanisms were assumed to be capable of solving entrenched socio-economic problems in communities (Webb, 2010).

Rather than examining the impacts of long-term structural inequality, the right-leaning thinktank ResPublica has suggested that these kinds of schemes failed where community engagement was not taken seriously enough (Kaszynska et al, 2012). This has not just been a critique of the political Right, with a clear tension between the New Labour rhetoric on community engagement in regeneration and a policy framework that fostered displacement and gentrification (Lees, 2014). The discourse that emerged under the Coalition 2010-15 was one of arguing that communities should be able to take much greater control over developments within their neighbourhoods. In some ways, this is a classic neoliberal move – emphasising individual choice to solve collective problems – and few politicians would want to come out against people being given more power. Thus, while the Localism Act 2011 represented a sea change in English spatial planning for many reasons, it was explicitly positioned against the perceived failures of New Labour-era top-down planning by apparently placing communities at the heart of the process. The problem is that while the neighbourhood's totemic power as the seat of community policy has been reinforced by the Localism Act, this has been accompanied by a shift in approach from an at least nominal commitment to redistribution toward self-help without any additional resources being devolved down to the neighbourhood (Bailey and Pill, 2011: 940). Thus, the context for the Localism Act was not demands for greater democratic accountability over local decision-making, but a desire to enforce swingeing central government cuts to public expenditure, particularly targeting regional and local government, and asking communities to solve their own problems (Westwood, 2011).

Governing the local

The Localism Act contained a number of policy innovations that alter the relationship between local government, communities and urban development. In this chapter, we focus on just one: the introduction of Neighbourhood Plans. The Localism Act gives power to communities to produce statutorily binding spatial plans for development in their neighbourhood. Although this is a powerful symbol of devolving control to communities, in practice, this transfer of power is somewhat less clear-cut. Neighbourhood planning as it emerged in the Localism Act was developed in *Open source planning*, a Conservative Party policy paper published before the 2010 general election (Conservative Party, 2010). Bishop (2010) argues that this paper drew on false assumptions that the system of parish and market town plans promoted under New Labour could be a model for more devolved planning structures. In practice, it was highly unusual for these rural planning documents to engage with one of the key tenets of spatial planning – determining what kinds of development should happen on which sites – yet this would be at the core of the proposed new Neighbourhood Plans (Bishop, 2010: 620).

Transferring an approach to planning conceptualised for rural areas into complex urban contexts is also problematic from a governance point of view. Although parish councils exist for small settlements in rural areas, there is no equivalent structure below the level of the local authority for neighbourhoods in urban areas. The Localism Act thus created a new governance structure – the Neighbourhood Forum – for coordinating activity at this scale. Neighbourhood Forums are intended to be established through grassroots efforts by communities in order to gather at least 21 people from across the geographic area that they seek to control, write a constitution and then apply to the local authority to create a new Neighbourhood Forum. From the outset, therefore, this privileges those with the time, money and education to determine that they want to write a Neighbourhood Plan and organise themselves to do this. It also raises the possibility of conflict as rival groups seek to draw boundaries around the same areas in different ways. In practice, larger local authorities like Birmingham City Council have therefore taken a lead on coordinating the establishment of Neighbourhood Forums, although in Birmingham, these still only covered around 40% of the population by the end of 2013 – and many of these remain inactive.

Even assuming enough interest in a community to sustain a Neighbourhood Forum, there are still considerable barriers to establishing a Neighbourhood Plan. Neighbourhood Plans need to conform to both the local authority's own statutory plans and the National Planning Policy Framework (NPPF). Given that the NPPF places an emphasis on growth and removing the barriers to development, in practice, Neighbourhood Plans are about saying 'yes' to development rather than resisting it. No matter how much local opinion might want to stop supermarket chains moving in to the neighbourhood, might prefer affordable housing over luxury flats or might want to keep out undesirable facilities such as bail hostels and strip clubs, this cannot be written into the Neighbourhood Plan. Thus, bottom-up, community-led planning is very clearly delimited. Haughton et al (2013) have referred to new governance structures like Neighbourhood Forums as being 'soft spaces' and argue that they are complicit in reinforcing neoliberal growth imperatives. Although there is some apparent community control, they only 'allow for particular demands to be voiced and negotiated, as long as they do not question and disrupt the overarching framework of market-led development' (Haughton et al, 2013: 222).

Neighbourhood Plans also need to be produced in a format that fits with the formal strictures of the planning system since they will be given statutory weight. This requires considerable expertise both to gather local opinion on what the priorities should be and to then condense this into a formal document. Finally, if approved by the local authority, the Neighbourhood Plan must then be passed in a referendum held in the area it covers. Given this level of complexity, Colenut (2012: 15) has suggested that the majority of the money given to local authorities to facilitate neighbourhood planning will need to be spent examining the submitted plans and running local referendums, leaving little to give direct assistance to the Neighbourhood Forums attempting to actually draw these up in the first place.

It becomes clear that putting a Neighbourhood Plan together is an exceedingly time-consuming process, requiring considerable expertise and being highly limited in what it can achieve. Unsurprisingly, therefore, the wider Localism Act has elicited considerable cynicism. Durman (2012: 680), for example, argues that it can:

> be read as an indicator of a state disillusioned with its capacity of fulfilling its role as long-term mediator and fair arbiter of social processes to such an extent that it outsources to its own citizens the capacity of mediating those conflicts without providing a structurally sound platform of social justice on which such mediations and adjudication can take place.

The issues around mediating conflict are exceedingly important and the ways in which discursive spaces are constructed poses a critical challenge facing more participatory approaches to governance (Fischer, 2006). This is a point we will return to later. Nonetheless, in the pilot project described here, we wanted to move away from a somewhat despairing discourse of cynicism about the reforms to planning. We chose instead to try to engage more positively with the potential that Neighbourhood Plans offer, in theory at least, to give communities more control over their immediate environment, attempting to produce a tool that at least partly mitigated the lack of resources being offered to undertake this process.

MapLocal: facilitating localism?

From the outset, however, the MapLocal project deliberately dodged the issue of mediating between different priorities for action within a community. The reason for this decision was pragmatic. As a small-scale project funded by the 'Connected Communities' programme, we simply did not have the resources to take on the wicked issue of reconciling community views. Instead, we concentrated on producing a tool that would help communities that lacked external resources and expertise to undertake the first stage of drawing up a plan: gathering information from residents about their understanding of the neighbourhood, the issues they perceive to be problematic and their ideas for change.

MapLocal is an application designed for Android smartphones and tablets that is available to download from the Google Play store. It allows people to walk around their neighbourhood recording audio clips and taking photos that are tagged with GPS coordinates and uploaded to a community map. The app design emerged from conversations with two social enterprises, MADE and the Chamberlain Forum, which work on the built environment and community engagement. The interface was designed by Chris Speed and programmed by Chris Blunt of Plymouth Software.

The app links to a website that hosts maps displaying the contributions from different community members. Photos and audio clips gathered by the app are uploaded to this website without user intervention so there is a low skill threshold to adding material to the community map. Smartphones are by no means ubiquitous, particularly in low-income communities, but market penetration within the UK is such that they form by far the majority of phones being purchased today. This means that the technology is much more familiar, much less intimidating and much less likely to make someone using a smartphone in public space a target for mugging than even five years ago. Users of the app look unremarkable, appearing as though they are chatting into their phone, texting or taking photographs as they walk through their local area.

We worked across two different neighbourhoods in Birmingham. Balsall Heath is an ethnically diverse, densely populated inner suburb, which scores highly on the English indices of multiple deprivation. It received central government funding to act as a pilot ('pathfinder') for the neighbourhood planning process, which paid for local architect and urban designer Joe Holyoak to undertake a conventional participatory planning exercise and draw up a draft plan for submission to the local authority. In contrast, the Jewellery Quarter, just to the west of the city core, has a small, mostly white, professional residential population and is home to service and creative businesses, as well as small-scale jewellery manufacture. A Neighbourhood Forum was not established in the Jewellery Quarter until mid-2014, meaning that at the time we did the data collection in November–December 2012, there was no active plan-making process.

Holman and Rydin (2012: 77) have noted that participation suffers from a 'collective action problem': individuals do not see the value of engaging in participatory processes because the likely outcomes of engagement are not commensurate with the time spent. The neighbourhood planning process is a clear case in point here: the reward is a plan that may or may not respond to specific local concerns and the cost is attending a great many meetings. More than this, the processes of engagement can itself be quite intimidating – with familiar problems of confident people dominating discussions and hard-to-reach groups being excluded from these processes (see, eg, the specific case of local sex workers discussed by Sagar and Croxall, 2012).

The intention with MapLocal was to produce something that had fairly low barriers to use and would be a relatively inexpensive way of collating a large quantity of material from people in the neighbourhood, without demanding that they come to meetings at fixed times and have to speak in front of other people. We also intended to develop something that could offer a relatively fun exercise, attempting to give an added value to participation in a process that might only distantly result in changes to the neighbourhood. Within the pilot, there was the added complication that we were asking participants to act, effectively, as co-researchers, testing an unproven interface and giving us feedback. We therefore felt that it was important to pay participants for their time as they were making a substantial contribution to undertaking the research itself (a similar position to that adopted by Thomas and O'Kane, 1998). Although payment made it easier to recruit participants, many commented afterward that they had enjoyed the experience and would have taken part even without the cash incentive.

All the participants were briefed about how to use the app and loaned either a smartphone or a slightly larger tablet (depending on preference) to undertake their survey of the neighbourhood. In total, 50 people took part across the two study sites, producing 626 audio clips and over 1,000 geotagged photographs during the four weeks of data collection. The material within the audio clips falls into three broad categories. The first, like the photographs, describes and documents sites within the neighbourhood. The second category consists in noting issues/problems that participants would like to see addressed – by no means limited to things that can be resolved through spatial planning. The final category comprises suggestions for actions that would make a positive change to the neighbourhood.

Knowing the local

The description/documentation category of the materials produced is interesting in terms of how it taps into local knowledge. Often, this is quite banal, but it provides a grounded view of neighbourhood features that would be broadly invisible from a top-down perspective. For example: "We have 115 Ladypool Road, it's a dental surgery. It's a very popular surgery because these people can speak at least, three, four foreign languages as well and the community really appreciates …" (transcribed audio clip, Balsall Heath).[1] The speaker tails off and changes direction at the end of this quote, which typifies some of the stream-of-consciousness commentary that this technique can generate. One can see material like this as fitting into the broad 'citizens as sensors' mode described by Goodchild (2007). Here, participants are simply acting as the eyes and ears of decision-makers, giving them information that they might be unaware of – the presence of a useful multilingual dental surgery in an area with a great many first-generation migrants.

This kind of local, grounded knowledge can be highly valuable within a planning process. Nonetheless, from our perspective, the more interesting comments fall into the second two categories: identifying issues and suggesting strategies for changing the neighbourhood. For example:

> "This is the River Rea, which crosses through the boundaries of Balsall Heath and crosses through the Calthorpe Estate as well. It could be more positive because the way it's built, it's not really visible to the residents, and if it was, if it was created and designed better, it could actually be a really nice, scenic part of Balsall Heath, with steps coming down and making it a bit more beautiful. But it's a really nice bit of river with a lot of potential." (Transcribed audio clip, Balsall Heath)

The Rea is a heavily engineered river of a design now out of step with best practice in environmental science; today, flood management emphasises the socio-environmental benefits of creating more recreation-friendly and aesthetically pleasing natural-looking watercourses (Wild et al, 2011). 'Daylighting' engineered rivers is quite an expensive process, but it is a good example of the kinds of longer-term aspirations that it would be appropriate to include in a Neighbourhood Plan, especially where it can be demonstrated that there is community buy-in to such an idea.

A number of people came up with suggestions for these larger-scale interventions that could only occur over the longer term and with significant financial backing, such as reopening the local train station in Balsall Heath. Other suggestions were more modest and achievable in the short term. As one participant commented:

> "the reason for this photo is right at the top on the gable, another architectural detail, which from here says H.A. Wronsburg Brothers, Goldsmiths and Jewellers. We really do need to preserve things like that, make a trail of them or something like that. It's not just the buildings, it's not just the people, it's the little features that make this place what it is." (Transcribed audio clip, Jewellery Quarter)

This was one of many comments relating to the Jewellery Quarter that reflected on the rich architectural heritage of the area, one of the few parts of Central Birmingham that was not comprehensively redeveloped during the post-war reconstruction. Things like heritage trails can be quite inexpensive to establish, but validate a particular way of viewing the environment. This can be a low-cost means of agenda-setting within a Neighbourhood Plan, for example, highlighting heritage value and thus establishing an atmosphere favouring the refurbishment of existing building as against demolition and reconstruction.

Other suggestions related to the environment but were not so easily tied to what is achievable within a spatial plan. There were clear concerns, for example, about problems related to litter in parts of Balsall Heath ("lots of rats around there ... this is very disgusting"). In many ways, these are conventional socio-environmental justice issues, with insufficient public resources made available to meet the challenges of waste management in a neighbourhood with a very high population density – not something a Neighbourhood Plan alone could solve. In other cases, these kinds of everyday issues of maintaining the environment could have distinct implications for spatial planning:

> "I like to come to walk around Key Hill Cemetery. It's a nice peaceful green space in the Jewellery Quarter. However, the state of some of the graves and the gravestones is quite poor really and I think it gives a poor impression. The council

needs to improve the maintenance and look after this area more because I think it could be more valuable space for recreation in the Jewellery Quarter." (Transcribed audio clip, Jewellery Quarter)

Here, one can perceive a shortage of local authority funds for maintaining its public spaces as a barrier to an existing green space being given a more prominent role in the spatial planning of the neighbourhood. A poorly maintained open space is not necessarily a selling point to developers looking to invest in the neighbourhood.

Funding localism: winners and losers

The spatial planning process is potentially one route for tackling some of these maintenance-type issues. Section 106 (S106) agreements are negotiated between developers and local planning authorities as a mechanism for leveraging benefits into a community in exchange for granting planning permission. This could be anything from developers paying for a new access road or enforcing a proportion of affordable housing, to mitigating environmental impacts. S106 remains, however, a somewhat blunt instrument for bringing additional funding into an area. They are only ever paid by a small proportion of development projects that take place in a local authority area and the local authorities have been under no obligation to demand that the new infrastructure paid for in an S106 agreement be located in the neighbourhood where development was taking place. The Community Infrastructure Levy (CIL), introduced in the Planning Act 2008, applies to a much greater range of developments but comes with a fixed tariff – giving certainty about the charges that will be applied to a development – and guarantees that a proportion of the money raised should be spent in the neighbourhood where the development takes place. Communities that have a Neighbourhood Plan in place are given 25% of the CIL raised on developments in their areas, as against 15% otherwise (Crabtree and Mackay, 2013).

Thus, there is the possibility that the CIL mechanism could be used to tackle everyday neglect of the built environment in tandem with promoting new development through a Neighbourhood Plan. This represents a certain amount of joined-up thinking at the neighbourhood scale. However, this returns us to a key problem with how localism is being implemented within planning, in that it favours those who already have the skills and capacity to organise (Matthews et al, 2014). If you have enough resources to write a Neighbourhood

Plan, then you will get still more resources from the CIL. Similarly, the CIL generates more returns for a neighbourhood where more and higher-quality development is taking place, which is likely to be in already relatively well-resourced areas. In our case study, there are far greater opportunities for undertaking high-value developments such as luxury flats for professionals in the fashionable Jewellery Quarter than in the somewhat run-down Balsall Heath, thus raising more CIL resources for general environmental improvements in an area that, arguably, needs it less.

More broadly, these kinds of issues highlight the ways in which the 'local' is being constructed within the policy discourse. As Layard (2012: 135) has noted:

> the legal construction of these locals, with each apparently having a single purpose and separate from the rest, is interesting. It appears to create rather fixed, static, territorial units rather than reflecting an inter-linking network of scales of decision making.

The emphasis on creating fixed boundaries around a neighbourhood planning unit ignores the ways that localities overlap and intersect. This perhaps reflects the origins of the neighbourhood planning policy in the more coherent planning units of rural villages and smaller market towns. This fixing of the local within a set of legally binding boundaries is also significant because of the ways in which the local has become almost fetishised as the most appropriate seat of decision-making for issues affecting communities. Indeed, as Featherstone et al (2012: 179) have noted, localism tends to be constructed as inherently positive, which closes down discussions about how this localism is being constructed. Fracturing local governance into a series of small, fixed, neighbourhood territories erodes the potential for thinking more strategically about resource allocation with an eye on redistribution. Simply moving some decision-making to the neighbourhood scale cannot be seen as a solution to the structural inequalities that come hand in hand with the neoliberal agenda (Purcell, 2006).

Conclusions

As the MapLocal pilot demonstrated, communities have no shortage of knowledge and concerns about their neighbourhoods, nor ideas for their transformation. Converting this into action is, of course, quite a different matter. There is also an issue about the valorising of local knowledge over external expertise. There is a danger that the volume of material from the 'ground up' creates almost a reversal of the modernist, top-down paradigm, where 'expert' knowledge was always privileged over local. It would be too easy to make claims that systems like MapLocal generate more 'authentic' knowledge because they are embedded in the local. This is an issue that Mohan and Stokke (2000) have identified in relation to the developing world and it plays into a particular neoliberal trap that starts to downgrade the importance of the state playing a coordinating role.

Padley (2013: 345) argues that it is simply spurious to assume that the removal of bureaucratic structures at the local authority scale will stimulate 'the burgeoning of locally authored innovative solutions within communities'. Let us consider the proposal for de-engineering the River Rea as it passes through Balsall Heath. It is possible in theory (though highly unlikely in practice) that people within the neighbourhood would be able to persuade a developer to bring cash to the table to upgrade the river because of the potential uplift in sales values to any new development in the area. However, there is no way that such a scheme could take place without considering wider implications for catchment management at the city scale, which, frankly, requires coordination by the state. Fine-grained local knowledge of a neighbourhood is simply insufficient when an issue cuts across multiple locals within the wider city and requires particular technical expertise in issues like hydrology, ecology and flood management.

In practice, Neighbourhood Plans do not represent a substantial transfer of power to communities. Instead, they give a place to articulate local aspirations, very much within the confines of a planning system that has been recast to maximise economic returns for developers. Haughton et al (2013: 231) lament the fact that for all the rhetoric of community control, the system does not see 'a return of healthy democratic disagreement at the heart of the planning system'. As a tool, MapLocal offers the possibility of airing very different points of view without those opinions being shouted down or otherwise closed out in a public meeting or facilitated participatory planning exercise. As such, it does allow a more prominent role for multiple, contradictory views.

Where MapLocal is less successful is in resolving the paradox identified by Durman (2012) earlier in this chapter. People have different views about the future planning of their neighbourhoods. Writing a Neighbourhood Plan means attempting to reconcile these different views. Communities are being asked to take on the task of mediating disagreement without necessarily having the resources (financial, educational, cultural) devolved down to the neighbourhood scale in order to do this. MapLocal made it easier for people to express dissenting views. What it failed to do was provide a mechanism for collating those views, allowing people to rank those ideas that seemed most important, to explain why they disagree with someone else's position and so on. MapLocal does not itself create a space for analysis, reconciliation and the development of a course of action.

Of course, MapLocal was never intended to do this, and were it to be further developed, it would need to find ways of providing tools for sifting through the mass of material collected by participants, to start to crowdsource analysis as well as data collection. Even a simple ranking mechanism for prioritising particular issues raised or suggested solutions would be a way to move this forward. Clearly, however, when one starts to go beyond learning about the problems to setting out collective solutions, the limitations on neighbourhood planning as offered by the Localism Act 2011 become starkly apparent. When there is no possibility of dissent – and Neighbourhood Plans cannot challenge a centrally dictated agenda for growth – then there is no need to mediate conflict. This problem is at the heart of discussions around the post-political. A community's agreed compromise over a preferred course of action does not suddenly generate the resources to undertake such action at the neighbourhood scale. More so, if the preferred approach does not fit within a neoliberal growth paradigm, it will not even get as far as a local referendum. So much for community-led decision-making. These wider and more difficult issues require a much greater public debate than can be offered by interactions with a smartphone while exploring one's neighbourhood.

Acknowledgements

Thank you to all of the participants in Balsall Heath and the Jewellery Quarter for their time, hard work and feedback, as well as the Chamberlain Forum, MADE and Joe Holyoak for ideas and facilitation. We are grateful to have received funding from the Arts and Humanities Research Council's 'Connected Communities' scheme, grant number AH/J006580/1.

Note

[1] All the recordings are dated between mid-November and mid-December 2012. We made a deliberate choice to keep recordings made via the app anonymous, although friends/neighbours are able to identify individuals' voices.

References

Bailey, N. and Pill, M. (2011) 'The continuing popularity of the neighbourhood and neighbourhood governance in the transition from the 'big state' to the 'Big Society' paradigm', *Environment and Planning C: Government and Policy* 29(5): 927–42.

Bishop, J. (2010) 'From parish plans to localism in England: straight track or long and winding road?', *Planning Practice & Research* 25(5): 611–24.

Cameron, S. (2006) 'From low demand to rising aspirations: housing market renewal within regional and neighbourhood regeneration policy', *Housing Studies* 21(1): 3–16.

Colenut, B. (2012) 'A conditional right: the Localism Act and Neighbourhood Plans', in TUC (ed) *Localism: threat or opportunity*, London: TUC, pp 14–16.

Conservative Party (2010) *Open source planning*, Policy Green Paper No 14, London: Conservative Party.

Crabtree, P. and Mackay, I. (2013) 'Neighbourhood planning: a new approach to consensus building?', *Journal of Urban Regeneration and Renewal* 7(1): 34–41.

Durman, A. (2012) 'Dispatches from "the frontline of gentrification"', *City* 16(6): 672–85.

Featherstone, D., Ince, A., Mackinnon, D., Strauss, K. and Cumbers, A. (2012) 'Progressive localism and the construction of political alternatives', *Transactions of the Institute of British Geographers* 37(2): 177–82.

Fischer, F. (2006) 'Participatory governance as deliberative empowerment: the cultural politics of discursive space', *The American Review of Public Administration* 36(1): 19–40.

Goodchild, M. (2007) 'Citizens as sensors: the world of volunteered geography', *GeoJournal* 69(4): 211–21.

Haughton, G., Allmendinger, P. and Oosterlynck, S. (2013) 'Spaces of neoliberal experimentation: soft spaces, postpolitics, and neoliberal governmentality', *Environment and Planning A* 45(1): 217–34.

Holman, N. and Rydin, Y. (2012) 'What can social capital tell us about planning under Localism?', *Local Government Studies* 39(1): 71–88.

Imrie, R. and Raco, M. (2003) 'Community and the changing nature of urban policy' in R. Imrie and M. Raco (eds) *Urban renaissance? New Labour, community and urban policy*, Bristol: The Policy Press, pp 3–36.

Jones, P. and Evans, J. (2013) *Urban regeneration in the UK* (2nd edn), London: Sage.

Kaszynska, P., Parkinson, J. and Fox, W. (2012) 'Re-thinking neighbourhood planning: from consultation to collaboration'. Available at: http://www.architecture.com/Files/RIBAHoldings/PolicyAndInternationalRelations/Policy/RIBAResPublica-Re-thinkingNeighbourhoodPlanning.pdf (accessed 25 August 2014).

Layard, A. (2012) 'The Localism Act 2011: what is "local" and how do we (legally) construct it?', *Environmental Law Review* 14(2): 134–44.

Lees, L. (2014) "The urban injustices of New Labour's "new urban renewal": the case of the Aylesbury Estate in London', *Antipode* 46(4): 921–47.

Matthews, P. and Hastings, A. (2013) 'Middle-class political activism and middle-class advantage in relation to public services: a realist synthesis of the evidence base', *Social Policy & Administration* 47(1): 72–92.

Matthews, P., Bramley, G. and Hastings, A. (2015) 'Homo economicus in a Big Society: understanding middle-class activism and NIMBYism towards new housing developments', *Housing, Theory and Society* 32(1): 54–72.

Mohan, G. and Stokke, K. (2000) 'Participatory development and empowerment: the dangers of localism', *Third World Quarterly* 21(2): 247–68.

Padley, M. (2013) 'Delivering localism: the critical role of trust and collaboration', *Social Policy and Society* 12(3): 343–54.

Purcell, M. (2006) 'Urban democracy and the local trap', *Urban Studies* 43(11): 1921–41.

Sagar, T. and Croxall, J. (2012) 'New localism: implications for the governance of street sex work in England and Wales', *Social Policy and Society* 11(4): 483–94.

Thomas, N. and O'Kane, C. (1998) 'The ethics of participatory research with children', *Children & Society* 12(5): 336–48.

Webb, D. (2010) 'Rethinking the role of markets in urban renewal: the Housing Market Renewal initiative in England', *Housing, Theory and Society* 27(4): 313–31.

Westwood, A. (2011) 'Localism, social capital and the "Big Society"', *Local Economy* 26(8): 690–701.

Wild, T.C., Bernet, J.F., Westling, E.L. and Lerner, D.N. (2011) 'Deculverting: reviewing the evidence on the "daylighting" and restoration of culverted rivers', *Water and Environment Journal* 25(3): 412–21.

TWELVE

Translation across borders: exploring the use, relevance and impact of academic research in the policy process

Steve Connelly, Dave Vanderhoven, Catherine Durose,
Liz Richardson, Peter Matthews and Robert Rutherfoord

Introduction

Complex social and governance problems have engaged academic researchers ever since the closely linked emergence of public welfare policy and associated academic disciplines in the post-Second World War era (Lindblom and Cohen, 1979; Fischer, 2003). In the UK's recent past, governments' demand for research rose as both New Labour and the post-2010 Conservative–Liberal Democrat Coalition sought to portray their policies as being based on objective analysis, rather than ideology (Nutley et al, 2007; HMG, 2013). In parallel, pressure rose on academia to demonstrate the utility of its research, constructed as having 'demonstrable economic and social impacts' (HEFCE, 2009: 7) and requiring the planning of 'pathways to impact' (RCUK, 2011). The 2007 economic crisis, and ensuing public sector austerity measures, further increased the pressure on academia to justify its cost to the public purse through its contribution to solving society's problems. As discussed in Chapters One and Three, this prompted new relationships between academics and policymakers: programmes such as 'Connected Communities' were devised with government priorities in mind, and cuts in government research budgets reinforced other trends promoting the co-production of policy-relevant knowledge.

This chapter draws on four 'Connected Communities' projects: three that produced 'policy briefings' (Connelly et al, 2013; Durose et al, 2013; Richardson and Durose, 2013) for the Department for Communities and Local Government (DCLG)[1] and the 'Translation Across Borders' 'legacy' project (2014–15). All reflected the DCLG's desire for new knowledge to guide post-regeneration policy development and delivery. The move away from area-based initiatives towards the decentralisation of budgeting and planning, as part of a fundamental rescaling and reimagining of the relationships between citizens and the central and local state, has heightened the importance of grappling with some very old political theory problems of how to understand and reinforce accountability and representation. This has provided fertile ground for new relationships with the academy, and some researchers – ourselves included – have stepped into this arena, aiming not only to help solve problems, but also to shape agendas by influencing how key issues are understood.

However, the emphasis on evidence-based policy and impact has brought to the fore long-standing mutual frustrations over academics' perceived inability to produce usable outputs, and policymakers' perceived inability to use academic research in appropriate and responsible ways (Lindblom and Cohen, 1979; Owens, 2005; Smith and Joyce, 2012). While diagnoses of the roots of these problems differ, most emphasise the differences between academic and policy worlds – their individual and organisational interests, cultures and 'languages' (Orr and Bennett, 2012). Perhaps because the policy world is seen as the more resistant to change, and because the pressures to engage effectively bear harder on academics (since policymakers have alternatives to universities as sources of evidence), the cures tend to be prescribed to academics. They may involve learning more about the policy world and its needs and 'rhythms' (Stoker, 2013) and to learn its language better – to 'speak in human' (Flinders, 2012). Even more strongly, though, academics are encouraged to work with the putative users of research on the assumption that such co-production will overcome the barriers between the worlds and produce robust, yet useful, knowledge. In practice, these are not straightforward prescriptions, nor are they necessarily successful (Walker, 2010; Orr and Bennett, 2012).

In this chapter, we contribute to a growing literature that problematises straightforward analyses and prescriptions, and builds on a long tradition that recognises the complexity of the policy world. However, our approach is symmetrical in that we pay equal attention to the complexity of the academic world. Our focus is on the practices by which research 'findings' are taken up and used within and by government. In common with others in this field (eg Lendvai and Stubbs, 2007; Nutley et al, 2007; Freeman, 2009), we find the notion of 'translation' fruitful.

We take translation seriously; rather than using it as a loose metaphor, we draw on ideas from the concept's home in the humanities, in particular, translation studies, which illuminate the complexities of collective processes of (re)interpretation and meaning-making. In particular, theories of translatorial action (Schaffner, 1998) emphasise the active and purposeful role of translators, emphasising their situated practices and institutional constraints (Sullivan 2011; Orr and Bennett, 2012), which are our principal concern. Further, translation between communities implies the presence of borders: translation takes place between the 'languages' of different groups. The nature of these borders – their effects on translation, their permeability and the extent to which they can be challenged and repositioned – are thus also important to our analysis.

The 'Translation Across Borders' project was developed by academics and civil servants within the DCLG to investigate how research is translated from the academy into the department and out to neighbourhood projects. It focused on the production and subsequent fate of the three policy briefings prepared by the current authors (among others) for the DCLG in 2012/13 on local representation, the co-production of services and accountability in the context of decentralisation and fiscal austerity. We combined interviews, participant observation and interactive workshops with elements of action research to explore the influence of these projects on the DCLG and how future research could be made more useful to the civil service. Our unusually symmetrical focus and practice – which involved civil servants interviewing academics – produced a rich understanding of the practice of translation as applied to the very varied policy briefing project outputs, which included films, reports, 'slide packs' and a poem (see Chapter Six in this volume). The almost inevitable limitation of such an in-depth approach is narrowness of empirical scope, and the likelihood that relationships between academics and analysts elsewhere in the civil service may be very different. Nevertheless, while the nature of the relationships we uncovered may be very context-specific, it seems likely that both the analytical approach and the kinds of processes we uncovered are more general in their relevance.

In conclusion, we neither deny the enduring reality of the borders between academic and civil service domains, and so the ongoing necessity for translation, nor accept that their impermeably and resistance preclude effective research. We do not, however, conclude that the co-production *of knowledge* is necessarily the solution as this overemphasises the possibility of merging the domains. Rather, we suggest that a focus on fostering collaborative translation under the aegis of a 'shared endeavour' is more productive, emphasising the different environments and practices involved and the work required in creating useful meaning.

Theorising translation

In this project, we have adopted an interpretive approach to understanding policy processes, 'based on philosophical presuppositions that put human meaning and social realities at their heart', and recognising that 'all actors in a policy situation (as with other aspects of the social world), interpret issue data as they seek to make sense of the policy' (Yanow, 2000: 5, 6). This emphasis on subjectivity and meaning-making, and the resultant multiplicity of meanings in any setting, leads naturally to an interest to the processes of *translation* of meanings between people and groups, and so also to the ways in which translation is theorised in the humanities (Freeman, 2009). In his overview of the ways in which policy scholars make use of the concept, Freeman draws attention to the negative literary connotations of translation being less than the original – a sentiment which parallels that at the heart of academic worries over the need to translate academic research into policy prose. Overall, he concludes that linguistic and literary studies show that translation 'is not merely change but conscious change' (Freeman, 2009: 434), which involves work, choices and thus judgements by the translator. Furthermore, 'translation emphasises the production of a new semantic object. Translation has a more active sense [than "interpretation"] of re-writing, re-production' (Freeman, 2009: 435).

We dissent from Freeman's valuable insights in two significant ways. The suggestion that translation involves creating *shared* meaning seems unnecessarily restrictive. Despite current pressures to co-produce, translation does not have to be collaborative, nor is it necessary for meaning to be agreed as translators *rewrite* their texts. Freeman's conclusion that 'translation' may be no more than a helpful 'boundary practice', because there *is* no 'translation itself' (Freeman, 2009: 441), seems unnecessary. Rather, 'translation' captures the ideas of combined transfer-plus-creation and of something (perhaps 'meaning') crossing between bordered domains.

Here, we use elements of the theorising in translation studies to investigate this process. This is a complex academic field in its own right, which has developed in recent decades from a historical focus on texts towards seeing translation as a sociocultural act (Munday, 2012), with striking parallels to the development of interpretive, political understandings of policymaking. To organise our necessarily selective engagement with the discipline, we start from the practices of translation, and the role of the translator. Recognising their situated agency then leads to concern with the ways in which this is enabled and constrained by institutions at societal and organisational levels. Our interest in practices then draws our attention in the other direction, to the way in which translation is shaped by the nature of the 'stuff' through which meaning is generated and communicated.

Translation studies' early theoretical concerns were with what gets carried over in translating a religious source text. Fidelity to the source was the central goal, but debate raged over whether this meant fidelity to the (sacred) language of the text or to its (sacred) meaning – the latter requiring more interpretation, creativity and sensitivity to the world of the audience on the part of the translator (Steiner, 1998). (Analogues with academics' concerns are clear: in communicating findings to a non-academic audience, how much has to be rewritten in a new idiom and what is therefore lost?) In the 20th century, the latter position was radically developed. Theories of translatorial action and *skopos* (i.e. function) theory emphasised the primacy of function over fidelity: a good translation is one that is functionally appropriate and adequate (Schaffner, 1997). This privileges the audience over the author, pointing to 'usefulness' as the primary criterion for quality (c.f. Lövbrand, 2011). Unsurprisingly, these departures from traditional conceptions of translation prompted much (unresolved) debate, as they imply the downplaying (even abandonment) of fidelity to the source, and potentially unconstrained freedom for the translator to reinterpret the original in the quest for relevance. These theories also draw attention to the way translations are likely to simultaneously communicate content *and* perform a range of other communicative and strategic functions, and that the latter may be the more important (Reiss, 1989 [1977]; Schaffner, 1998). The possibilities for miscommunication and conflict are obvious: for instance, it is perhaps reasonable to assume that the academy would privilege fidelity to source and policymakers would privilege usefulness, thus contributing to the frustration noted earlier.

These theories also emphasise the agency of the translator in assessing what function(s) the translation has to fulfil and how best to do this. Thus, who translates is important. Whether an academic is second-guessing their users' needs in translating their own findings, or a government policy analyst is translating an academic paper for a minister, clearly affects what takes place as translators always act in a social and institutional setting.

Freeman also draws our attention to the branch of translation studies concerned with power and manipulation (Hermans, 1985), in particular, to concerns with 'what norms are at work in selecting any given text … for translation, and translating it in a certain way' (Freeman, 2009: 433). For translators, Toury (1995: 55) took these norms to be 'the translation of general values or ideas shared by a group – as to what is conventionally right and wrong, adequate and inadequate – into performance instructions appropriate for and applicable to particular situations', and differentiates between formal rules, sanctions, less stringent norms and conventions, and 'idiosyncrasies'. Some specifically concern the nature of translation, whereas others are broader, originating in and policed by the elite, who control broader systems of ideology, economic sanctions and rewards and status (Lefevere, 1992; Chesterman, 1997).

Usefulness is not the only important criterion for acceptability from a user's perspective: there are also criteria associated with the nature of the translation as a 'thing' in itself. Here, we depart from translation studies per se, as that discipline's principal focus on translating texts between languages is too constraining, and use Kress's theorising of communication in general. Whereas both policy and translation studies tend to privilege the cognitive content of a text, Kress (2010; Kress and Van Leeuwen, 2001) shows that a communication always involves three further dimensions: design, the substance that bears the content and the processes through which it is produced and distributed. For instance, Flinders's 'speaking in human' is a case where a single dimension – design in choice of language – is invoked as key to success. In other cases, design, materiality and practice all play a role; consider the differing likelihoods of successful communication between sending a dense statistical report to a civil servant and explaining its content, orally and with projected graphics, in a seminar. This is not just about making communication easier, as personal, technical, institutional and social norms all affect a communication's acceptability, and these norms will vary between and within institutions, such as academia and the civil service.

Finally, by adopting the lens of 'translation', we invoke the idea of borders between communities with different languages. Much of the academic and policy literature on research transfer takes these borders as a given but overstates the problems they create (Orr and Bennett, 2012: 3–4). In contrast, Smith and Joyce (2012) point to theories of networked policymaking which show that much policymaking spans boundaries rather easily. We suggest that this overstates the opposing case: there *are* real normative and structural differences in people's organisational contexts which mean that boundary-crossing involves work, and often translation. However, while the expertise of 'boundary spanners' (Williams and Sullivan, 2009) or those with boundary-crossing professional biographies (Lewis, 2008; Milligan et al, 2011) has received attention, the everyday challenges of making meaning across boundaries are less well-explored.

'Translation Across Borders'

In this section, we discuss preliminary findings of our interpretive investigation of these challenges through the 'Translation Across Borders' project. At the time of writing (autumn 2014), we had completed interviews with civil servants in the DCLG (by Vanderhoven) and with most of the academics in the policy briefing teams (carried out jointly by Matthews and a policy analyst from the DCLG). Vanderhoven had also spent two separate weeks within the DCLG, observing, interviewing and participating in routine work. The material in this section draws on this fieldwork, with quotes unattributed except where a role is specified to clarify meaning. We write of 'the academics' in the third person rather than the first as the interviewees included colleagues involved in the policy briefings but who are not authors of this chapter.

Two important points emerged from the outset. First, there are many forms of researcher–civil servant engagement, from conventional research relationships to informal, unfunded advice and conversation. Second, *three* (not two) key domains are involved. Within the civil service, important organisational and cultural distinctions exist between policy teams and the economic, statistical and social research analysts whose primary functions are to provide 'evidence for policy' and 'ensure policy debate is informed by the best research evidence and thinking from the social sciences' (Civil Service, no date). Many civil service analysts have professional biographies that have crossed the border from academia, and have a level of experience and intercultural competence (Byram, 1997) less common in either the policy teams or the academy. In their role as intermediaries, analysts *are* translators (Mulgan, 2013). As one put it in the context of a discussion about how to promote evidence to influence more 'principle-based' positions:

> "[the policy teams] need to get some pretty compelling evidence if they need to try and change [a] minister's mind. And so our role and academia's role, I would say, is in that

translation. And if we both do that, then it will have more impact."

The practising translators

For the analysts, the overriding emphasis is on making research useful for the policy teams. Their expertise is crucial: to transform research-based texts, they both have to make sense of them in their own terms ('What does the research say?') and know enough of the policy environment to judge what might be useful:

> "Having an easily accessible and then relatively easily digestible evidence base to inform [our] thinking is valuable.... Shaded by the need to kind of respond to the political realities. There is little point us putting up advice that says 'One of our best ideas ... is to vastly increase taxation'."

Creating something that meets their audience's expectations may involve reworking a whole report, creating a single slide, providing a few lines in an email or creating a table of data. To an extent, this is exactly about 'writing in human'. One analyst said:

> "What I probably find the most challenging is I have to strip back a lot of the narrative, the academic over-elaboration and floweriness of the language because that is important for the academic publications and the narrative across academia. But here it's seen as noise."

However, what forms of communication count as acceptable changes: in 2014, "there's a big demand for infographics, so I've got a [number] of people that work on producing infographics".

Research-based knowledge may be deployed immediately as 'evidence', but it is also synthesised and banked by the analysts, whose expertise shapes their strategic use of knowledge in policymaking. Function does not entirely trump fidelity, however, as the research base has to be reliable. The policy team members trust their analyst colleagues to judge this, and are thus able to take for granted some 'coherence' (Munday, 2012: 122–3) with a robust empirical base, and focus on utility: "People want to see the function, they don't want to see the wiring underneath it. They want to know that that product works. They don't want to understand all of the kind of minutiae behind it".

The academics' principal concern was with communicating a message – to introduce new ways of thinking that would change government action in line with their own agendas. Their translations of their own research were thus 'operative' as well as 'communicative' (Reiss, 1989 [1977]), and they were open about this, even though they were being interviewed by a DCLG analyst. One academic said: "I think there was a space to come in and be a sort of critical friend. But I think wanting to be policy-relevant isn't the same as going along with whatever the government agenda is."

The translations were also deliberately aimed at developing and maintaining relationships (Nord, 1997) with the DCLG, primarily because 'making a difference' was a personal agenda for all of us. Mainly, this manifested in sharing the civil servants' concern for usefulness. In contrast, the representation team deliberately used unusual modes of communication (film, poetry) to disrupt civil servants' expectations – both hoping to communicate better in this way and also to maintain an arts-based approach in reaction to the perceived dominance of social science norms in the policy research world (see Chapter Six, this volume). As Kate Pahl put it:

> "Because I think part of it, in a very intentional way, was I was disrupting modes. By modes, I mean ways of representing things. So it was almost a mimetic project ... we were mirroring issues around representation in what we gave you [i.e. DCLG]. So we made it harder for you not easier."

In both academia and the civil service, the concern for being useful was complemented rather than challenged by notions of academic quality. Producing good translations is a way in which individuals prove their worth, and ultimately keep their jobs. For civil service analysts, this means providing reliable and useful information in a 'marketplace' crowded with sources. For academics, it is partly about producing highly rated articles and being seen to have impact, although in contrast to Smith's (2010) findings in the health policy sector, these were secondary functions. Their primary commitment was to creating and reproducing research that would 'make a difference' – which goes beyond simply being useful to include promoting change. Yet, being overtly political is problematic in the civil service context (Civil Service, 2010), and another of the analysts' translatorial tasks is thus to depoliticise academics' messages – not necessarily to exclude innovation (*pace* Smith, 2014), but to make potentially challenging new ideas palatable. As one analyst put it:

"Ministers or policymakers ... are interested in, you know, the key succinct messages and why it's relevant ... OK, if you [academics] want to rail against [their] philosophy, you can do, but then you've got to understand that you're not going to have that influence."

The context for situated practice

Here, we consider further how the DCLG and academic environments shaped the process of translation. The closest thing to Toury's 'formal rules' is the Civil Service Code, which requires a 'commitment to the Civil Service and its core values: integrity, honesty, objectivity and impartiality' and excludes the influence of personal or party politics (Civil Service, 2010: 1, 2). The Code is highly respected and regarded but underlain by assumptions of the objectivity of evidence and the possibility of impartiality, and hence assumes 'invisible' translators. However, if translators are necessarily and actively exercising judgement, then adhering to the Code requires constant care and reflexivity. Academia has no corollary to the Code. Peer review and ethics review enforces some 'quality' norms on some academic outputs, but, in general, academics' daily lives are much freer, at least in this sense.

In contrast, the domains are similar in the importance of reward and sanction structures, enforced through performance management processes. Individual civil servants must deliver in accordance with individual objectives that are explicitly linked to departmental and ministerial goals and priorities. Academics have publishing and funding targets, and therein lies some of the importance of the relationship-building functions of doing translation work 'for' government – it often leads to another grant application and further research. This can create competition: in our policy briefing teams, we were conscious of the others as competitors for the prizes of relationships with the DCLG and future work. These contexts are dynamic, yet this crucial aspect is largely absent from translation studies, and, indeed, from much policy science. While Stoker's (2013) notion of policy rhythms begins to address this, there is much more going on. Long-term policy drifts – for instance, towards service integration or governance decentralisation – are superimposed on to electoral and budgeting cycles. At even shorter timescales, weekly rounds of questions to ministers in Parliament create unpredictable workloads. Academic cycles are perhaps more predictable: demands for outputs (articles and 'impact statements') are highly structured by the Research Excellence Framework,[2] while internal workloads follow annual, termly and weekly cycles. Again, however, the interactions of these are unpredictable, vary between institutions and are overlain by the more linear timelines of research projects and publishing, and even longer trends in research fashions.

Modes of communication

The key issue here is the extent to which an intended communication actually communicates – whether it *will* be read at all, and whether it *can* be understood. In practice, this is complicated, and we illustrate it here through the key outputs from two of the policy briefings (Connelly et al, 2013; Richardson and Durose, 2013). These projects were unusual in that although they were funded by the Arts and Humanities Research Council (AHRC), there was significant DCLG input. At the inception meeting, attempts were made to agree what and whom the outputs were principally for, and what format was preferred, and the DCLG positioned itself as the primary audience. Their expectation was a report with two summaries – described by the meeting's chair as a 1:4:20-page format. In contrast to the other teams, Pahl (in line with how she describes her position earlier; see also Chapter Six, this volume) explicitly rejected this and appealed to the AHRC's involvement to justify using arts–practice-based modes of reporting, which were less familiar to the DCLG. Modal choice was thus woven into an enduring pattern of relationships between the DCLG and the three teams, with Pahl and her colleagues much less engaged with their policy (as opposed to AHRC) audience throughout. (It should be noted, however, that none of the teams produced a 1:4:20-page report, and members of each went on to work closely with the DCLG on 'Translation Across Borders'.)

The briefings produced ideas that clearly had relevance and potentially broad use for the DCLG: that communities represent themselves in ways that are not conventionally political (Connelly et al, 2013); and that accountability within localism can be understood in five different ways, which can be used both heuristically and normatively to promote community control (Richardson and Durose, 2013). They were explicitly normative as well as analytic, presenting frameworks through which the academics thought that the DCLG could *and should* understand their concerns and practice – frameworks that promote a particular, participatory democratic politics. Yet, the two outputs had very different fates within the DCLG. A table of accountability models from the five-page summary section of Richardson and Durose's (2013) 2:5:58-page format report was enthusiastically embraced, reproduced and reused. Pahl's representation team produced a 33-page report (without a summary, although the introduction does include an 'Outline of the core argument'; see Connelly et al, 2013: 1) and a DVD of a set of short films that included a youth group representing their crime and safety concerns through shadow puppets and one made in an artistic community in Troyeville, Johannesburg. None were taken up by the DCLG, and as a result, the ideas, the cognitive content, failed to permeate across the border and change DCLG practice.

We suggest that while the content of each was equally relevant, and equally challenging, at least part of the explanation lies in Kress's other communicative dimensions. Design was clearly crucial. Success came from clarity and simplicity. A summary text organised in tabular form was *relatively* easy to comprehend, with clear implications, and could also be easily reproduced as a single slide (without Richardson and Durose's accompanying 64 pages), eliminating the need for much further translation – although comments have also been made about its academic-text heaviness, and the consequent need to 'talk it through'. Generally, though, the table fits with anticipated, known and acceptable ways of presenting information. In contrast, films with little commentary require interpretation, which, in turn, require a combination of time and prior insight, which the analysts did not have. Primarily, what the films achieved was to represent the views of a youth group and present evidence of the value of arts in urban regeneration to the DCLG, rather than provide a usable narrative on how to think differently about representation. The accompanying report was less opaque, though dense and academic in style, and equally demanded time to comprehend and further work to translate into something useful for policy teams.

The material nature of the outputs played a role in reinforcing these differences in design. Commonly used formats – PDFs, Word and PowerPoint files – made for easy access to the reports, and, in particular, the extraction of the key table. The DVD containing films was unfamiliar, requiring a different approach to access and use its content.

Such shortcomings could perhaps have been overcome by a different approach to communicative practice. During and following the projects, Durose and Richardson were in frequent contact with the DCLG. This opened opportunities not just for aligning their projects' outputs with the DCLG's needs, but also to actively promote them in successful exercises in policy entrepreneurship. In contrast, there was virtually no dialogue between the representation team and the DCLG once the project started. The exception was at a seminar at which draft findings were presented: the opportunity to show and talk about the films (prefaced by a poem!) opened up a conversation between academics and civil servants that built new relationships and led to the current project.

Running through the preceding is a common thread: ease of access – ideally enhanced by dialogue – is key to acceptability and utility. This is far more than simply an issue of the language used, although that is important. Time is again a significant factor. For analysts and policy teams alike, there is a premium on being able to extract relevant information quickly – as one policy team member said "we're not thick – I read at 10 p.m. on the train home, that's the test". This is not identical to either familiarity with or the legitimacy of one kind of data over another. While the fate of the policy briefings might suggest that unusual visual communication is likely to be less successful than text, the current success of infographics (mixing graphic design with text and numbers) within the civil service tells a different story. Accessibility is the key, achieved through a mix of content and design, coupled with dialogue that presents opportunities for clarification and interpretation. The contrast is clear in this final quotation from one of the analysts:

> "Poems, I'm not sure about … it comes down to getting across really clear, really simple messages. You'll have seen our infographics work, you know, they're quite deceptive actually; they look simple but underpinning them is a huge amount of intelligence and thought and analysis. And actually what gets presented in that, again, it's just the tip of the iceberg."

Conclusions

As we suggested at the outset of the chapter, among the many aspects of the restructuring and rescaling of citizen–state relationships is the need for new knowledge to address the political challenges posed by post-regeneration policies at the neighbourhood level. Under the twin pressures towards academic impact and evidence-based policymaking, the onus is largely on academics to change their practices and become more societally useful. We argue that while this opens opportunities for (at least some) academics, it also requires a sophisticated understanding of the long-standing barriers to government's effective use of academic research.

Conceptualising research 'uptake' as practices of translation seems fruitful: the creation of useful meaning from a source text captures much of what is going on, compared to the idea of the simple transfer of research-based knowledge ('evidence') from one domain to another. The humanities discipline of translation studies has much to offer in the detail of its analysis, in particular, drawing attention to translation as a social act and the significance of the translation of meaning rather than just content. For us, though, the fundamental issue is the function of translation, and the possible conflicts between differing functions. We have found that the possibility, and likelihood, of the effective translation of academic research depends on whether an analyst – or, more rarely, an academic – can translate a research 'output' in order to make it useful to the policy teams and politicians. Such translation is a complex, skilled process of recognising content, making sense of it in the DCLG's own terms, judging what is useful and knowing how to convert it into something useful to others within the resources available.

This process is influenced by a range of institutional and communicative factors in both academic and government spheres. In consequence, these environments are multidimensional and dynamic – 'complex' in the sense of being created by interactions of different systems (Goodwin, 1994). They thus contains elements of both predictability and unpredictability in ways that, we suggest, are more challenging to engage with than the more one-dimensional cycles and rhythms of policy theory.

Given the formidable boundaries posed by these factors, is better, more effective translation possible? Clearly Flinders' 'speaking in human' would be a useful step, though not in itself sufficient. Better understanding of the processes in each domain would also help, though, again, only partially. Detailed knowledge of the complexity of these contexts and practices would require something like an ethnographic approach – embedding an academic researcher in government and vice versa – but the usefulness of this would be hampered by variation across organisations and the rapidity of change. Further, much of the requisite knowledge is know-how and the capacity for situated judgement – both very inaccessible to an outsider researcher and hard to communicate to non-participants in the research.

We suggest that a solution may lie in a particular way of co-producing knowledge across the border between the academic and policy analyst domains. Researching together does not lead unproblematically to the creation of shared knowledge (Orr and Bennett, 2012) – institutional differences are real and cannot be wished away. Even if a new identity could be created in which researchers and users shared enough to remove the boundaries between them, this would inevitably create new borders across which they would have to translate back to their respective domains.

Rather, what we suggest is collaboration around translation. This shifts the emphasis to explicitly recognising the existence of borders between domains with different cultures, languages and needs, and the necessity for translators to actively reinterpret and recreate 'research' in order to move it across these borders. Such recognition is potentially challenging, both to academics' care for the quality of their research and to civil service emphases on the neutrality and objectivity of evidence. It is also challenging in practice – as we have found in the 'Translation Across Borders' project. It requires communication to establish mutual understanding of the needs of the three domains – academic, analyst and policy – in order that practices can be developed that better align with all of these. This is easier said than done, mitigated against by academic and civil service career pressures, the need for time and nurturing to develop trust, misalignment of the timescales of change in each domain, and simply because the primary functions and values of the academy and civil service may be hard to align. There must also be a willingness to engage in this way, and we were fortunate that the civil servants in the DCLG shared with the academics an interest in exploring these issues. We recognise that the possibilities for such working almost certainly vary greatly across the civil service. Yet, it is not impossible. Further research is needed to understand how successful translation is achieved, where usefulness has been combined with fidelity to the original research, and to understand better what institutional changes and techniques would support academics seeking to have their work understood by a policy audience.

So, we are not arguing for the dissolving of borders, and therefore the removal of the complex processes of translation. This would be both undesirable and impossible. Rather, we suggest the importance of recognising the need for and possibility of collaboration – of dialogue and meaning creation across borders. The necessary commonality is not one of culture, but one of mutual respect and the sense of a shared endeavour, jointly oriented towards a common understanding of usefulness as at least one of the principle functions of the translation of research.

Notes

[1] The central government department principally responsible for localism, local government, planning and urban regeneration in England.

[2] The UK's national system for assessing the quality of research in higher education institutions (see: http://www.ref.ac.uk/).

References

Byram, M. (1997) *Teaching and assessing intercultural communicative competence*, Bristol: Multilingual Matters.

Chesterman, A. (1997) *Memes of translation: the spread of ideas in translation theory*, Amsterdam: John Benjamins Publishing.

Civil Service (no date) 'About the Government Social Research Service', Civil Service, London. Available at: http://www.civilservice.gov.uk/networks/gsr/about-the-government-social-research-service (accessed 2 September 2014).

Civil Service (2010) 'Civil Service Code', Civil Service, London. Available at: http://resources.civilservice.gov.uk/wp-content/uploads/2011/09/civil-service-code-2010.pdf (accessed 3 September 2014).

Connelly, S., Dabinett, G., Muirhead, S., Pahl, K., Vanderhoven, D. and Pool, S. (2013) *Making meaning differently: policy briefing for DCLG – community governance in the context of decentralisation*, Sheffield: University of Sheffield.

Durose, C., Mangan, C., Needham, C., Rees, J. and Hilton, M. (2013) *Transforming local public services through co-production*, Birmingham: University of Birmingham.

Fischer, F. (2003) 'Beyond empiricism: policy analysis as deliberative practice', in M. Hajer and H. Wagenaar (eds) *Deliberative policy analysis: understanding governance in the network society*, Cambridge: Cambridge University Press, pp 209–27.

Flinders, M. (2012) 'Keynote speech', delivered at the Political Studies Association, Belfast, 12–14 April.

Freeman, R. (2009) 'What is "translation"?', *Evidence & Policy* 5(4): 429–47.

Goodwin, B. (1994) *How the leopard changed its spots: the evolution of complexity*, New York, NY: Touchstone.

HEFCE (Higher Education Funding Council for England) (2009) *Research Excellence Framework: second consultation on the assessment and funding of research*, London: Higher Education Funding Council for England.

Hermans, T. (ed) (1985) *The manipulation of literature: studies in literary translation*, London: Croom Helm.

HMG (Her Majesty's Government) (2013) *What works: evidence centres for social policy*, London: HM Government.

Kress, G. (2010) *Multimodality: a social semiotic approach to contemporary communication*, London: Routledge.

Kress, G. and Van Leeuwen, T. (2001) *Multimodal discourse: the modes and media of contemporary communication*, London: Arnold.

Lefevere, A. (1992) *Translation, rewriting, and the manipulation of literary fame*, London: Routledge.

Lendvai, N. and Stubbs, P. (2007) 'Policies as translation: situating transnational social policies', in S.M. Hodgson and Z. Irving (eds) *Policy reconsidered: meanings, politics and practices*, Bristol: The Policy Press, pp 173–89.

Lewis, D. (2008) 'Crossing the boundaries between "third sector" and state: life-work histories from the Philippines, Bangladesh and the UK', *Third World Quarterly* 29(1): 125–41.

Lindblom, C.E. and Cohen, D.K. (1979) *Usable knowledge: social science and social problem solving*, Cambridge, MA: Yale University Press.

Lövbrand, E. (2011) 'Co-producing European climate science and policy: a cautionary note on the making of useful knowledge', *Science and Public Policy* 38(3): 225–36.

Milligan, C., Kearns, R. and Kyle, R.G. (2011) 'Unpacking stored and storied knowledge: elicited biographies of activism in mental health', *Health & Place* 17(1): 7–16.

Mulgan, G. (2013) 'Experts and experimental government', in R. Doubleday and J. Wilsdon (eds) *Future directions for scientific advice in Whitehall*, Cambridge: Centre for Science and Policy, pp 32–8.

Munday, J. (2012) *Introducing translation studies: theories and applications* (3rd edn), London: Routledge.

Nord, C. (1997) *Translating as a purposeful activity: functionalist approaches explained*, Manchester: St. Jerome.

Nutley, S.M., Walter, I. and Davies, H. (2007) *Using evidence: how research can inform public services*, Bristol: Policy Press.

Orr, K. and Bennett, M. (2012) 'Public administration scholarship and the politics of coproducing academic–practitioner research', *Public Administration Review* 72(4): 487–95.

Owens, S. (2005) 'Making a difference? Some perspectives on environmental research and policy', *Transactions of the Institute of British Geographers* 30(3): 287–92.

RCUK (Research Councils UK) (2011) *RCUK impact requirements*, Swindon: Research Councils UK.

Reiss, K. (1989 [1977]) 'Text types, translation types and translation assessment', in A. Chesterman (ed) *Readings in translation theory*, Helsinki: Finn Lectura, pp 105–15.

Richardson, L. and Durose, C. (2013) *Who is accountable in localism? Findings from theory and practice*, Manchester and Birmingham: Universities of Manchester and Birmingham.

Schaffner, C. (1997) 'From "good" to "functionally appropriate": assessing translation quality', *Current Issues In Language and Society* 4(1): 1–5.

Schaffner, C. (1998) 'Action', in M. Baker (ed) *Routledge encyclopedia of translation studies*, London and New York, NY: Routledge, pp 3–5.

Smith, K.E. (2010) 'Research, policy and funding – academic treadmills and the squeeze on intellectual spaces', *British Journal of Sociology* 61: 176–95.

Smith, K.E. (2014) 'The politics of ideas: the complex interplay of health inequalities research and policy', *Science and Public Policy* 41(5): 561–74.

Smith, K.E. and Joyce, K.E. (2012) 'Capturing complex realities: understanding efforts to achieve evidence-based policy and practice in public health', *Evidence & Policy* 8(1): 57–78.

Steiner, G. (1998) *After Babel: aspects of language and translation* (3rd edn), Oxford: Oxford University Press.

Stoker, G. (2013) 'Why policymakers ignore evidence', interdisciplinary blog, Southampton, University of Southampton. Available at https://generic.wordpress.soton.ac.uk/multidisciplinary/2013/09/17/why-policymakers-ignore-evidence/ (accessed 1 July 2015.)

Sullivan, H. (2011) '"Truth" junkies: using evaluation in UK public policy', *Policy & Politics* 39(4): 499–512.

Toury, G. (1995) *Descriptive translation studies – and beyond*, Philadelphia, PA: John Benjamins Publishing.

Walker, D. (2010) 'Debate: do academics know better or merely different?', *Public Money & Management* 30(4): 204–6.

Williams, P. and Sullivan, H. (2009) 'Faces of integration', *International Journal of Integrated Care* 9 (online).

Yanow, D. (2000) *Conducting interpretive policy analysis*, New York, NY: SAGE.

THIRTEEN

Conclusion

Dave O'Brien and Peter Matthews

The central argument of this book has been that Britain, and particularly England, faces an era of urban policy very different to what has come before. This idea has multiple bases, from the backdrop of 'austerity' and central government spending retrenchment, through the Coalition's rescaling of policy from regional to city and parish level, to the specificity and particular situations in spaces and places across the UK. The central planks of the regeneration era, of buildings, property and state investment, are seemingly replaced by a demand from the state that society and atomised communities should simply deal with urban problems themselves. These trends will only continue under the Conservative administration elected in May 2015.

This, therefore, is a curious conclusion to write. In making the case for a post-regeneration era, *After urban regeneration* has sought to bring together a range of approaches that are seemingly far from each other, from locally specific artistic interventions that seek disruption by co-production, through to wide-ranging, large-scale analyses influenced by a more positivist social-scientific tradition. A simple description of each chapter would not do justice to the eclectic nature of the book. As a result, this conclusion will not attempt a neat synthesis. Indeed, this would be to miss the key points of the text and the common themes running across the multiple ways of thinking about community in urban regeneration exhibited in the text. Rather, this conclusion will consider *where* the book's discussions leave the study of urban regeneration and *how* the problems, issues and debates identified in the text might better be dealt with following the experiences of the researchers working on this collection.

The post-regeneration era

The key thrust of the text has been to argue for a post-regeneration era. This requires new thinking from academics studying regeneration as well as the associated new modes of urban practice and governance. One route into a consideration as to the status of studying urban regeneration is to situate the post-regeneration era between those seeking to overturn the conception of regeneration itself, specifically seeking to argue that it is merely gentrification, with all of that phenomenon's associate evils (Lees et al, 2007), and those seeking to trumpet the possibilities of success found in urban interventions, whether cultural or on the level of more generic social, economic or built environment impacts (Shaw, 2009; Matthews, 2012). Of the two poles, the gentrification school is perhaps the more important, particularly as *After urban regeneration* has sought to both raise attention to questions of power in the construction and practice of the local, and demonstrate how the intervention, or lack of intervention, by the state is shaping conditions that may well further gentrification processes at the local scale.

Gentrification scholars have sought to demonstrate the structural conditions, most notably the role of capital-seeking rents, underpinning the dynamics of urban life and its associated policies (Lees, 2000; Smith, 2005). The interesting question raised by *After urban regeneration* is how these structural conditions will be affected by the rescaling and redefinition of the role of the state. It is likely that the demands of property speculation will continue to be held as more important than the lives of place-based communities. Indeed, these tensions can be seen from the struggles over local institutions, as in Cohen and McDermont's chapter, through attempts to make visible urban control strategies in Pool and Pahl's case study, to the robustness (or not) of local media in Harte and Turner's chapter. The reconfigured role of the state may well see an acceleration of gentrification as even the most cursory mechanisms of consultation and its association with participation in decision-making are removed in favour of governance mechanisms that favour those already well-resourced to take advantage, as Jones et al demonstrated in Chapter Eleven.

However, and in keeping with the activist nature of much gentrification scholarship, the projects discussed in *After urban regeneration* do much to demonstrate the existing capacity for resistance to the revanchist urban agendas now confronting communities. The projects demonstrate this not only through the examples they offer of good or best practice, but also through a reassertion of the expertise that exists in communities and the different ways in which this has been expressed.

The reassertion of expertise is present across almost all of the chapters. Most interestingly, it plays out in Nathan's and Wilks-Heeg's more macro-discussions of urban policy. Their discussions both stress, implicitly and explicitly, one of the great failures of regeneration policy, a failure that underpins the rhetoric of Coalition discourse, was the act of doing *to* communities, rather than doing *for*, let alone the much more appropriate act of doing *with*.

The recognition of existing resources and capacities within communities points to a valuable lesson: that these resources and capacities require sustenance, nurturing and organisation. Organisation must come around the politics of decision-making, the practices of making everyday life in communities work and also at the symbolic level of what, and what is not, the community itself. Bernstein et al, in Chapter Seven, show this very clearly, demonstrating how the local is constructed, struggled over and, in turn, requires construction if it is to be brought into the realm of policy outlined by Connelly et al in Chapter Twelve.

Thus, narrating the community is vitally important, whether an estate in Cardiff or Edinburgh, young people in Rotherham, infrastructure in Birmingham, or a government department. The narration of a community can act as a form of mapping, bringing the community's assets, capacities and expertise to light, as well as demonstrating potential partnerships (Yanow, 2000). The act of storytelling about a community is a clear contrast to the practice of the era of urban regeneration, dominated as it was by the process of doing regeneration *to* communities. Indeed, the act of doing to was prevalent as much within the academy as it was within policy. Social science was telling communities' stories for them, as Nathan's and Wilks-Heeg's considerations on the basis for knowledge in urban policy show.

The role of the academy

If *After urban regeneration* is right to share a pessimism that the inequalities at the root of Lees et al's (2007) critique will worsen as a result of the emerging settlement that the book has identified, what are the implications for those in the academy seeking to engage with the communities at the sharp end of this change? Indeed, as the state reconfigures its role as shaping the conditions for civil society to deliver urban policy, there is a clear need for other institutions to support the range of communities, in all their different forms, with the task that the state has set.

There is a case to be made for a re-conceptualisation of the role of the academy in the post-regeneration era, but what will that re-conceptualisation involve? Gentrification scholars, among others, have shown that there is a venerable tradition of activist partnerships between academics and communities. However, this was within an era before the radical changes facing the contemporary British university. These changes are shaping both teaching and research and point towards a different landscape of both arts and humanities and social science in the coming years. Indeed, the work explored by Nathan in Chapter Four was part of this landscape, with its consequences felt in the shape of communities and places described across the case studies in the rest of the book, for example, Harte and Turner's work in Birmingham. We can characterise this previous model of research, particularly state-led university research, as part of the doing *to* rather than the doing *with*.

In some ways, the development of 'what works' centres will continue this approach. However, the 'what works' idea takes place against the background of an academy adapting to the impact agenda. Impact, as previously mentioned, is 'defined as an effect on, change or benefit to the economy, society, culture, public policy or services, health, the environment or quality of life, beyond academia' (HEFCE, 2011: 26). This agenda is designed partially with an eye to the cost-effectiveness of research in an era where the state is questioning a whole range of investments. It also reflects a broader audit and surveillance society. It has faced detailed criticisms (for a recent example, see Knowles and Burrows, 2014), but because it sets the framework for the conduct of British academic research, it is important to take seriously its demand for research to be conceptualised as 'beyond academia'.

'Connected Communities' is clearly part of this agenda. It is also part of the failures of previous research interventions structured by the division between *on* and *with*. The projects discussed in this book have shown a way for the university to be part of both the support, and also the resistance to, a localist agenda that, in its present form, may well deepen inequality. However, as the chapters have shown, universities require a new form of academic identity (Graham et al, 2014) that takes seriously the act of researching *with* and not *on* communities. Universities need the right bureaucratic and career structures to support these academics, from the act of paying project participants promptly, through to supporting a career that may produce radical social change that is difficult, if not impossible, to distil into the prevailing disciplinary and performance management structures of the university (a point made by Pool and Pahl in Chapter Six).

Most notably, there is the question of what is undervalued by universities if the state is offering the carrot of both bureaucratic affirmation and funding through the filter of 'impact'? One element here can be the link between capacity-building within those communities facing the demands of localism, and the way in which universities formally recognise this activity. The Caerau and Ely

Rediscovering Heritage project, detailed in Chapter Eight, shows how lifelong learning and short courses can be crucial to developing community skills. Universities need to show faith in these forms of learning in an era where full-time study with its attendant fee income may seem more attractive than capacity-developing work expressed in formal qualifications that do not necessarily raise the same revenue.

A space is being created for the university to become an anchor institution, across its research and teaching, and the academic to become a translator and intermediary. However, this space must not, under any circumstances, be filled by research projects and research funding as a way to carry on or conduct community development activity, which is the proper function of the state. This is for reasons of democracy, for reasons of transparency and for reasons of research ethics.

It is wrong, as this book has repeatedly argued and demonstrated, to use a community, in whatever form, as a collection of subjects for academic experimentation, just as it has been wrong, as Wilks-Heeg has shown, for public policy to experiment on communities for the purposes of urban policy.

It is wrong for academic funding and projects to intervene for a six-, nine- or 12-month period to produce a single output, paywalled within a peer-reviewed journal, which participants and partners will never read and have no ownership over.

It is wrong for the academic community, governed by its capacity for disciplinary-specific expertise, to become a major source of funding for communities, unless the academy is willing to recognise the expertise of the communities that it will work with.

It is wrong for the system of peer review of research proposals, again governed mainly by academic expertise, to supplant open democratic debates about the purpose, focus and function of regeneration funding. This is most severe in those places that have been deemed to be problematic by the intersection of academic research and vengeful public policymaking (Slater, 2014).

Finally, and most fundamentally, it is wrong that some of the most vulnerable, yet resilient and potentially powerful communities in the UK should see their capacities translated into profit for universities and individual academics. It is only by offering guarantees of genuine partnership that universities can avoid repeating the inequalities engendered by the profiteering of consultants, businesses and government ministries that prevailed during the era of urban regeneration. This profiteering came at the expense of the very people and places that this work was meant to be for.

It is time, therefore, for the academy to consider what, exactly, it can do right. *After urban regeneration* is merely the beginning of, not the conclusion to, this conversation, a conversation that must learn the lessons of co-production and participation, both possibilities and limitations, offered by the 'Connected Communities' programme.

References

Graham, H., Hill, K., Matthews, P., O'Brien, D. and Taylor, M. (2014) 'Connecting epistemologies'. Available at: www.earlycareerresearchers.wordpress.com (accessed 29 November 2014).

HEFCE (Higher Education Funding Council for England) (2011) *REF: assessment framework and guidance on submissions*, Bristol: HEFCE.

Knowles, C. and Burrows, R. (2014) 'The impact of impact', *Etnographia* 18(2): 237–54.

Lees, L. (2000) 'A reappraisal of gentrification: towards a "geography of gentrification"', *Progress in Human Geography* 24(3): 389–408.

Lees, L., Slater, T. and Wyly, E. (2007) *Gentrification*, London: Routledge.

Matthews, P. (2012) 'From area-based initiatives to strategic partnerships: have we lost the meaning of regeneration?', *Environment and Planning C: Government and Policy* 30(1): 147–61.

Shaw, K. (2009) 'Rising to a challenge', in K. Shaw and L. Porter (eds) *Whose urban renaissance? An international comparison of urban regeneration strategies*, London: Routledge, pp 253–60.

Slater, T. (2014) 'The myth of "Broken Britain": welfare reform and the production of ignorance', *Antipode* 46: 948–69.

Smith, N. (2005) *The new urban frontier: gentrification and the revanchist city*, Taylor & Francis.

Yanow, D. (2000) *Conducting interpretive policy analysis*, London: Sage.

Index